The dynamics of company profits

The dynamics of company profits

An international comparison

Edited by DENNIS C. MUELLER

Contributors

John Cubbin
Paul A. Geroski
Frederic Yves Jenny
Ioannis N. Kessides
R. Shyam Khemani
Talat Mahmood

Dennis C. Mueller
Hiroyuki Odagiri
Joachim Schwalbach
Daniel M. Shapiro
André-Paul Weber
Hideki Yamawaki

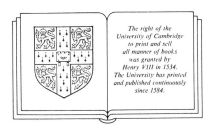

The right of the
University of Cambridge
to print and sell
all manner of books
was granted by
Henry VIII in 1534.
The University has printed
and published continuously
since 1584.

CAMBRIDGE UNIVERSITY PRESS

Cambridge
New York   Port Chester   Melbourne   Sydney

WZB -Publication
WISSENSCHAFTSZENTRUM BERLIN

Published by the Press Syndicate of the University of Cambridge
The Pitt Building, Trumpington Street, Cambridge CB2 1RP
40 West 20th Street, New York, NY 10011, USA
10 Stamford Road, Oakleigh, Melbourne 3166, Australia

First published 1990

Printed in Canada

Library of Congress Cataloging-in-Publication Data

The Dynamics of company profits : an international comparison /
editor, Dennis C. Mueller ; contributors, John Cubbin ... [et al.].

p. cm.
ISBN 0-521-38372-2

1. Corporate profits. I. Mueller, Dennis C. II. Cubbin, John.
HG4028.P7D96 1990
658.15'5 – dc20   89-25184
                                                                        CIP

British Library Cataloguing in Publication Data

The dynamics of company profits: an international
comparison.

1. Companies. Profitability
I. Mueller, Dennis C. 1940–
338.5'16

ISBN 0-521-38372-2

Contents

Preface

This project began when I visited the International Institute of Management, a member of the Science Center Berlin, during the years 1981-3. I was working on my study, *Profits in the Long Run,* and in visiting with people in Europe and presenting portions of that work the idea arose to do some of the same hypotheses testing for other countries as I was doing for the United States.

A project of this scope requires the enthusiastic participation of a large number of people, and this project was fortunate in there being such a group to be found. A couple of meetings were held on methodological issues, data problems, and the like, and things sailed along from then on rather smoothly – with the inevitable delays of a project with twelve participants drawn from six countries and three continents.

The gratitude of all of us goes to the Science Center Berlin, which sponsored the research of myself and several others on portions of this project, as well as a conference in 1987 to discuss preliminary results. We also thank the Center for Economic and Policy Studies (CEPS) of Brussels for sponsoring one of our earlier meetings.

Rebecca Flick provided invaluable assistance on putting the manuscript together, typing not only my work but redrafts of the work of others, and to her I owe a special note of thanks.

College Park, Maryland   Dennis C. Mueller

vii

Contributors

JOHN CUBBIN
Reader
Queen Mary College
London, United Kingdom

PAUL A. GEROSKI
Senior Lecturer
London Business School
London, England

FREDERIC YVES JENNY
Professor of Economics
ESSEC
Cergy, France

IOANNIS N. KESSIDES
Assistant Professor of
    Economics
University of Maryland
College Park, Maryland

R. SHYAM KHEMANI
Director, Economics and
    International Affairs
Bureau of Competition Policy
Ottawa, Hull, Canada

TALAT MAHMOOD
Research Fellow
International Institute of
    Management
Berlin, West Germany

DENNIS C. MUELLER
Professor of Economics
University of Maryland
College Park, Maryland

HIROYUKI ODAGIRI
Associate Professor of Economics
University of Tsukuba
Sakura, Ibaraki, Japan

JOACHIM SCHWALBACH
Research Fellow
International Institute of
    Management
Berlin, West Germany

DANIEL M. SHAPIRO
Associate Professor of Economics
Concordia University
Montreal, Canada

ANDRÉ-PAUL WEBER
Professor of Economics
ESSEC
Cergy, France

HIDEKI YAMAWAKI
Research Fellow
International Institute of
    Management
Berlin, West Germany

CHAPTER 1

Profits and the process of competition

DENNIS C. MUELLER

I Two views of competition

Two views about competition exist. The first sees competition as a process for allocating resources to their optimal uses. The price mechanism is the instrument for achieving this goal, and when it functions properly, equilibria emerge with prices equated to marginal social costs of production. When it malfunctions, equilibria exist with some prices above marginal costs, and society suffers a welfare loss from the underconsumption of these goods. Such malfunctions are usually attributed to an insufficient number of buyers or sellers. Monopoly is seen as the antithesis of competition. Thus, under the first view, competition is seen as a process for determining prices and quantities, the allocation of resources for a given set of tastes and technological opportunities. At its zenith, competition produces an equilibrium set of prices that induce a Pareto optimal allocation of the economy's goods and services. Such equilibria are anticipated so long as monopolistic elements are absent.

The other view of competition sees it not as a process for allocating a given stock of resources but as a process for transforming these resources into new products and production techniques. Competition takes the form not of lower prices for an existing set of products but of new and improved ideas, and these in turn are the property of the individual(s) who created them and his/her/their employer. In the first instance, competition for a new product is competition for a newly created monopoly. With time the monopoly disappears as other firms imitate and improve upon the new product. Thus, monopoly is an integral part of a dynamically competitive process, a passing stage in an industry's evolution whose presence might signify progressive good performance just as readily as poor performance.

When competition is viewed as a dynamic process of new product and process creation, the concept of equilibrium does not play an important role. What is of interest is not the constellation of prices and allocation of resources at a particular point in time but their movements over time. The

1

perspective is that of a system in flux, of constant disequilibria evolving through time, rather than of a system in a state of equilibrium at a particular point in time.

It is the first view of competition that informs most economic analysis and underlies most model building. And it is the first view of competition that is predominant in the economics classroom. Yet it is arguably the second view that more accurately describes actual competition. The essays in this volume attempt to model and test this second view of the competitive process.

II   The static model

The origins of the first view of competition can be traced back to Adam Smith (1776) or more directly to Augustin Cournot (1838). From Cournot we obtain a clear definition of a market equilibrium and a prediction that price and number of sellers are inversely related at the equilibrium. The Cournot model might be regarded as the theoretical foundation for a generation's empirical research in industrial organization relating firm or industry profitability to industry concentration levels.

This research established fairly conclusively that profitability and concentration are positively correlated, as the Cournot model or a small numbers-collusion hypothesis predicts (Weiss, 1974). Given the assumptions underlying the Cournot-collusion hypothesis, the inference must be drawn that the divergence between price and costs is greater in concentrated industries, and from this it follows that welfare losses must be greater in more concentrated industries.

The assumptions underlying these inferences leading to a positive correlation between profit and concentration have been challenged, however. Yale Brozen (1971a, b) argued that firms with efficiency advantages over their competitors tended to grow faster than their competitors. Therefore, it would be these more efficient firms that would grow to fill the ranks of the largest firms in an industry. At any point in time, the most concentrated industries in an economy would contain many that had become so through recent, rapid growth due to efficiency advantages. Brozen argued that the normal process of competition and imitation would eliminate the efficiency advantages of these firms, reducing both industry profitability and concentration. Brozen thus reasoned that the positive association between profit rates and industry concentration levels was a transitory, disequilibrium phenomenon. He presented empirical evidence indicating that the positive association between these variables that Bain (1956) had observed did disappear in a few years.

Brozen's critique of Bain's early results and of the generation of research it spawned raises two fundamental objections to the underlying assumptions of this model. The first questions whether the costs and prices of all firms within an industry can be assumed to be the same. The second questions whether the relationship between a firm or industry's profitability at a given point in time and other firm–industry characteristics can be assumed to represent a stable, long run equilibrium relationship. Both objections indirectly question the applicability of the first view of the competitive process to the study of company profitability. To investigate efficiency differences across firms, which change over time, one must adopt a dynamic view of the competitive process.

III   The Schumpeterian perspective

The second representation of the competitive process owes its origin to Joseph Schumpeter (1934, 1950), of course. The salient feature of Schumpeter's description of the capitalist process is its dynamic nature. Iconoclastic entrepreneurs introduce innovations – new products, new production processes, new marketing techniques, new organizational structures – that create temporary monopolistic advantages over their competitors. These transitory monopolies create pockets of profits, which in turn provide the incentive for imitators to step forward and thereby drive these profits back to zero. Thus, the "process of creative destruction" proceeds: innovation creating monopoly, monopoly creating profits, profits creating imitators until a state of normalcy returns, only to be followed by new innovations and a repeat of the cycle.

This Schumpeterian image of the competitive process often seems to underlie more informal arguments by economists in favor of capitalist institutions over socialist institutions, unregulated markets over regulated markets, or an explanation for why some developed countries outperform others over the long run. Yet the Schumpeterian perspective has had little impact on the development of more formal models of market behavior. Efforts to move the profession in this direction (e.g., Clark, 1961; McNulty, 1968; Kirzner, 1973), although often applauded, do not launch a subsequent stream of research that develops their initial insights. The Schumpeterian perspective remains just that, a perspective on the nature of competition rather than a model of the competitive process.

The most important exception to this generalization is perhaps the evolutionary model of capitalism of Nelson and Winter (1982).[1] Nelson and

---

[1] A second important exception might appear to be the contestable market theory of Baumol, Panzer, and Willig (1982). Entry and exit are the heart of Schumpeter's process of creative destructive, just as the conditions of entry and exit are central to defining the contestability of a market. But in contrast to Schumpeter's dynamic depiction of the competitive process, the contestable market theory is entirely static. It relates *conditions*

Winter consciously eschew standard neoclassical models of profit-maximizing firms operating in competitive markets and the notion that these markets are in equilibrium. Rather, they trace the evolution of firms and industries over time using simulation techniques. Although these simulations trace out a rich mosaic of a capitalist economy's evolution, a mosaic that accords well with actual experience in many ways, they do not constitute a formal test of a Schumpeterian or evolutionary model against, say, a neoclassical model. They raise rather than answer the question of how to test a Schumpeterian model of the competitive process.

Such a test would seem to have to consist of at least two elements: first, an examination of the histories of various industries to see whether they follow the innovation–imitation–maturity cycle sketched by Schumpeter and, second, an examination of the profit histories of firms and industries to see whether the process of dynamic competition does indeed erode abnormal profits over time.

Case study evidence on product and industry life cycles seems to support a Schumpeterian description of an industry's evolution (see, e.g., Gort and Klepper, 1982; Klepper and Graddy, 1984). Initial innovations are followed by the entry of numerous "imitators," which in turn leads to a shake-out phase in an industry's evolution, which might be likened to Schumpeter's gale of creative destruction. Whereas this general pattern accords with the Schumpeterian view of industry dynamics, industry life cycles appear to enfold at substantially different speeds, and exceptions do exist (e.g., Gort and Klepper, 1982; Klepper and Graddy, 1984). Moreover, the studies of product life cycles have not investigated the profit performances of the innovating and imitating firms. Indeed, very little is known about the intertemporal patterns of profitability for individual firms and industries in general. This void will be filled to some extent by the essays in this volume.

We seek to test two main tenets of the Schumpeterian thesis: (1) that the competitive process does successfully erode positions of excess profits, that is, in the long run all economic rents tend toward zero, and (2) that the erosion process proceeds quickly. Although the first hypothesis can be clearly formulated and tested – rents are either zero or they are not – the second hypothesis is more equivocal. How quick is quick? We shall not actually try to answer this question but rather present evidence of the speed of adjustment of profits to their long run equilibrium values.

of entry to *levels* of profit in equilibrium. The dynamics of attaining equilibrium are not addressed. Testing the contestable market theory has proceeded in the tradition of other empirical work in industrial organization by relating profit rates to market structures in cross-sectional analyses.

IV   Previous research

Yale Brozen's (1971a, b) critiques of Joe Bain's work were the first studies to raise, if only indirectly, the question of the intertemporal pattern of profitability and its relationship to market structure characteristics. David Qualls (1974) responded to Brozen's attack on Bain by pointing out that high concentration was a necessary but not sufficient condition for persistent above normal profits. Where entry barriers are low, high profits attract new entrants, which in turn drive profit rates down. Thus, Qualls argued that one should expect a stable concentration-profits relationship only in industries with high entry barriers. He presented evidence of a continuing positive association between profits and concentration for those firms and industries having high entry barriers.

Although the profits-concentration relationship remained significant after a decade, Qualls's estimates indicated a weakening of the relationship and thus were consistent with an eventual disappearance of all above normal profits. Indirectly, his results posed the salient questions of this study. Do profits converge on a common, normal rate of return, and how is this convergence process related to firm and industry characteristics?

A large literature dating back a half century has been concerned with the intertemporal variability of profit rates in response to business cycle factors. These studies have predicted changes in profit rates or price-cost margins over the business cycle, with these changes being related to industry characteristics like concentration and capital intensity. In general, the studies have assumed that price-cost margins change with varying business cycle conditions due to changes in the abilities of oligopolists to coordinate behavior (e.g., changes in conjectural variations; see Qualls, 1979). They have not been concerned with the long run equilibrium values of firm and industry profit rates and the adjustment process to this equilibrium as a result of the entry and exit of firms and intraindustry shifts of resources – the concerns of the present set of studies. Thus, we do not attempt to build off of this previous research, but rather we adjust the data to mitigate the influence of business cycle factors on our results.

The first direct test of the hypothesis that individual profit rates converge on a common normal value was presented by myself (Mueller, 1977). Using data for 472 firms from 1949 to 1973, I rejected the null hypothesis of convergence on a common rate of return. Subsequent research on a sample of 551 companies confirmed this earlier conclusion and presented evidence on the relative importance of various firm and industry characteristics in explaining permanent differences in company profit rates (Mueller, 1986).

Connolly and Schwartz (1985) raised several objections to the methodology of my 1977 study and presented alternative tests of the competitive environment hypothesis. Their evidence supported the hypothesis for below normal profit firms. In the long run, the profits of companies that are at one time below the normal level do tend to rise toward that level. But for a substantial fraction of firms with above normal returns, the process is incomplete. These firms appear to earn above normal rates of return indefinitely.

David Levy (1987) estimated the adjustment rates to long run equilibrium values for profit rates measured at the industry level using U.S. data and a model similar to that used in this study. He estimated very slow adjustment rates when he did not include separate industry intercepts and fairly rapid adjustment rates when he did include them. His results at the industry level are similar to those reported by Kessides in Chapter 4 and to those of the other studies at the firm level. Significant differences in permanent profit rates exist across industries, but adjustments to these permanent rates are rather quick (less than five years in Levy's results).

Geroski and Jacquemin (1988) present estimates of permanent rents and the speeds of adjustment to long run equilibrium for France, West Germany, and the United Kingdom. Their findings, based on a smaller sample of firms, are somewhat at variance with those reported in this volume for these three countries. Geroski and Jacquemin find a greater degree of profits persistence in the United Kingdom than in France and West Germany, whereas the results in this volume indicate that permanent rents are higher in France, with West Germany and the United Kingdom being relatively similar.

The first test of whether persistent differences in profit rates exist across firms for a country other than the United States was the Odagiri and Yamawaki (1986) study of Japan. They found persistent differences in profit rates across Japanese companies and that a significant component of these differences can be explained by industry characteristics.

V   The present, international comparison

Regardless of which view of the competitive process one takes, the question of whether profit rates converge on a common, normal return and the measurement of the speed of convergence are central to both a positive and normative discussion of economic competition. If convergence is quick and complete, then competition among existing firms within an industry, the entry and exit of firms, and the threatened entry of firms must be presumed to be sufficiently swift and strong to bring firm and industry profit rates quickly back to their long run competitive equilibrium levels. Although deviations from this equilibrium at any point in time exist, the competitive process can be seen as functioning rapidly enough so that substantial and permanent welfare losses from price–cost deviations do not exist. Similarly, if one thinks in terms of dynamic competition, the entry of imitators and exit of failed firms must be presumed to proceed rapidly enough so that even innovators' profits are relatively short-lived.

The existence of permanent rents and/or a slow adjustment to long run competitive equilibrium values raises some troubling questions, however. Measured in static terms, the cumulative welfare losses from deviations between prices and costs could be large. The knotty question then must be faced as to whether these welfare losses from allocative inefficiency are somehow offset by the welfare gains from innovations that create long-lived monopoly positions.

Although industrial organization economists have certainly been aware of the importance of these dynamic competition issues, this awareness has generally not informed empirical studies of firm and industry profitability. The existing literature consists of but a few studies of the movements of profits over time, and these employ disparate methodologies.

The present volume seeks to help fill this void by presenting a set of studies of intertemporal patterns of company profitability in different countries, all of which build from a common methodological foundation. This foundation is developed in the next chapter. It is followed by separate studies for the United States at the firm and industry level. These in turn are followed by individual chapters of profitability at the company level for Canada, the Federal Republic of Germany, France, Japan, and the United Kingdom. The original plan was to include also a chapter on Sweden, but it was not completed in time for inclusion in the final volume. Preliminary results were supplied by Gunnar Eliasson and are included in the overview, Chapters 10 and 11, however. These two chapters summarize the results for the individual countries and draw some implications from them.

The countries studied differ in size, progressivity, and international competitiveness. With respect to size, they range from Canada up to the United States. The United States for the period studied (1950–72) and Japan are relatively closed economies. Others were quite open to international competition. Japan has been the world's pacesetter in productivity, income, and export growth. The United Kingdom has been at the other pole, epitomizing slow growth and economic retardation.

These contrasts raise several interesting questions concerning the intertemporal profit patterns of the different countries. Are permanent profit differences greater and adjustments to equilibrium slower in the relatively closed economies of Canada, Japan, and the United States than in the other countries? Has Japan's spectacular performance in international markets been led by a group of dynamically progressive firms, which have been able to translate this success into persistently above normal profits? Is the sluggish overall performance of the United Kingdom evident in individual company profit rate patterns, for example, in relatively slow adjustment speeds to long run equilibrium levels? These and other questions are addressed in this volume.

Almost all of the analyses in this book are based on rates of return on corporate assets. These accounting measures of performance have been subject to substantial criticism in recent years, and their usefulness has been the topic of a hot debate. We do not wish to join this debate here but feel some discussion of the issue is warranted. The appendix of this chapter discusses the major questions. Those willing to accept accounting measures of profitability as legitimate measures of performance can move directly to Chapter 2.

Note to the reader: Chapters 3–9 make use of the methodology of Chapter 2. Each is written more or less as a self-contained entity, however, so that following Chapter 2, the reader can read from the ensuing seven chapters in any order and number(s) he or she chooses. Chapters 10 and 11 overview the results and conclusions of the book.

Appendix

Accounting returns versus economic returns

All of the studies in this book use accounting profits and assets data. Although accounting data have various well-known deficiencies, it has generally been felt that they can be used with caution to analyze company performance. Recent papers by Fisher and McGowan (1983) and Benston (1985) have questioned whether accounting profit rate data can tell us anything at all about economic performance or its determinants. As Fisher and McGowan put it, "there is no way in which one can look at accounting rates of return and infer anything about relative economic profitability or, a fortiori, about the presence or absence of monopoly profits" (1983, p. 90). If Fisher and McGowan are correct, then the reader need go no further. We think they overstate their case, however.

Fisher, McGowan, and Benston give several reasons for why accounting profits and accounting assets are incorrect measures of their ideal economic counterparts. Fisher and McGowan present several examples suggesting extremely high measurement errors. The basic point they make is surely valid. Accounting returns *may* deviate from true economic returns by large magnitudes. Whether they do in fact deviate by wide margins is a separate question, however, a question that cannot be answered by presenting hypothetical examples.

The Fisher–McGowan critique focuses upon problems arising in the calculation of the internal rate of return on a single investment project due to variations in the patterns of returns over time and depreciation schedules. As Edwards, Kay, and Mayer (1987, hereafter EKM) point out, however, for most questions in industrial organization, it is the return on assets for the *entire firm* over a particular *interval of time* that is of interest (pp. 32–6).

They derive the following equation that estimates the deviation of the one period accounting rate of return, π_t, from the true economic return of the entire firm over its lifetime, r, as

$$\pi_t = r + (g_a - g_m) + (\pi_t - g_a)\frac{M_{t-1} - A_{t-1}}{A_{t-1}}, \qquad (A.1)$$

where A_{t-1} and M_{t-1} are the book value of the firm's assets and their value derived as the present value of future profits and g_a and g_m are the growth rates of these two variables (derived from EKM, 1987, eqs. 2.4, 2.6, and 3.5). We shall use annual observations on π_t to estimate long run projected or permanent profit rates for each firm, π_p, and speeds of adjustment $(1 - \lambda)$ to these π_p.

With respect to the two bias terms in (A.1), it is difficult to believe that g_a could permanently exceed or fall short of g_m. Were such the case, the book value of a firm's assets would increasingly diverge from its present value based on future profits. Considering the market value of a firm as an estimate of the latter, one would expect to see the ratio of market to book value converging on zero or infinity, something one does not regularly observe. It is likely, however, that $g_a \neq g_m$ each year but rather sometimes exceeds and sometimes falls short of g_m. Thus, $g_a - g_m$ can be expected to impart a nonsystematic error in the measurement of r using π_t.

If the book value of assets correctly measured the present value of these assets $(A_{t-1} = M_{t-1})$, the last term in (A.1) would be zero. But, as EKM note (p. 35), conservative accounting conventions should result in the book value understating the present value so that $M_{t-1} - A_{t-1}$ is generally positive. The bias introduced by the third term in (A.1) should have the same sign as $\pi_t - g_a$.

We measure π_t for each firm as a deviation of a firm's profit rate in year t from the sample mean for that year. It is likely that $\pi_t - g_a < 0$ for firms with low π_t and $\pi_t - g_a > 0$ for firms with high π_t. An upward bias in π_t as a measure of r is introduced for high π_t's, and a downward bias for low π_t's.

One of the findings of this book will be that some firms have persistently high accounting profit rates and others persistently low accounting rates. Given the likely signs of the third terms in (A.1), it is possible that this finding is at least in part due to systematic bias in the measurement of r using π_t. In some of the country studies, we shall relate π_p estimates to economic variables that are hypothesized to explain r. The support we find for these hypothesized relationships suggests that all of the deviations in long run projected profit rates that we observe are not due to accounting induced biases.

We also measure the speeds of adjustment of π_t to our estimates of permanent profits π_p. We shall interpret these speeds of adjustment as measures of the rapidity with which market forces eliminate short run deviations from a firm's permanent profit levels. Equation (A.1) suggests that short run biases in the measurement of r may also affect these speeds of adjustment. If $g_a - g_m > 0$ for several periods but converged back on zero, then π_t would tend to fall toward r, with the speed of adjustment a measure of the speed with which this component of the accounting bias is eliminated. Although we shall interpret our measures of π_p and $1 - \lambda$ as estimates pertaining to underlying economic profits, these possible accounting biases must be kept in mind.

One way to judge the seriousness of the biases from accounting data is to estimate the same types of relationships using data free from or containing smaller biases. Many writers have argued that the market value of a firm is an unbiased measure of a firm's economic performance and have employed Tobin's q as a substitute for accounting rates of return in structure–performance studies. It is defined as the ratio of the market value of the firm to the replacement value of the firm's assets. In comparison to accounting profits over total assets as a measure of economic performance, Tobin's q differs in both the numerator and the denominator. Of these two differences, the change in the numerator is the greatest innovation.

By definition, the market value of the firm is the sum of the market values of its outstanding shares of common stock, debt, and other forms of securities. Each of these in turn should equal the present discounted value of expected future dividends, interest payments, and so on. The argument that the market value of the firm is superior to accounting profits rests on two assumptions, neither of which is obviously true: (1) dividends and interest are paid out of economic profits not accounting profits and (2) the securities markets can accurately predict future economic profits.

The pioneering study in this literature was by Lindenberg and Ross (1981). After an elaborate development of the methodology for measuring

Tobin's q, they present but three regressions: q regressed on the accounting-profits-to-sales ratio, a measure of the four-firm concentration indexes in the firm's industries, and the two variables together. Concentration and q were uncorrelated. Thus, if one believes that concentration and economic profits should be positively correlated, q would not appear to be a good measure of economic returns from Lindenberg and Ross's tests. Several recent studies have also failed to find a positive relationship between accounting profit rates and concentration (Shepherd, 1972; Ravenscraft, 1983; Mueller, 1986), so this result does not really distinguish q from accounting returns as a measure of economic returns.

Lindenberg and Ross do find a strong positive association between q and the accounting-profits-to-sales ratio ($t = 19.59$). This result certainly implies that the stock and bond markets regard current accounting profits as a good indicator of a firm's future ability to pay dividends and interest. If Tobin's q is a good measure of economic returns, then accounting profits as a ratio to sales appears from Lindenberg and Ross's study to be likely to be one also.

Smirlock, Gilligan, and Marshall (1984) seek to demonstrate that Tobin's q is "a more appropriate measure of firm rents than more standard measures such as accounting profit rates" (p. 1058) and claim to have done so. In a footnote, they present the results for one regression using accounting profit returns on invested capital (n. 12, p. 1057). These results are presented here along with the comparable results using Tobin's q as the dependent variable (Table 1.1). The fit to the data with q as dependent variable is somewhat better as indicated by the higher F-statistic. But the same variables are significant and insignificant in both equations. Exactly the same qualitative picture of the determinants of economic returns emerges. Market share and growth in market share have a significant impact on economic returns; concentration and entry barriers do not. The most important difference between the two regressions is the much stronger performance of growth in market share in the q equation. This difference may be because rapid growth in market share signals larger future market shares and economic rents. But this does not imply that accounting profits are a bad or worse measure of *current* economic rents than q. Indeed, π's relationship to measures of current market structure – market share and concentration – is stronger than for q. The difference between q and π's performance in the work of Smirlock et al. seems largely due to q's measuring future economic returns whereas π measures only current economic returns rather than that q is a superior measure of economic returns per se.

Salinger finds "results in the profitability regressions are significantly different from the results in the q regressions" (1984, p. 167). Two representative equations from his paper are presented in the bottom half of

Table 1.1. *Structure-performance results using accounting profits and Tobin's q*

Dependent variable	Independent variables Smirlock, Gilligan, and Marshall (n = 132)						
	Int	MS	CR	MBTE	HBTE	MSG	F
q	-2.60 3.51	0.055 3.61	0.009 1.05	0.261 0.40	0.380 0.95	2.67 4.50	17.07
π	-1.14 0.36	0.177 5.27	0.047 1.48	0.703 0.69	-0.141 0.10	5.38 2.07	11.72

	Salinger (n = 252)									
	Int	A/K	RD/K	MES·CR	K·CR	(A/K)CR	(RD/K)CR	CR	G	F
q	0.481 2.36	2.08 2.11	4.86 3.40	2.89 0.26	-0.004 0.03	-2.32 0.89	-1.02 0.27	-0.291 0.57	0.349 4.28	0.43
π	0.229 4.81	5.92 2.60	0.593 1.77	5.05 1.96	-0.008 3.05	-1.14 1.89	-0.795 0.91	0.027 0.22	0.031 1.61	0.19

Variables used:

q = Tobin's q
π = accounting profit rate
Int = intercept
MS = market share
CR = four-firm concentration ratio
MBTE = moderate barriers to entry
HBTE = high barriers to entry

MSG = market share growth
A = stock of advertising
K = replacement value capital stock
RD = stock of research and development
MES = minimum efficient size measure
G = growth of firm

Note: t values below coefficient.

Table 1.1. The results are different. But whether the results for the q equation are better than those for the π equation or indicate that q is a better measure of economic returns is less clear. The q equation has a fairly high R^2 despite its having only three significant variables in it suggesting multicollinearity. The variables MES·CR and K·CR are prime candidates for this problem. They have the lowest two t values in the q equation but are both significant in the π equation with opposite signs. Both variables should have positive coefficients. Whether one finds the performance of these two variables in the q equation "better" than in the π equation strikes me as very much a matter of taste. Beyond these two variables, the qualitative nature of the results in the two equations is the same. The biggest improvement in fit between the π and the q equations, and the strongest overall performance, is for the growth in firm size. Growth's appearance in the equation is in Salinger's words an "*ad hoc*" adjustment for demand growth (1984, p. 164, n. 10). Salinger finds the relative strength of this variable in the q equation "surprising" (p. 167), and yet it would appear to be largely because of this variable that the q equation gets a higher R^2. Assuming that growth in Salinger's model, as in that of Smirlock et al. (1984), is capturing future increases in economic rents reflected in current market values, it is difficult to see how these results indicate that q is superior to π as a measure of *current* economic rents.

Connolly and Schwartz (1985) obtain qualitatively similar results for their tests of the disappearance of economic rents over time for both accounting profits and market value measures of economic returns. Of particular interest is the asymmetric nature of their conclusions with respect to positive and negative rents. Although it is difficult to perceive how firms can earn negative rents indefinitely, it is certainly possible that they might earn positive rents indefinitely. Thus, if accounting profits and Tobin's q did accurately measure true economic returns, one might expect that negative rents would disappear over time but positive rents would, or at least might not, which is exactly the pattern Connolly and Schwartz observed. On the other hand, if persistent differences in accounting rates of return were solely due to systematic biases in estimating economic returns, one would expect below normal profits to be as persistent as above normal returns. The asymmetry in the test results Connolly and Schwartz report is inconsistent with the assertion that all differences in accounting returns are merely reflections of biases in estimating economic returns.

We conclude that accounting profits are not obviously inferior to market value measures of economic returns like Tobin's q, at least as measures of current economic returns. This is not to deny what I take to be the basic point of the Fisher–McGowan–Benston position. Accounting conventions can and probably do introduce substantial errors of observation when using accounting returns as measures of economic returns. These errors tend to obscure the true relationships between profits and other economic variables our theories predict. We can expect low R^2 for equations that use accounting profits as the dependent variables, and the economic relationships we uncover are likely to be stronger than our econometric tests might suggest.

CHAPTER 2

Modeling persistent profitability

PAUL A. GEROSKI

I   Introduction

The structure–conduct–performance model has long attracted the attention of industrial economists interested in the empirical analysis of monopoly. The most notable characteristic of that model is that much of the theorizing underlying it is static, and virtually all of the associated empirical work has been cross-sectional in character. Standing at a slight distance to the structure–conduct–performance paradigm are evolutionary and Schumpeterian arguments. Focusing on innovation, imitation, and adaptation, they are concerned not so much with monopoly as with its persistence. Both of these alternative lines of thought are fundamentally dynamic in character, and both are concerned with analyzing competition as a process. To date, neither have generated much empirical research, much less a full-blown empirical methodology. However, as industrial economists gradually come to perceive more and more limitations in static models and cross-sectional empirical analysis, so the attractiveness of developing alternative methodologies will grow. Under the circumstances, it is natural to think that extending the empirical analysis of monopoly to examine its persistence will be placed high on the research agenda.

In this chapter, we shall make a case for extending traditional static, cross-sectional empirical models to include market dynamics. In the main, we shall examine a particularly simple type of dynamic model whose major characteristic is an autoregressive structure that emerges as the solution to a latent variables problem. Aside from any other virtues, the

This chapter was originally circulated under the title "The Persistence of Profits: Some Methodological Remarks on Measurement and Explanation." I am obliged to D. Allard, J. Cubbin, J. Scott, H. Odagiri, A. Jacquemin, R. Schmalensee, T. Mahmood, R. Masson, D. Mueller, J. Schwalbach, H. Yamawaki, and J. Walters for helpful comments on that draft and on related work. It has also benefited from discussions at several group meetings with members of the "Persistence of Profits" team, from the financial assistance of CEPS, Brussels, and from the support and hospitality of the IIM, Berlin. The usual disclaimer applies.

model does enable one to see clearly that latent variables are a major difficulty that must be faced when modeling market dynamics. The problem is that many of the forces that propel movement toward long run equilibrium take the form of threats or expectations to which agents respond, and these threats or expectations are not generally observable. To solve this problem, one can link these unobservables to their causes (high profits) and consequences (profits bid away) and substitute the latent threat or expectations variables out of the structural equations. This leaves one with a reduced form equation that, in the examples we shall examine, is essentially an autoregression in profits. The object of this chapter is to explore the properties and interpretation of this particular type of model.

Section II motivates the whole exercise by examining two reasons why one might wish to push beyond static models of firm or industry performance and consider dynamic models. Section III compares structural and reduced form dynamic models, isolating the latent variables problem and outlining its solution. We extend the model in Section IV to examine heterogeneities in dynamics within industries, and in Section V, we relate its parameters to several different notions of "competition." A brief summary and a sketch of several further extensions conclude the chapter.

II   Static and dynamic market models

Conventional cross-sectional analyses of the variation in profits across industries are commonly seen as examining propositions about the character of long run equilibrium positions. First order conditions describing the appropriate oligopoly pricing equilibrium are often used to guide the specification of the empirical model (e.g., Cowling and Waterson, 1976), and a concern with testing various comparative static predictions generates an interest in the size, sign, and significance of various estimated parameters. An example of such a model is as follows. Let π_{ip} be the equilibrium (permanent) level of returns of some firm i (or the return on average in some industry i), let the values of the "explanatory" variables (market share, advertising, concentration, etc.) be described by a vector $\mathbf{x}_i$ with associated unknown parameters β, and let μ_i^1 be an error with classical properties. Then, it is usually posited that

$$\pi_{ip} = \mathbf{x}_i \beta + \mu_i^1. \tag{2.1}$$

The object of estimating (2.1) is to make inferences about the unknown parameters β and, in particular, about those associated with market share or industry concentration.

Although a great many economists have used equations like (2.1) to make inferences about the existence of monopolistic resource misallocation,[1] its informativeness has been somewhat exaggerated. Of several caveats that must be kept in mind, we wish to focus on two. Both are shortcomings that arise from the neglect of market dynamics. The first problem is that whereas (2.1) is an equation describing long run equilibrium, the data used in estimation may not have been generated from long run equilibrium configurations. This mismatch between theory and data can, if not properly controlled for, generate biased estimates of the unknown parameters, leading to incorrect inferences about the association between market structure and performance. The second problem arises because static cross-sectional models do not contain enough information to enable one to draw policy recommendations from raw observations of market structure and performance in any particular industry. The difficulty here is that apparent monopolistic distortions may not be permanent, and the rationale for antitrust intervention must acknowledge the complementary role played by inbuilt market "error correction" mechanisms (e.g., entry and intraindustry mobility). Let us consider each problem in turn.

The first problem is one of interpreting estimated parameters. What seems to be crucial to the appeal of cross-sectional work is the notion that the data used are generated from long run equilibrium positions or, at worst, are generated only during temporary and purely random departures from equilibrium, departures that can be corrected by easy controls (like measures of industry growth). Were this presumption to be true, the cross section of industries contained in a random sample ought to generate enough variation in the data to measure unknown parameters common to all the various industry long run equilibrium configurations. What is controversial about this presumption is the assertion that any observations not drawn from long run equilibrium positions will differ from them only randomly, or in a way that can be completely controlled for using additional exogenous variables. This effectively assumes that the incidence and extent of disequilibrium is unaffected by those factors that determine the character of equilibrium positions. If this assumption is incorrect, then biased estimates of the characteristics of long run equilibrium states may result.

To see this point more clearly, suppose that (2.1) has only one explanatory variable (say, market share or industry concentration) denoted S_i, so that it can be written as

$$\pi_{ip} = \beta_0 + \beta_1 S_i + \mu_i^1. \tag{2.2}$$

---

[1] Despite a controversy initiated by Demsetz (1974), the estimated coefficient on concentration is usually interpreted as the ratio of some measure of *imperfectly competitive behavior* (as reflected, say, in the conjectural variations of firm i) to an appropriate elasticity of demand. Recent surveys of this literature include Schmalensee (1987), Geroski (1987), and Cubbin (1986).

The problem with estimating β_1, the parameter of interest in (2.2), is that long run equilibrium returns π_{ip} are not observable. Current period returns π_i are observable but unfortunately are not the same as π_{ip} unless every industry is in long run equilibrium when observed. If, as is commonly the case, one nevertheless uses π_i to proxy π_{ip}, then the empirical model

$$\pi_i = \beta_0 + \beta_1 S_i + \mu_i^2 \tag{2.3}$$

differs from the model derived from theory. If (2.2) is the "true" model as assumed, then μ_i^2 contains a measurement error $\pi_i - \pi_{ip}$ in addition to any stochastic term inherent in (2.2); that is, $\mu_i^2 \equiv \mu_i^1 + (\pi_i - \pi_{ip})$. The existence of this additional noise inflates standard errors and so biases t-statistics downward. What is worse, it can introduce bias if $\pi_i - \pi_{ip}$ is correlated to S_i; that is, if S_i not only explains the level of equilibrium returns π_{ip} but also helps to govern dynamic movements around equilibrium. Suppose that this is true and, for example, that the deviation from equilibrium at any given time is proportional to S_i,

$$(\pi_i - \pi_{ip}) = \alpha S_i + \mu_i^3, \tag{2.4}$$

where μ_i^3 summarizes all other determinants orthogonal to S_i. Then, neglecting (2.4) in the estimation of (2.3) yields an estimated slope coefficient of $\alpha + \beta_1$, clearly a biased estimate of the parameter of interest in (2.3), β_1. The only way to recover estimates of α and β_1 separately is to analyze (2.3) and (2.4) together. To put it another way, one can only have confidence in estimates that purport to measure β_1 if either the hypothesis that all units i are in equilibrium ($\pi_i = \pi_{ip}$ for all i) or the hypothesis that x_i has no effect on disequilibrium motion ($\alpha = 0$) cannot be rejected by the data or if a control variable (like market growth) captures the non-random variation that causes bias.

There are at least two instances in the structure–performance literature where this type of bias may have arisen. Negative correlations between profits and concentration using the 1975 Line of Business data (e.g., Martin, 1983; Ravenscraft, 1983; Scott and Pascoe, 1986; the effect is also present in Schmalensee, 1985) have been attributed to the effects of recession and energy price shocks on capital intensive, highly concentrated industries. Such industries are likely to have had their 1975 returns depressed below equilibrium levels ($\alpha < 0$), and so, despite the "fact" that the true $\beta_1 > 0$, the estimated slope coefficient ($\alpha + \beta_1$) attracts a negative sign. Similarly, Weiss (1974) observed that slope coefficients in regressions of profits on industry concentration were generally insignificantly different from zero during periods of inflation. Since it is well known (e.g., Scherer, 1980, ch. 13; Encaoua and Geroski, 1986) that firms in more highly concentrated industries are slower to adjust their prices to cost and demand shocks, their returns are depressed relative to those in more competitive industries during highly inflationary periods. It is, therefore, hard to avoid the conclusion that $\alpha < 0$, and so that $\alpha + \beta_1 \cong 0$ despite $\beta_1 > 0$. In both examples, it is clear that a cross-sectional empirical analysis may not cast reliable light on the parameter of interest, β_1, and that when cross-sectional models cannot be fully specified in a manner that is consistent with the way the data are actually generated, they ought to be supplemented by dynamic models.

The second reason for turning toward more dynamic empirical models arises from the difficulty of trying to make antitrust policy recommendations from data that may not have been generated from long run equilibria. Suppose that one observes an industry with high profits and high industry concentration and suppose that $\beta_1 > 0$ and that one is sure that this is only because of monopolistic pricing (and not, say, differential efficiency). The difficulty with using results from the static, cross-sectional model to recommend intervention policies to lower prices in high profits, high concentration industries is that, in principle, this effect may already be occurring. Markets have inbuilt error correction mechanisms that function to bid away excess profits, and the alternative to policy action is to allow competition from entry and intraindustry mobility to erode the monopolistic output restriction that high concentration apparently induces. This observation implies that a case for intervention cannot rest on estimates from a model like (2.3) since (2.3) does not indicate the extent to which "monopoly power" persists in the face of market forces. Thus, to the observations of high concentration, high profits, and $\beta_1 > 0$, one must add the assurance that antitrust intervention can correct the apparent resource misallocation more quickly and cleanly than the market itself can before one can make a case for intervention. To the extent that the important antitrust policy problem is "persistent monopoly," the static cross-sectional empirical relationship embodied in equation (2.1) is not sufficient for policy decision making, and a more dynamic empirical analysis is necessary.

In short, there seems to be a reasonable case to be made for extending static structure–performance models to include consideration of both long run equilibrium configurations and the systematic motion around them that is induced by market forces. This necessarily creates an interest in extending cross-sectional empirical analyses to include a times series dimension. Observed market data cannot be generally presumed to be generated by economic activity in equilibrium, and empirical analyses using such data must be based in part on modeling the process – equilibrium or disequilibrium – that generated the data.

III   A time series model of profits

Extending traditional structure–performance models like (2.2) to describe market dynamics is, in principle, straightforward and requires the addition of equations describing the market-induced feedback to disequilibrium. Such feedback is likely to take the form of entry, exit, and intra-industry competitive mobility occurring in response to positive or negative excess profits. Entry is likely to respond to positive excess profits created by monopoly pricing, and entrants are likely to undercut the prices set by incumbents, displacing those who are inefficient and slow to respond. Similarly, high excess profits earned by one firm on the basis of some superior efficiency or new product are likely to induce imitation by rivals and entry by new firms, leading, in due course, to a return to normal profits. Thus, to extend (2.2), one needs to add equations describing the response of entry, exit, or intraindustry mobility to deviations of current returns from their long run equilibrium levels and, in turn, to trace the effects of entry on subsequent industry performance.

However, although a multiequation model describing this process enables one to handle the shortcomings of the static structure performance model discussed in Section II, dynamic models have their own peculiar drawbacks. The major problems include not only the difficulty of measuring entry flows, imitation rates, and intraindustry mobility in practice but also the more fundamental problem that "entry" (hereafter considered broadly to include all competitive responses to excess profits) need not actually occur to have an effect on market performance. This second observation springs from a long tradition of theorizing [culminating recently in Baumol, Panzar, and Willig (1982)] that suggests that the mere threat of entry may be enough to provide discipline on pricing conduct. That is, the expectation of new competition may lead incumbents to attempt to preempt entrants by limit pricing, capacity installation, and other strategic actions. Whereas most of these strategic initiatives will reduce the returns earned by incumbents, the difficulty from the point of view of econometric modeling is that this anticipatory behavior induces a systematic movement in profits without any corresponding change in an observable variable like "entry." Thus, potential entrants drawn to a market by the high excess returns occasioned by monopoly pricing may induce a limit pricing response from alert incumbents that both lowers the returns incumbents enjoy and discourages the potential entrants from actually attempting entry. As potential entry never actualizes in this case, the observer has no systematic determinant for the movement in returns toward equilibrium.

There is thus a strong case for thinking that "entry" may have many of the characteristics of a classic latent variable and that latent variable problems may be at the center of many dynamic market models. The solution to this kind of problem is to model around the latent variable, linking its causes and consequences in a manner that allows knowledge of the entire structure of the model to cast light on one unknown component of it. Precisely how this can be done depends a good deal on the characteristics of the model and on the information (or set of observables) available for analysis. In what follows, we shall focus on a particularly simple case in which only the profits of individual firms are observable.[2]

Let $\pi(t)$ be firm i's profits at time t, and let $\pi p(t)$ be the long run competitive rate of return. Then $\rho(t) \equiv \pi(t) - \pi p(t)$ is the level of excess profits enjoyed by firm i. We start by partitioning the forces inducing changes in profits into two types: systematic factors, which we refer to as "entry" $E(t)$, and all other factors, which are collectively referred to as "luck" $\mu(t)$ and are, by construction, orthogonal to $E(t)$. All variables are taken to be firm specific and are implicitly indexed by i unless otherwise stated. The distinction between $E(t)$ and $\mu(t)$ is that entry, potential or actual, is the outcome of decisions made by market participants and so is a consequence of high profits. Luck includes all factors that affect profitability but are exogenous to market participants' decisions, that is, do not respond to changes in profits.

The effects of entry on profits can make themselves felt through any of several channels. Entry can alter industry pricing conduct by causing changes in the form and intensity of nonprice conduct (e.g., by sparking an advertising war); "entrants" can physically displace incumbents in the market and so alter tacit or overt collusive patterns; entry may spark a price response by incumbents, predatory or otherwise; or finally, the anticipation of entry may lead incumbents to sacrifice some profits prior to entry in the form of strategic entry preventing investments made to avoid even larger expected losses should entry actually occur [for a survey of the theory underlying such strategic investment behavior, see Geroski and Jacquemin (1984)]. The simplest possible description of the net effect of all these forces is the equation

$$\Delta\rho(t) = \theta_0 + \gamma_0 E(t) + \gamma_1 \rho(t-1) + \mu(t), \qquad (2.5)$$

[2] Gabel (1979), Yamawaki (1984), and Geroski and Murfin (1987) are all multiequation structural models of industry evolution; Hannan (1979) is a relatively rare attempt to measure the extent of potential entry. Geroski (1987) and Geroski and Masson (1987) consider reduced form models of varying complexity that attempt to overcome the latent variables problem. In these models, the dynamics of market processes are tracked by variations in market structure over time.

where $\gamma_0 < 0$, $\gamma_1 < 0$, and $\Delta\rho(t) \equiv \rho(t) - \rho(t-1)$. The parameter γ_0 measures the effect that entry has on $\rho(t)$ as entrants bid away excess returns, and it clearly varies inversely with the level of entry (and mobility) barriers surrounding firm i. The term $\mu(t)$ summarizes a variety of exogenous factors whose collective impact is most simply characterized as a normally distributed i.i.d. (independently and identically distributed) stochastic process with zero mean and variance δ_μ^2.[3] The permanent advantage enjoyed by firm i (relative to a perfectly competitive firm), θ_0, persists in the long run; that is, in equilibrium, when $\Delta\rho(\tau) = 0$ at some time τ, $\pi(\tau) = \theta_0 + \pi p(\tau)$. Finally, γ_1 is a necessary feedback control parameter that ensures that steady state values of $\rho(t)$ remain finite.[4]

The consequences of high positive or negative excess returns include the entry of new firms, the expansion of existing fringe firms, and the expansion of incumbents (collectively, *entry*). Most of these actions will probably be based on the returns anticipated as a consequence of such action, but as a first approximation, it seems natural to imagine that entry responds to preentry excess returns. To focus ideas, let ρ^* be the equilibrium value of $\rho(t)$, that is, that value at which all entry is zero. Clearly $\rho^* = -\theta_0/\gamma_1$. Since positive excess profits $[\rho(t) - \rho^*]$ can be expected to attract entry $[E(t) > 0]$ and low profits to induce "exit" $[E(t) < 0]$, it is natural to write

$$E(t) = \phi[\rho(t-1) - \rho^*] + \epsilon(t), \tag{2.6}$$

where $\phi > 0$.[5] The parameter ϕ reflects the speed with which entry is attracted by those excess profits that can be bid away, thus measuring the alertness of individual entrants, the size of the potential "entry pool," and the ability of entrants to penetrate into markets. The term $\epsilon(t)$ is, by construction, the exogenous flow of entry or exit that would occur where $\rho(t-1) = \rho^*$. For simplicity, we take it to be a normally distributed i.i.d. stochastic process with zero mean and variance σ_ϵ^2.

The parameters ϕ and δ_ϵ^2 in (2.6) are, like γ_0, γ_1, and δ_μ^2 in (2.5), not estimable since entry $E(t)$ is a latent variable. However, one can use the

---

[3] Assuming that luck is not serially correlated amounts to assuming that the occurrence of an innovation affecting i's profits at time t does not raise the likelihood of another innovation occurring at time $t+1$. It is a straightforward exercise to assess how persistent luck is.

[4] Were $\gamma_1 = 0$, (2.5) reduces to $\Delta\rho(t) = \theta_0 + \gamma_0 E(t) + \mu(t)$, and when $E(t) = 0$, $\Delta\rho(t) = \theta_0$ plus a stochastic term. Clearly it is possible that $\rho(t) \to \infty$ as $t \to \infty$, not a very satisfactory property for a zero entry equilibrium to have. If $\gamma_1 \neq 0$, then (2.5) yields a long run equilibrium value of $\rho(t)$ equal to $\theta_0/-\gamma_1$.

[5] This is, in fact, the empirical model of Orr (1974), who proxies $\pi_{ip}(t)$ by a series of observable determinants (i.e., various measurable entry barriers); for a survey of this literature, see Geroski (1983).

that the fortunes of the leading firms in most industries are liable to be somewhat divorced from those of the industry as a whole. The profits of an enterprise operating in several industries is bound to move somewhat differently from those of specialized firms in any of those several industries. Any one of these empirical observations (see also Scott and Pascoe, 1986) is probably enough to raise the suspicion that the fortunes of various firms in particular industries may diverge from each other considerably, and this in turn leads one to suspect that the intraindustry variation in excess profits (or in the time paths of excess profits) may be more interesting to examine than interindustry variations in average industry profitability.

To address these concerns, it is necessary to isolate those movements in the $\rho(t)$ of firm i that firm i shares in common with other members of industry I from those movements in $\rho(t)$ that are i specific.[9] We have already distinguished the effects of two types of factors on $\rho(t)$: "systematic" factors summarized in $\rho(t-1)$ and "unsystematic" ones captured in $v(t)$. Independence between the $\rho(t)$ of firms i and j in the same industry I can also be expressed in these terms. Firms i and j respond to systematic forces in different ways if the value of their λ's differ and are buffeted by different sets of unsystematic factors if their $v(t)$'s have a zero covariance. If firms i and j are independent in either sense, then clearly an analysis of the profits of firm j will be of little help in predicting what happens to the profits of firm i. Since whatever is common in the movements of their profits over time must originate in common industrywide factors or forces, observing independence between the profits of firms i and j would lead one to conclude that "industry" effects are unimportant relative to "firm specific effects."

To make the discussion more precise, we need to extend the model of Section III to include both firm specific and industrywide determinants of profit dynamics. The procedure that we shall follow is to separate $\rho(t)$ into firm specific and industrywide components and then to model each. Let $\pi(i, t)$ be firm i's profit at time t, let $\pi p(t)$ be the common long run competitive return for all firms in all industries, let $\pi(I, t)$ be the profits on average across all members of firm i's industry I at time t, and define $\rho(i, t) \equiv \pi(i, t) - \pi(I, t)$ and $\rho(I, t) \equiv \pi(I, t) - \pi p(t)$. Clearly, $\rho(t) \equiv \rho(i, t) + \rho(I, t)$. There are two types of systematic forces that affect i's

---

[9] Although developed independently, the spirit of the technique to be discussed shares much in common with that of Schmalensee (1985). He makes an analysis of variance across firms in a given year to sort out firm and industry effects in much the same way that we shall analyze the covariance in movements of $\rho(t)$ over time. In view of the preceding arguments in the text, it is worth recording that Schmalensee found industry effects to be very important.

profits: "entry," $E_I(t)$, which affects all firms i in industry I (although perhaps to differing degrees), and "mobility" $M_i(t)$, which affects only firm i and no others in industry I. Thus, should firm i earn positive excess returns, both industry I as a whole as well as i's niche within I in particular will become attractive to other firms. Entry forces are those attracted to industry I in general, and although possibly attracted only by i's excess returns, they affect all firms to some greater or lesser degree. Mobility is the activity both within and outside industry i that is attracted to and affects only i's market niche or strategic position. As before, both entry and mobility are to be thought of as latent variables.

The model of $\rho(I, t)$ is similar to that discussed in Section III, although now the two equations refer to a "representative," or average, member of industry I and not to firm i. Profits on average are affected by entry,

$$\Delta\rho(I, t) = \alpha_I E_I(t) + \phi\rho(I, t-1) + \mu_I(t), \tag{2.8}$$

and entry into the industry as a whole is related to average profits,

$$E_I(t) = \beta_I \rho(I, t-1) + \epsilon_I(t). \tag{2.9}$$

Movements in $\rho(i, t)$ are slightly more complex. Entry is likely to affect i's profits relative to the average and may do so to a different degree for firms i and j. Furthermore, mobility into i's niche will also affect $\rho(i, t)$. Putting both factors together,

$$\Delta\rho(i, t) = \alpha_i M_i(t) + \gamma_i E_I(t) + \phi_i \rho(i, t-1) - \mu_i(t). \tag{2.10}$$

Finally, mobility, like entry, is attracted by excess profits, and this yields

$$M_i(t) = \beta_i \rho(i, t-1) + \epsilon_i(t), \tag{2.11}$$

where $\alpha_I, \phi_i, \alpha_i, \phi_I, \gamma_i < 0$ and $\beta_i, \beta_I > 0$.

Taking entry and mobility to be latent requires transforming the structural model (2.8)–(2.11) into a reduced form analogous to (2.7). Combining (2.10) and (2.11) yields

$$\rho(i, t) = (1 + \alpha_i \beta_i + \phi_i)\rho(i, t-1) + \gamma_i E_I(t) + \mu_i(t) + \alpha_i \epsilon_i. \tag{2.12}$$

Substituting (2.9) into (2.12) yields

$$\rho(i, t) = (1 + \alpha_1 \beta_i + \phi_i)\rho(i, t-1) + \mu_i(t)$$
$$+ \alpha_i \epsilon_i + \gamma_i \beta_I \rho(I, t-1) + \gamma_i \epsilon_I(t), \tag{2.13}$$

and (2.8) and (2.9) together yield

$$\rho(I, t) = (1 + \alpha_I \beta_I + \phi_I)\rho(I, t-1) + \alpha_I \epsilon_I(t) + \mu_I(t). \tag{2.14}$$

Finally, since $\rho(t) \equiv \rho(i, t) + \rho(I, t)$, (2.13) and (2.14) can be added together, producing

$$\rho(t) = \Gamma_0 + \Gamma_1 \rho(i, t-1) + \Gamma_2 \rho(I, t-1) + \omega(i, t), \tag{2.15}$$

where Γ_0 is the expected value of the quantity

$$\{\mu_i(t) + \alpha_i \epsilon_i(t) + \mu_I(t) + (\gamma_i + \alpha_I) \epsilon_I(t)\},$$

$\Gamma_1 \equiv (1 + \alpha_i \beta_i + \phi_i)$, $\Gamma_2 \equiv (1 + \alpha_I \beta_I + \phi_I + \gamma_i \beta_I)$, and $\omega(i, t)$ is a zero-mean, white noise residual equal to the sum of the residuals in (2.13) and (2.14) less their means. Equation (2.15) is the desired generalization of (2.7).

To interpret (2.15), it is useful to consider two extreme cases: first, where only firm specific factors are important and, second, where firm specific factors are unimportant. If only firm specific factors matter and firm i's fortunes are divorced from those of its rivals, then $\gamma_i = 0$ and (2.10) and (2.11) jointly yield a first order autoregression in $\rho(i, t)$. Further, in this case, $\mu_i(t)$ will be uncorrelated to $\mu_j(t)$. Clearly, in these circumstances there is no information in the movements of firm j's profits to use in predicting movements in i's profits. In this sense, "industry effects" are unimportant, and there is no fundamental link between the fortunes of rival firms i and j. By contrast, if $\gamma_i = \gamma$ for all i, then all firms are equally affected by entry and Γ_2 takes a common value across firms. This common response to the common variable $\rho(I, t-1)$ links together movements in the profits of firms i and j to some degree and makes observations of $\pi(j, t)$ useful in predicting $\pi(i, t)$. If, in addition, the $\mu_i(t)$ are correlated within industry I or if Γ_1 is common to all firms i in I (i.e., if α_i, β_i, and ϕ_i take common, industrywide values, as would be the case in a homogeneous goods industry), then the usefulness of $\pi(j, t)$ for predicting $\pi(i, t)$ is enhanced. In this sense, the industry "matters," and various exogenous and endogenous factors have a common, broad impact on the fortunes of rival firms.

Thus, (2.15) is a simple vehicle that can be used to analyze the independence in the fortunes of firm i from those of its fellow industry members (for further details, see the Appendix). If all firms display profits that follow a common dynamic motion and move toward similar long run equilibrium positions, then an analysis of a typical or average industry member is sufficient. Averaging across relatively homogeneous firms loses no essential information, and interindustry analysis is likely to be informative. However, should firm i's excess returns follow a different dynamic to other industry members (or take a different long run value, Γ_0), then it is clear that intraindustry variations in excess returns are as interesting and probably of as much importance as interindustry ones (dynamics aside) and that models like (2.1) should be generalized to allow both types of variation.

V   Three notions of "competition"

The goal of much work in industrial economics is the evaluation of just how competitive markets are. In view of its antecedents, it is clear that (2.7) can be informative on this issue. What is interesting is that there are at least three distinct senses of the adjective "competitive" to which the parameters of (2.7) can be related. For simplicity, in what follows we shall take (2.7) to apply equally to all firms in any given industry, and we shall refer to values of α, λ, and δ_v^2 as if they described markets and not particular firms.

The conventional, *neoclassical* definition of "competition" is static. Competition is that equilibrium state that would prevail were entry free and firms price takers. The consequence, of course, is zero excess profits. It is usual to argue that a market is competitive not so much if it is actually in this state as if it is capable of reaching this state in the long run. Either way, competition, in this sense, requires that $\alpha = 0$. There are, however, other notions of competition in the literature. A rather different, more *classical* (or Austrian) view is less tied to particular states and views competition as a process with certain characteristics (principally free entry). To be sure, it would generally be expected that this process converged to something like the neoclassical competitive state, but the stress of this tradition is very much on the properties of the process and not on the characteristics of the final state. A classically competitive process is one in which the forces of entry are strongly and rapidly attracted by excess profits (i.e., ϕ is "large") and in which they rapidly bid these profits away (i.e., γ_0 is large in absolute value). Adding the presumption that the process is stable leads one to identify competition by the parameter value $\lambda = 0$. Thus, a test of whether competition in the neoclassical sense prevails is a test of the properties of the long run steady state of (2.7), whereas a test of whether a competition in the classical sense prevails amounts to a test of whether the market process is stable and quick.[10]

---

[10] The test $\lambda = 0$ is difficult to make since the classically competitive state is strictly identified only by a boundary value in the parameter space [an analogous problem exists in the disequilibrium econometrics literature; cf. Quandt (1978) and, for a survey, Quandt (1982)]. In fact, one would be happy to call a market competitive for λ "sufficiently close" to zero, and this suggests that one might try to divide the parameter space $\lambda \in [0, 1]$ into two regions, corresponding to what one might think is "reasonably" or "workably competitive" and what is not. This requires using a priori information in the following manner. Suppose one thought that in a truly competitive market excess profits on the order of 10% would be reduced to about 1% within three years. Since a starting value of ρ_1 is reduced to ρ_2 after T years when $\alpha = 0$ and $\lambda = (\rho_2/\rho_1)^{1/T}$ in (2.7), these orders of magnitude suggest $\lambda \leq 0.500$ might correspond to "reasonably competitive."

A third definition of competition that might attract interest is suggested by considering Simon's (1959, pp. 2–3) famous analogy:

> Suppose we were pouring some viscous liquid – molasses – into a bowl of very irregular shape. What would we need in order to make a theory of the shape molasses would take in the bowl?... With (the assumption that, under the force of gravity, it minimized the height of its centre of gravity), the equilibrium behavior of a perfectly adapting organism depends only on its goal and environment: it is otherwise completely independent of the internal properties of the organism.

One thinks of economic theory as describing the actions of agents and of competitive markets as those where the environment strongly and systematically constrains agents' choices and actions. However they make their choices and no matter what these are, economic natural selection in a competitive market ensures that only certain types of agents survive [Alchian (1950) and Winter (1964) are classic expositions and evaluations of this argument]. But this implies that the survivors we observe act as if they had no discretion; their actions are, in effect, completely determined by those forces that determine the market's dynamic motion and eventual equilibrium. It seems natural to call this an *ecological* definition of competition and to identify these discretion-eliminating market forces with the entry mechanism of equations (2.5) and (2.6). If, in (2.7), $v(t) = 0$ for all t, then movement in firm i's profits over time is completely described by α and λ. On the other hand, $v(t)$ contains the multitude of firm specific events, shocks, and innovations that operate on $\rho(t)$ independently of the fundamental market forces that α and λ reflect. If $v(t)$ is, on occasion, large, then it is clearly not enough to know only the nature of the firm's market environment if one wishes to accurately predict its profitability. Since $E\{v(t)\} = 0$ by construction, $\delta_v^2 = 0$ corresponds to a competitive state of affairs in an ecological sense. Regardless of the precise values of α and λ, all choices and outcomes are, in effect, determined exogenously to firms and independently of their idiosyncrasies if $\delta_v^2 = 0$. How market forces affect each firm may differ from firm to firm (i.e., α and λ may take firm specific values), but in an ecologically competitive market, the only thing that affects firms' profits are these market forces. That is to say, competitive behavior is predictable by outsiders who understand how markets operate.[11]

---

[11] The parameter $\delta_v^2 = 0$ is also a boundary value, thus creating testing problems analogous to those discussed in footnote 10. A reasonably informative procedure might be as follows. From (2.7), the model's prediction of $\rho(t)$ is $P\{\rho(t)\} = \alpha + \lambda\rho(t-1)$, and one might insist that a reasonably competitive ecological environment is one where the probability of prediction error was less than some specified amount, say, 2ζ, that is, where the likelihood that $|\rho(t) - P\{\rho(t)\}| > 2\zeta$ was less than 5% for some $\zeta > 0$ [i.e., one's predictions

It is worth closing this section with a brief remark on the somewhat different notion of "persistence" and on its relation to notions of competition. It is natural to measure the persistence l of $\rho(t)$ as the likelihood that $\rho(t) > 0$ given that $\rho(t-1)$ takes some value $\bar{\rho} > 0$. That is,

$$l \equiv \text{Prob}\{\rho(t) > 0 \mid \rho(t-1) = \bar{\rho}\}. \tag{2.16}$$

This amounts to defining l as the probability that $v(t) > \bar{v} \equiv -\alpha - \lambda\bar{\rho}$, and since $v(t)$ is normally distributed with density function $\phi(v)$, it follows that

$$l = \int_{\bar{v}}^{\infty} \phi(v)\, dv = 1 - \Phi\frac{\bar{v}}{\delta v}, \tag{2.17}$$

where $\phi(v)$ is the standard normal cumulative distribution function (e.g., Mood, Graybill, and Boes, 1974, p. 110, Theorem 14). Since $\bar{v} = 0 \Rightarrow l = 0.5$, profits are "persistent" if l is "sufficiently" above that value. Simple calculations reveal that l, the likelihood of positive profits persisting, rises with α, λ, and $\bar{\rho}$ and rises (falls) with δ_v if $\bar{v} > 0$ ($\bar{v} < 0$).

The two points to draw from this argument are the following. First, persistence is a notion that cannot be identified with any one parameter taken alone (as was the case with the different notions of competition); rather, it depends on all three parameters in a precise way. Second, a situation of persistent positive profits is not inconsistent with competition prevailing in any of the three senses noted. The probability $l > 0.5$ can arise if $\alpha = 0$ but $\lambda = 1$, $\alpha \neq 0$ but $\lambda = 0$, or $\alpha, \lambda \neq 0$ but $\delta_v^2 = 0$, respectively. It follows that whereas competition and departures from it can be given a normative evaluation, this is less clearly true for persistence. That firm i's profits are persistently high is interesting as a statement of fact and as a summary of the forces of market dynamics as they affect firm i; as a normative statement relating to notions of competition, it is not very compelling unless one can explain why they are persistently high.

VI   Some final remarks

In this chapter we have been concerned to make a case for extending familiar static structure–performance models to look at market dynamics. Of the many arguments that one might advance in support of this

of $\rho(t)$ has a 95% chance of being within 2ζ of $P\{\rho(t)\}$, the prediction given by the competitive model]. Since $\rho(t) - P\{\rho(t)\}$ is normally distributed with variance δ_v^2, clearly if $\sigma_v^2 \leq \zeta^2$, the market process under consideration is reasonably competitive. Thus, if one thought that one ought to expect a less than 5% chance of observing $|\rho(t) - P\{\rho(t)\}| > 0.10$ (which is surely a huge error, for, practically speaking, $\rho(t) \in [0, 0.5]$), then $\zeta^2 = 0.025$ is the appropriate cutoff point.

enterprise, we have focused on those that emerge from the econometric problems created by omitting consideration of disequilibrium dynamics in static cross-sectional models and those that arise from antitrust policies that are concerned as much with the persistence of monopoly power as with its existence. Both lines of argument lead one to think that examining the pattern and speed of disequilibrium dynamics is a natural next step for empirical work in this tradition.

One of several difficulties that such work is likely to present arises from the fact that many of the factors to which firms respond are difficult to observe or, what is worse, are fundamentally unobservable. Indeed, in many ways, entry is the quintessential latent variable. The mere threat of entry can lead actual competitors to take strategic actions that both drive profits toward competitive levels and, at the same time, discourage potential entrants from actually entering. Any structural model that attempts to track profit dynamics using observed actual entry flows runs the risk of omitting an important dynamic force whose nonappearance is endogenous to the process. Consideration of this problem has led us to examine the use of reduced form models to track market dynamics, and we have concentrated here on a particularly simple model in which the only observable variable is profits. This reduced form model was derived from an unsophisticated structural model relating profits and entry. The two-equation structural model transforms itself into an autoregression in profits, with parameters that cast light on both the speed of the competitive process and the character of its long run equilibrium. A relatively straightforward variant of the model enables one to assess the extent to which rival firms within industries attract and experience fundamentally different dynamic forces. This, in turn, casts light on the persistence of profitability differences between firms and on whether analyzing interindustry variations in average profitability omits interesting information on their intraindustry variability.

It is natural to close a polemic with an exhortation, and to that end, we shall conclude by briefly sketching three extensions to the basic methodology discussed in this chapter. These are concerned with asymmetry, complexity, and further information.

The structural model (2.5)–(2.6) implicitly assumes that entry, $E(t) > 0$, and exit, $E(t) < 0$, are symmetric; that is, that any level of excess returns, $\bar{\rho}(t) \equiv \rho(t) - \rho^*$, produces a volume of entry equal to $\phi\bar{\rho}(t)$ if $\bar{\rho}(t) > 0$ and equal to $-\phi\bar{\rho}(t)$ if $\bar{\rho}(t) < 0$. However, it is conceivable that the size and timing of the response of agents to positive excess returns may differ from their response to negative excess returns (if only because different agents are likely to be involved) and that the effect of entry and exit on $\rho(t)$ may differ in the short and/or long run. Allowing asymmetric effects essentially transforms the simple autoregression (2.7) into one with a time-varying parameter. Thinking of λ as the "response" of the system to excess returns $\rho(t-1)$, one wishes to allow the response to positive excess returns λ^ρ to differ from the response to negative excess returns λ^N. Constructing an indicator variable,

$$I(t) = \begin{cases} 1 & \text{if } \rho(t-1) \geq 0, \\ 0 & \text{if } \rho(t-1) < 0, \end{cases} \tag{2.18}$$

the appropriate generalization of (2.7) is

$$\rho(t) = \alpha + \{\lambda^N + (\lambda^\rho - \lambda^N) I(t)\} \rho(t-1) + v(t). \tag{2.19}$$

Estimates of (2.19) yield all the information produced by (2.7) plus, in addition, a test of the assumption of symmetry in response.

Equation (2.5) implicitly assumes that entry responds relatively rapidly to excess returns and, in particular, that the entry response mechanism only has a one-period memory. Similarly, the effects of entry at any date t in equation (2.6) are assumed to persist for only the duration of the period in which they occur. The two assumptions together are responsible for the simple one-period autoregressive structure of (2.7). One of the less immediate consequences of this pair of assumptions is that they impose a structure of gradual, monotonic convergence to equilibrium (if $0 \leq \lambda \leq 1$). Yet entry is potentially a destabilizing force, and extended postentry price wars are likely to generate an overshooting of equilibria in the first instance. Hence, it is natural to specify more carefully and extensively the nature and the timing of the response of entry to excess profits as well as to explore the timing of its effects. Work in either direction will clearly complicate the lag structure of the reduced form (2.7), producing more complex autoregressive structures. Thus, estimating a generalization of (2.7) such as

$$\rho(t) = \alpha + \sum_{l=1}^{L} \lambda_l \rho(t-l) + v(t) \tag{2.20}$$

will yield all the information generated by (2.7) plus, in addition, information on the incidence over time of the causes and consequences of entry.

Finally, and most speculatively, it is natural to contemplate bringing more information to bear on the analysis of market dynamics. Focusing only on profits produces a fairly simple reduced form but sacrifices much information. The obvious extension of the model is to examine the interdependent dynamic motion of both profits and market structure (e.g., industry concentration). A comparison between the two is likely to be revealing because profits are affected by both actual and potential entry, but market structure is affected only by actual entry. This, in turn, implies that differences in their dynamic motion might be attributable to the unobservable, potential entry. Such a comparison may also give some indication of the relative size of actual and potential entry flows and thus of the extent to which persistent monopoly positions imply persistent monopoly power.

Appendix

One can develop a more precise feel for the relative importance of firms and industry effects by examining the extent to which (2.15) exhibits common parameters when applied to individual members i of some industry I. To simplify the exposition, consider an industry I with two members, $i = 1, 2$. A regression model of (2.15) is a system

$$\begin{aligned}
\rho_1(t) &= \Gamma_0^1 + \Gamma_1^1 \rho(1, t-1) + \Gamma_2^1 \rho(I, t-1) + \omega(1, t), \\
\rho_2(t) &= \Gamma_0^2 + \Gamma_1^2 \rho(2, t-2) + \Gamma_2^2 \rho(I, t-1) + \omega(2, t),
\end{aligned} \tag{2.21}$$

where $\eta(i, t) \equiv \Gamma_0^i + \omega(i, t)$, and so $\omega(i, t)$ is a zero-mean white noise stochastic process. Clearly, $\rho_1(t)$ and $\rho_2(t)$ are not independent as they share a common term, $v(I, t)$. This interdependence is reflected in a nonzero covariance between $\omega(1, t)$ and $\omega(2, t)$ in (2.21). There are two restrictions that weaken even this limited interdependence between $\rho_1(t)$ and $\rho_2(t)$. First, it may be that there are virtually no unsystematic factors (like macroeconomic events or other industrywide changes unrelated to entry) that have a common effect on both $\rho_1(t)$ and $\rho_2(t)$. This corresponds to a situation in which the two streams of profits satisfy

$$\text{equation (2.21)} \quad \text{plus} \quad \text{cov}[\omega(1, t), \omega(2, t)] = 0. \tag{2.22}$$

Second, the response of $\rho_1(t)$ and $\rho_2(t)$ to industrywide factors $\rho(I, t-1)$ may be the same as their response to firm specific factors $\rho(i, t-1)$, yielding

$$\text{equation (2.22)} \quad \text{plus} \quad \Gamma_1^i = \Gamma_2^i. \tag{2.23}$$

These two restrictions jointly reduce (2.21) to a first order autoregression in $\rho(t)$ like (2.7) and imply that $\pi_i(t)$ moves with reference only to $\pi \rho(t)$ and not to $\pi_I(t)$. In this situation, firm i's profits follow a dynamic path truly independent of those rivals in I, and so information about the movement in profits of any of i's rivals will not prove helpful in predicting movements in i's own profits.

By contrast, if mobility barriers are low, then firms will respond in a similar fashion to the competitive forces that affect them. The restriction that $\gamma_i = \gamma$ implies that entry affects all industry members in the same way, so that all the $\rho(t)$ react in a similar fashion to the common value $\rho(I, t-1)$. In this case, (2.21) becomes equation (2.21)   plus $\Gamma_1^i = \Gamma_2^i$. $\hspace{3cm}$ (2.24)

If mobility affects all firms in I to the same degree, then firms will respond to firm specific forces in the same manner. This situation can be captured with restrictions on (2.21) that transform it into

equation (2.24)   plus $\Gamma_1 = \Gamma_2$. $\hspace{3cm}$ (2.25)

Like (2.23), (2.25) reduces (2.21) to a first order autoregression in $\rho(t)$ analogous to (2.7). However, unlike (2.23), *the system* (2.25) models individual firms as experiencing common effects from the occurrence of unsystematic factors $(\text{cov}[\omega(1, t), \omega(2, t)] \neq 0)$ and as responding in identical fashion the systematic forces captured by $\rho(t-1)$. If, in addition to (2.21), $\Gamma_0^i = \Gamma_0$, then individual firms i in industry I have profits that differ only randomly. In this case, aggregation of (2.25) to industry level or application of (2.7) to a representative firm involves no sacrifice in information. Further, information on movements in the profits of any of i's own rivals will be useful in predicting movements in i's profits.

Thus, in models (2.21)–(2.23) "industry effects" are relatively unimportant, whereas in (2.24)–(2.25), the industry "matters." Firms in industries classified in the first three models exhibit substantial firm specificity in their dynamics of a degree that differs slightly between (2.21), (2.22), and (2.23). On the other hand, firms in industries classified in the second three models display a certain homogeneity within industries, the degree of which also varies slightly between (2.24) and (2.25).

CHAPTER 3

The persistence of profits in the United States

DENNIS C. MUELLER

This chapter extends the recent work of the author on company profitability in the long run (1986). We adopt a slightly different methodology in the present work to conform to the other studies in this volume. We begin by briefly reviewing this methodology.

I   Intertemporal patterns of profitability

Assume that firm i's return on capital in year t, π_{it}, is composed potentially of three components: (1) a competitive return c common to all companies; (2) a permanent rent r_i specific to firm i, which could be a premium for risk; and (3) a short run rent s_{it} with zero expected value:

$$\pi_{it} = c + r_i + s_{it}. \tag{3.1}$$

For a t sufficiently long s_{it} might be assumed to have mean zero and constant variance over time, and the hypothesis that competition eventually drives all profit rates to a common normal level could be tested simply by comparing mean profit rates across firms to see whether they are significantly different from one another, given their intertemporal variances.

Such a test would require, if t is measured in years, that any short run rents earned this year are independent of rents earned last year. A more reasonable assumption concerning the s_{it} is that they are intertemporally related but converge on zero. Let s_{it} be defined by

$$s_{it} = \lambda s_{it-1} + u_{it}, \tag{3.2}$$

where $0 < \lambda < 1$ and the u_{it} are distributed $N(0, \sigma^2)$. Assuming equation (3.2) holds in every period, it can be used to remove s_{it} from (3.1) to obtain

$$\pi_{it} = (1 - \lambda)(c + r_i) + \lambda \pi_{it-1} + u_{it}. \tag{3.3}$$

Financial support for this research was received from the Thyssen Foundation of West Germany. Talat Mahmood and Klaus Ristan helped with the calculations. Helpful comments on an earlier draft were received from Paul Geroski.

Letting $\hat{\alpha}_i$ and $\hat{\lambda}_i$ be the estimates from the autoregressive equation

$$\pi_{it} = \hat{\alpha}_i + \hat{\lambda}_i \pi_{it-1} + u_{it}, \tag{3.4}$$

one derives an estimate of the long run projected profits of firm i, π_{ip}, as

$$\hat{\pi}_{ip} = \frac{\hat{\alpha}_i}{1 - \hat{\lambda}_i}. \tag{3.5}$$

A test of the hypothesis that competition drives all profit rates to a common competitive level would be to test whether the $\hat{\pi}_{ip}$ differ significantly across firms. Were no significant differences found, one would accept the hypothesis that all long run rents r_i are zero.

Even if one were to accept that hypothesis, however, one might be interested in examining the magnitude of the $\hat{\lambda}_i$'s. The bigger $\hat{\lambda}_i$ is, the slower short run rents erode, and the more a firm's profits constitute a slowly moving average around $c + r_i$. To see the difference between $\hat{\pi}_{ip}$ and $\hat{\lambda}$ more clearly, consider the following two firms. Firm 1 has a very high $\hat{\pi}_{ip}$, but $\hat{\lambda} = 0$; firm 2's $\hat{\pi}_{ip}$ equals the competitive rate of return c, but its λ is very large, say, 0.9. The implications would be that firm 1 earns substantial permanent rents equal to $\pi_{ip} - c$ but that any short run rents it experiences are expected to disappear within a year. The second firm's short run rents are highly correlated, however, and induce moving averages of lengthy periodicity. But they cycle around and converge upon the competitive return. In the long run, it is this return toward which 2's dampening cycle is moving.

II   Empirical estimates: persistence of profits

We test for the existence of persistent differences in profitability using a sample of 551 manufacturing firms drawn from the surveys of the 1,000 largest firms in 1950 and 1972 conducted by the Federal Trade Commission (FTC).[1] Basically any firm from either of these lists for which there is complete financial data over the 23-year period is included in the sample. The sample includes all companies satisfying this criterion regardless of the extent of their merger activity and thus includes many firms with radically different product structures in 1972 than they possessed in 1950, a point to which we shall return.

We define a company's return on capital as its profits net of taxes and gross of interest divided by total assets. We use a net-of-tax definition of profits on the assumption that the convergence of profits to the competitive

---

[1] Data were taken from Standard & Poor's COMPUSTAT and *Moody's Industrial Manual*. For definitions of variables used and a list of sample firms, see Mueller (1986).

Table 3.1. *Summary of results from autoregressive profits equations,* $\pi_{it} = \hat{\alpha}_i + \hat{\lambda}_i \pi_{it-1} + u_{it}$, $\hat{\pi}_{ip} = \hat{\alpha}_i / (1 - \hat{\lambda}_i)$

	Mean	Mean standard error	Minimum	Maximum
$\hat{\pi}_{ip}$	0.002	0.017	-0.099	0.193
$\hat{\lambda}$	0.183	0.210	-0.262	0.935
$\bar{R}^2$	0.052	—	-0.062	0.855

return is driven by the exit and entry of other firms and that this entry and exit respond to after tax profit levels.

Although we have modeled the competitive return c as if it were a constant, it may vary over time as business cycle factors and long run trends raise and lower the average performance of firms in the economy. To allow for these common intertemporal patterns, we take each firm's annual profit rate as a deviation from the sample mean for that year. In effect, we assume that the relationship between the competitive return c and the average return on capital is invariant over time. Later we shall also allow for firm and industry differences in c due to risk.

Table 3.1 summarizes the results for the estimations of equation (3.4) for the 551 firms. Starting with the bottom row, we see that the average fit to the autoregressive equation was rather weak, with a mean $\bar{R}^2$ of only 0.052. Thus, the transitory component of a firm's profit rate would not seem to require more than a year to be eliminated in many cases. A similar conclusion is implied by the figures for $\hat{\lambda}$. On average only 18 percent of any deviation from last year's sample mean is expected to reoccur this year.[2] The distribution of $\hat{\lambda}$'s is obviously positively skewed, however, with the mean $\hat{\lambda}$ pulled down by the negative $\hat{\lambda}$'s. Of the latter, *none* of the 122 $\hat{\lambda}$'s that were negative had a value for $|\hat{\lambda}| > 1.72$ times its standard error (the critical value for a two-tailed, 10 percent level test). Thus, the $\hat{\lambda}$'s for these firms are consistent with the hypothesis that the short run rents of these firms vary independently over time. Of the $\hat{\lambda}$'s greater than zero, on the other hand, 120 exceeded their standard errors by more than a factor of 1.72. This figure is more than four times the 28 one expects under a 5 percent level, one-tailed test if all $\hat{\lambda}$'s are zero, but random factors

2 In Mueller (1986) firm profitability was measured as a deviation from sample mean divided by the sample mean. This definition of π_{it} gave mean $\hat{\lambda}$'s of more than double those reported here.

generate significant coefficients in 5 percent of the equations. Thus, (3.4) does describe the pattern of profits over time for a significant fraction of companies.

The fairly low mean value for $\hat{\lambda}$ across the sample combined with almost 80 percent of the $\hat{\lambda}$'s being insignificantly different from zero (5 percent, one-tailed test) draws our attention to the long run projected returns for the firms.[3] Of these, 274 exceed their standard errors by a factor of more than 1.72, the critical value for a 10 percent, two-tailed test.[4] Thus, almost half of the firms in the sample are projected to earn long run returns significantly different from the average firm in the sample. Assuming some positive rents exist due to market power, the sample mean should exceed c, however. The relevant question is really, what fraction of firms have profit rates significantly different from c, the competitive return on capital?

We answer this question in two ways. First, note that if all $\hat{\pi}_{ip}$ equal a common c, all will equal one another. The hypothesis that all $\hat{\pi}_{ip}$ converge to a common, competitive c can thus be tested by seeing whether restricting all firms to have the same $\hat{\pi}_{ip}$ results in a significant increase in the sum of squared residuals from the unconstrained estimates. It does. The F-statistic with (551, 11,020) degrees of freedom is 2.423, considerably above the critical value of 1.15 for a 1 percent level significance test.

An alternative way to approach the question, and one that sheds some light on the value of c, employs the following logic. Most firms in a competitive economy should either have returns on capital close to the competitive return or be converging on it. Thus, the number of $\hat{\pi}_{ip}$'s significantly different from c should be less than for any other arbitrarily chosen benchmark return on capital. We thus did a search for c over the range -0.020 to $+0.010$ at 0.001 intervals to find that return from which the minimum number of $\hat{\pi}_{ip}$'s was significantly different (10 percent, two-tailed test). Three values (-0.016, -0.014, and -0.012) all had the minimum number of significantly different $\hat{\pi}_{ip}$'s, 259. The intervening numbers, -0.015 and -0.013, had 262 and 260 significantly different $\hat{\pi}_{ip}$'s, respectively. The number of significantly different $\hat{\pi}_{ip}$'s rises steadily as one moves away from -0.016 and -0.012 in either direction, reaching 273 at -0.020 and 323 at 0.010. Thus, it seems reasonable to conclude, by the logic sketched in the preceding, that c falls in the range -0.016 to -0.012 with -0.014 being a good point estimate. The competitive return on capital is then 0.014 below the average, which for the 23-year period 1950–72 was 0.076. The competitive return on capital is thus estimated to

---

[3] Note that all of the $\hat{\lambda}$'s fall between -1 and 1, implying convergence on the $\hat{\pi}_{ip}$.

[4] Since π_{ip} is a ratio of two estimated parameters, its standard error must be calculated from the covariance matrix of the coefficients (Kmenta, 1971, pp. 442–8).

Table 3.2. *The magnitude of persistent profit rate differences with adjustment for mergers*

Equation	Interest	π_{50}	$\pi_{50}/(1+\text{GAQ})$	$\bar{R}^2$
1	−0.0009	0.542	—	0.317
	1.25	15.52		
2	−0.0009	—	0.691	0.334
	1.33		16.15	

Notes: Dependent variable: $\hat{\pi}_p$. t values under coefficients.

be 18 percent below the average return on capital, an estimate that is quite close to the lower of the two estimates made before using a totally different logical argument (Mueller, 1986, ch. 2).

If all π_{ip}'s equaled c, one would expect 55 $\hat{\pi}_{ip}$'s to differ from c by more than 1.72 times these standard errors (the critical value for a 10 percent level, two-tailed test) assuming a normal distribution around c. The distribution of $\hat{\pi}_{ip}$ around c is not normal; rather it is positively skewed. Nevertheless, the number of $\hat{\pi}_{ip}$ differing from c by more than 1.72 times these standard errors, 259, seems sufficiently more than 55 to allow us to conclude that there exists a sizeable number of firms with nonzero permanent rents. Whereas short run rents appear to erode quite quickly for most firms, there exist significant differences in long run rents across firms.

III The size of the rents

Although the results of the previous section reject the hypothesis that the returns on assets of all firms converge on a common competitive return, the qualitative nature of the test conceals the magnitude of the differences in $\hat{\pi}_{ip}$ across firms. How much of the deviation in profit rates observed at any point in time is permanent and how much is transitory? To answer these questions, we regress $\hat{\pi}_{ip}$ back onto the deviation of each firm's profit rate from the sample mean averaged over the initial three years of the time period, π_{50}.[5] Equation 1 in Table 3.2 states that over 50 percent of any deviation from the sample average in those first three years is projected to persist indefinitely.

[5] Since the dependent variable is itself a parameter, each equation is estimated using a form of generalized least squares (GLS) in which each observation is weighted by the standard error of π_p. The coefficient on the intercept is thus the coefficient on $1/\sigma_{\pi_p}$. For a discussion of this procedure, see Saxonhouse (1976).

IV   An adjustment for mergers

As noted in Section II, firms from the 1,000 largest manufacturing companies' lists of 1950 and 1972 are included in the sample if complete accounting data are available regardless of the extent of their merger activity. Mergers have an averaging effect on corporate profitability, however, which conceals the extent to which a firm's returns in a given line of business persistently differ from the returns of other firms. This averaging effect ensues because firms with below average returns are more likely to acquire companies with profit rates above their own, whereas firms with above normal returns are more likely to acquire companies with returns below their own. Thus, mergers should raise the profit rates of below average profit firms and lower the rates of above average profit companies. Moreover, when the acquired company's assets are entered into the acquiring company's books at the acquired firm's purchase price, any long run rents the acquired firm was earning should be capitalized into the purchase price, and its return on these assets equals the normal return on capital. Thus, the long run returns of a company are driven toward the normal return in direct proportion to the assets it acquires.

To allow for the averaging effect of mergers, the assets a firm acquired in year t were divided by its assets at the beginning of t and cumulated over the 23-year sample period. This summation, GAQ, measures the relative growth in the firm's assets from acquisitions. Now assume that r is the fraction of the deviation from the sample mean return observed in 1950–2, which will persist indefinitely. Assume further that all of the acquired assets have an average return equal to the sample mean. The expected return on the assets after mergers, r^*, is then a weighted sum of the return on the initial assets (r) and on the acquired assets (zero) with weights 1 and GAQ. That is,

$$r^* = \frac{r \cdot 1 + \text{GAQ} \cdot 0}{1 + \text{GAQ}}. \tag{3.6}$$

We can then obtain an estimate of r, the fraction of π_{50} that persists indefinitely, by regressing $\hat{\pi}_p$ on $\pi_{50}/(1 + \text{GAQ})$. The coefficient on this weighted π_{50} variable is the fraction of π_{50} projected to persist indefinitely when GAQ is zero. As GAQ increases, the estimated fraction of the initial deviation of a firm's profit rate that persists is driven to zero.

Equation 2 in Table 3.2 presents the results when π_{50} is weighted by $1/(1 + \text{GAQ})$. The coefficient on π_{50} is substantially higher, implying a permanent deviation in a company's profit rate from the sample average of 69.1 percent of that observed in 1950–2. The fit to the data is also improved. Had no mergers taken place between 1950 and 1972, we estimate that 69.1 percent of the profit differences that existed in 1950–2 would have persisted indefinitely. The averaging effect of mergers conceals to a considerable degree the extent to which profit rate differences across firm lines of business persist.

V   A firm effects model of profitability

We have established that there are significant differences in the long run profit rates of companies. What accounts for these differences?

To explain them, we develop a model that allows for both firm specific differences in efficiency and product quality and industry differences in the degree of cooperation among firms. Thus, we employ a model that incorporates both the "new" and the "old" learnings regarding market structure and profit performance.

Let i's demand schedule be approximated by the linear function

$$p_i = a_i - bx_i - b\sigma \sum_{j \neq i} x_j, \tag{3.7}$$

where p_i is i's price, x_i is output, and σ is an index of product differentiation running from zero (a pure monopolist) to 1.0 (a homogeneous product). The a_i capture quality differences across firms. The higher a_i, the more buyers are willing to pay for each unit of output due, presumably, to the superior quality they associate with the firm's product. Efficiency differences are represented by firm specific unit costs c_i. Cooperation among sellers is modeled by assuming that each seller maximizes an objective function equal to its profits and a weighted sum of the profits of the other firms in the industry[6]:

$$o_i = \pi_i + \theta \sum_{j \neq i} \pi_j, \qquad \pi_i = (p_i - c_i)x_i. \tag{3.8}$$

The weight placed on the other firms' profits parameterizes cooperation; $\theta = 1$ implies perfect collusion, $\theta = 0$ Cournot independence, and $\theta < 0$ rivalry. Maximizing (3.8) with respect to x_i and a little algebra yields

$$\frac{\pi_i}{S_i} \simeq \frac{1}{\eta}\left(\frac{m_i}{\sigma} - m_i\theta + \theta\right), \tag{3.9}$$

where S_i is i's sales, m_i its market share, and η the industry demand elasticity.

Following in the tradition of the industrial organization literature, we shall assume that the degree of cooperation is dependent on the four-firm

---

[6] This method of modeling oligopolistic interaction has been employed by Cyert and De-Groot (1973), Kuenne (1974), Shubik (1980), and Long (1982).

concentration ratio C_4. No consensus exists as to what the functional form relating θ and C_4 is, so let us assume that whatever the true functional form is, it can be approximated by the quadratic

$$\theta = a + bC_4 + cC_4^2.$$ (3.10)

The product differentiation parameter σ must range between zero and 1. It seems reasonable to assume that the products of an industry with no advertising and inventive activity are homogeneous and that those for industries with substantial advertising and inventive activity are differentiated. Thus, we seek a functional form for σ that takes on the value 1 when advertising and inventive activity are zero and falls as these activities increase in importance. A relatively simple functional form having this property, with ADV being the industry advertising-to-sales ratio and PAT industry patents over sales, is

$$\sigma = \frac{d}{d + e\text{ADV} + f\text{PAT}}.$$ (3.11)

Experimentation with more complicated functional forms for (3.11) did not produce a superior fit to the data.

Substitution from (3.10) and (3.11) into (3.9) yields[7]

$$\frac{\pi_i}{S_i} = \frac{1}{\eta}\left(a + (1-a)m_i + b(1-m_i)C_4 + c(1-m_i)C_4^2 \right.$$

$$\left. + \frac{d}{e}m_i\text{ADV} + \frac{d}{f}m_i\text{PAT}\right).$$ (3.12)

Estimates of (3.12) using an estimate of the projected profits-to-sales ratio as dependent variable and two alternative measures of demand elasticities as right hand side weights led to a performance of the model similar but slightly inferior to that when the projected return on assets, $\hat{\pi}_{ip}$, is the dependent variable and all η are assumed equal.[8] We report only the results for these regressions. Variables are defined in the appendix.

Table 3.3, row 1, contains the results from estimating (3.12). The first two coefficients can be used to solve for a and the assumed constant η. It is reasonable to assume that a from (3.10) is nonpositive; that is, an unconcentrated industry achieves at best a Cournot equilibrium. The estimate of a/η is negative (η is defined to be positive). But when one uses the intercept and the coefficient on m to solve for a and η, the latter takes on a value of over 100. Market share m appears in every term, and there would appear to be collinearity among the terms, driving the coefficient

[7] For details of the deviation, see Mueller (1986, ch. 4).
[8] Estimates using a slightly different measure of $\hat{\pi}_{ip}$ are presented in Mueller (1986, ch. 4).

Table 3.3. *Results from firm effect model* ($n = 551$)

Equation	Intercept	m	$(1-m)C_4$	$(1-m)C_4^2$	$mADV$	$mPAT$	AmC_4	AmC_4^2	β	$\sigma_{\hat{\pi}_p}$	LG	$\pi_{50}/(1+GAQ)$	GAQ	$\bar{R}^2$	n
1	-0.022	0.030	0.063	-0.079	0.023	0.067								0.122	551
	2.45	1.52	1.52	1.71	4.79	2.86									
2	-0.014	-0.005	0.058	0.010	0.041	0.060	0.014	-0.031						0.134	551
	1.55	0.22	0.13	0.19	4.45	2.59	2.59	2.99							
3	-0.016	-0.002	0.014	—	0.041	0.060	0.014	-0.030						0.136	551
	3.81	0.13	1.29		4.49	2.59	2.91	3.45							
4	-0.029	0.036	0.098	-0.118	0.023	0.069								0.120	472
	2.69	1.61	1.97	2.11	4.51	2.86									
5	-0.009	0.007	0.064	-0.076	0.021	0.097	—	—	-0.014					0.141	472
	0.70	0.29	1.28	1.34	4.01	3.85			3.52						
6	-0.028	0.042	0.066	-0.083	0.023	0.066	—	—		0.629				0.144	551
	3.10	2.09	1.63	1.80	4.89	2.85				3.89					
7	-0.029	0.004	0.052	-0.044	0.043	0.022	0.017	-0.038		0.205	0.006	0.631	-0.007	0.457	551
	3.71	0.20	1.42	1.01	5.77	1.17	3.93	4.59		1.53	5.93	15.84	4.13		
8	-0.028	—	0.048	-0.039	0.044	0.023	0.017	-0.039		0.201	0.006	0.631	-0.007	0.458	551
	4.22		1.52	1.10	7.16	1.35	4.12	5.09		1.52	5.93	15.87	4.14		

Note: Dependent variable: $\hat{\pi}_p$. LG = logarithm of growth in sales; t values under coefficients.

on m down and thus exaggerating the size of η. Both the market share–advertising and –patenting terms have positive and significant coefficients. Market share in conjunction with product differentiation is strongly associated with long run profitability.

The coefficients on the two C_4 terms imply an inverted-U relationship that peaks at a C_4 of 0.40, less than the sample mean of 0.45. Cooperation weakens beyond the middle range of concentration values. Above a C_4 of 0.80 industry behavior is more rivalrous than at $C_4 = 0$. These results are consistent with recent findings indicating a weak relationship, if any, between concentration and profitability in the presence of market share (note both t values are less than 2.0) (see Shepherd, 1972, 1975; Gale and Branch, 1982; Ravenscraft, 1983; Mueller, 1986) and a relationship that runs counter to the old learning with respect to concentration, collusion, and profitability.

The strong relationship between profitability and the market share–product differentiation variables suggests that the more profitable firms are those that succeed in differentiating their products in industries in which product differentiation is important; that is, they are more efficient than their competitors in utilizing the nonprice modes of competition.

This strong performance of market share and product differentiation leads one to question whether the somewhat perverse relationship between concentration and profitability may also be related to nonprice rivalry. Perhaps cooperation slackens as product differentiation becomes more important in an industry, and it is this nonprice rivalry that is somehow reflected in equation 1 of Table 3.3. As a rough test of this conjecture, I multiplied the two concentration terms by industry patent and advertising intensity. The former had no effect, but the addition of ADV times $(1-m)C_4$ and $(1-m)C_4^2$ (AmC_4 and AmC_4^2, respectively) did raise the $\bar{R}^2$ (equation 2). There is obvious multicollinearity among the four terms involving C_4, which is broken when $(1-m)C_4^2$ is dropped (equation 3). Equation 3 suggests a *weak* positive relationship between concentration and profitability in industries where there is no advertising and an inverted-U relationship when advertising is present. Moreover, the peak of the curve shifts leftward as advertising intensity increases, approaching a peak at a C_4 of 0.23 in highly advertising intensive industries.

To test properly for the interaction between advertising and concentration at the industry level, one must employ a model of behavior at the industry level. But the results of this section may help to explain the riddle in the recent literature regarding the impacts of concentration and market share on profitability. Neither variable has a strong impact by itself, but both have a significant relationship in the presence of product differentiation. Successful product differentiation as measured by market share is associated with high profitability. But high concentration and high product differentiation may lead to more intense rivalry and lower profitability, ceteris paribus.

VI   The effects of other firm level variables on firm profitability

We have until now ignored the impact of risk on company returns. As noted in the preceding, one interpretation of the r_i in equation 3.1 is that they are not permanent rents but risk premia.

No consensus exists in the industrial organization literature on how to measure risk, so four measures were constructed: (1) the mean slope coefficient from monthly stock returns' regressions on the market portfolio's returns for 5-year intervals over the 23-year sample period, (2) the coefficient from a regression of the firm's annual profit rate on the annual sample mean rate, (3) the variance of the firm's profit rate over the sample period, and (4) the standard error of the estimate of $\hat{\pi}_p$. The two risk measures using company profit rates (2 and 3) both had positive but insignificant coefficients when entered into the basic equation (1 in Table 3.3), and we do not report these results.

The stock market return β's could be calculated for only 472 of the 551 companies. The results for this subsample are presented in equation 4 in Table 3.3. The pattern of coefficients resembles equation 1, although the multicollinearity between the two concentration terms is weaker. The addition of $\bar{\beta}$ results in a significant improvement in the fit of the equation (5 in Table 3.3). But the variable takes on the opposite sign from what theory predicts. Higher β risk is associated with lower permanent returns on capital. One possible explanation for this result is that the causal relationship of the equation should be reversed. Firms that are persistently more (less) profitable are perceived by the stock market to be less (more) vulnerable to business cycle and other shocks. These firms experience less (more) volatile swings in their stock prices and thus have lower (higher) β's.[9] Regardless of the validity of this conjecture, equation 5 in Table 3.3 demonstrates that the other market structure relationships implied by equations 1 and 4 hold up once one controls for β risk.

Our confidence in the estimates of a firm's long run profitability is measured by the standard error of $\hat{\pi}_p$, $\sigma_{\hat{\pi}_p}$. If the market predicts long run performance using some sort of time series projection such as ours, then the risk that it will be wrong is measured by $\sigma_{\hat{\pi}_p}$. The addition of this variable to the basic equation (equation 6 in Table 3.3) increases $\bar{R}^2$ substantially,

---

[9] John Scott (1980) observed a similar, negative relationship between a firm's $\hat{\beta}$ and its required rate of return on capital using data for Canadian firms for the period 1962–74. He offers a different interpretation of this finding, however.

and its coefficient is of the correct sign.[10] Moreover, it is quite large. The range of values for $\sigma_{\hat{\pi}_p}$ is from 0.001 to 0.090. The difference in return between the most and least accurately measured $\hat{\pi}_p$ is predicted to be associated with a difference in return on assets of 0.056, considerably more than a standard deviation in the $\hat{\pi}_p$. Nevertheless, $\sigma_{\hat{\pi}_p}$ seems nearly orthogonal to the other variables in the equation, and no alteration of our inferences regarding the structure–performance equation is required. The strong performance of σ_{π_p} as a measure of risk alongside that of the other three measures further justifies the use of $\hat{\pi}_p$ to measure long run profitability.

The model developed here to explain company profit rate differences is rather streamlined by the standards of today's literature. Although their addition to the basic model is admittedly ad hoc, several additional company characteristics were added to facilitate comparisons between our measure of profitability, $\hat{\pi}_{ip}$, and those used in other studies. Specifically, company advertising, patenting, acquisitions, diversification, size, capital intensity, and growth were included as separate terms.[11] Of these, the logarithm of a company's growth in sales from 1950 to 1972 and its cumulated merger activity, GAQ, were the only variables to increase $\bar{R}^2$ appreciably. Including these variables, the adjustment for the averaging effect of mergers, $\pi_{50}/(1+\text{GAQ})$, and the $\sigma_{\hat{\pi}_p}$ measure of risk, one obtains the results in equation 7 (Table 3.3). The merger-adjusted lagged profits variable is by far the most significant right hand side variable indicating that there are many variables related to persistent profitability that are not among the others included in the equation. This variable detracts substantially from both the size and significance of $\sigma_{\hat{\pi}_p}$, suggesting that $\pi_{50}/(1+\text{GAQ})$ is capturing an important component of risk differences across firms.[12]

The logarithm of a company's growth is highly significant and reduces both the coefficient and the t value on mPAT. Growth is obviously related to technological success, which in turn is related to persistent profitability. In addition, rapid growth also captures elements of performance related to persistent profitability but not well approximated by the other variables in the equation.

---

[10] Since all variables (including the intercept) are weighted by $1/\sigma_{\hat{\pi}_p}$, the coefficient for $\sigma_{\hat{\pi}_p}$ is actually the constant term from an ordinary least squares equation.

[11] These variables are defined and discussed in Mueller (1986).

[12] If one believes that the deviations between true economic profit rates and accounting profit rates are invariant over time, then a fraction of the persistent differences in profits, which are not explained by market share and the other right hand side variables, may represent accounting differences. The inclusion of π_{50} in the profitability equation would control for persistent differences in accounting conventions. Here it should be noted that a major difference between the results reported here and in Mueller (1986) lies in the greater, relative explanatory power of π_{50} for the estimates of $\hat{\pi}_{ip}$ employed here.

Once one controls for the averaging effect of mergers through the inclusion of $\pi_{50}/(1+\text{GAQ})$, mergers are found to have a separate *negative* effect on company profitability. Although the coefficient on GAQ, -0.007 appears small, the mean profit rate was 0.076, and some firms made acquisitions totaling as much as 13 times their original size ($\text{GAQ}=13$). Thus, the negative synergy of mergers can reduce the projected profitability of the most acquisition-oriented firms substantially.

Both sets of concentration terms imply inverted-U relationships now, but only the coefficients on the terms weighted by industry advertising are significant at conventional levels. The performance of the market share–industry advertising interaction term is strengthened. Market share by itself nearly disappears from view. Dropping m, we obtain the best overall fit to the data using the firm effects model, as supplemented by other firm characteristics (equation 8 in Table 3.3). The economic implications of this equation are reviewed in the concluding section.

VII   Industry effects on profitability

The model of Section V emphasizes differences across firms within industries in product quality and costs. The traditional structure performance model in industrial organization focuses upon the industry, however, and implicitly assumes all firms within an industry have access to the same technology and benefit equally from industrywide collusion and entry barriers to the extent they exist. In the extreme, this industry approach presumes that what is important in explaining a firm's profits are the characteristics of the industries in which it sells. All firms within an industry should have the same profit rate.

To test for the importance of industry factors, we first construct a matrix of the percentage of each firm's sales falling in each industry, that is, a matrix with firms defined by rows and industries by columns and each set of row entries summing to 100. We then regress $\hat{\pi}_p$ on the set of industry participation vectors to determine what fraction of a firm's profitability is explained by knowledge of the industries in which it participates.

Ideally, we would like to measure industry participation at the same level of disaggregation employed when measuring market share and concentration, a mixture of four- and five-digit definitions that seems most reasonable as economic markets given that we can go as low as but no lower than the five-digit level. But this set of definitions gave us 771 economically meaningful markets, too many to use with 551 companies. A reasonable compromise with disaggregation and degrees of freedom seemed to be to aggregate up to the 141 three-digit industries that spanned the manufacturing sector. Using stepwise regression and a 0.25 confidence criterion for entering and deleting industries, 35 of the 141 industries were entered, and the final equation explained 0.317 percent of the variation in $\hat{\pi}_p$, a figure that might be compared with the 0.458 $\bar{R}^2$ in equation 8, Table 3.3. The number of industries entering the equation, 35, is precisely the expected number that would enter under a 0.25 criterion, when there are no significant differences across industries. Nevertheless, when one uses a 0.05 criterion, one finds 16 industries entering, which is considerably more than the 7 one expects to observe by chance. Thus, there do appear to be a few industries in which participation is associated with significant differences in long run rents.

Whereas the firm specific variables seem to explain more than the industry vectors do, less than half of the long run variability in profits across firms is explained by the firm specific variables, and it is of interest to see what the industry participation vectors add to the explanatory power of the final firm effects model (equation 8 in Table 3.3).

The answer is not much. When the variables of equation 8 in Table 3.3 are forced into the equation, 28 industry vectors are stepped in at a 0.25-level criterion. The $\bar{R}^2$ rises from 0.458 to 0.474. The F-statistic of whether or not constraining these vectors to have zero coefficients adds significantly to the explanatory power of the equation is 1.63 greater than the 0.05-level critical value of 1.50 but not by an impressive amount.

Of course, several of the variables in equation 8 are measures of industry characteristics – advertising and patent intensity, concentration – and the π_{50} variable might capture industry characteristics in part. But these general descriptions of industry structural characteristics that one derives from the firm effects model seem to capture most of the information one needs to predict long run differences in firm profitability.

These results appear to differ from those Schmalensee (1985) has reported recently. Schmalensee undertook an analysis of variance of line-of-business (LB) profit rates in 1975. Knowledge of the industry in which an LB appeared was found to be highly significant in explaining LB profits. Knowledge of the identity of the firm was found to be unimportant. Industry effects explained everything, firm effects nothing.[13]

The model employed here assumes that firm effects *within an industry* may be important, and when they are, both the profitability and market share of a firm are increased. Thus, the important firm effects are captured through market share. Moreover, market share is not assumed to have the same relationship to profitability across all industries. The more significant product differentiation is, the greater the potential gain in

---

[13] But see the findings of Scott and Pascoe (1986) and Kessides (1988b), also using FTC LB data that firm effects are important.

profitability. The seemingly weak performance of market share in Schmalensee's work may in part be due to the imposition of a common coefficient on market share across all industries.[14]

The model employed here makes no claim that a firm's profits in one market are correlated with its profits in another. Thus, the lack of significance of the firm dummies in Schmalensee's results does not contradict our results on the importance of market share. Moreover, the significant averaging effect of mergers corroborates Schmalensee's findings. Firms with above average profitability in a market do not appear able to impart this property to the assets they acquire, and vice versa.

The most important difference in Schmalensee's study and mine is the choice of dependent variable, however. It is well known that some industries (automobiles, copper, steel) are very vulnerable to business cycle shocks, whereas others (drugs, cigarettes, food) are not. The profit rates in a single year's cross section are going to reflect, to the maximum, industry-related business cycle influences. This point is particularly valid with respect to Schmalensee's study as 1975 was an unusually bad year for the U.S. economy.

In contrast, my annual profit data are measured relative to the sample mean. The dependent variable in the structural equations, $\hat{\pi}_p$, is a projection of long run profits that should be nearly devoid of cyclical influences. If firm effects are important, then it is in explaining differences in permanent rents that one is most likely to observe them.

VIII   Firm and industry effects on profit adjustment paths

The results of the previous section indicate that both firm and industry characteristics are important in explaining differences in the long run projected profit rates of firms but that firm characteristics appear relatively more important. We now examine the characteristics of the profit adjustment equations.

To apply the methodology developed in Chapter 2, we constructed a sample of industries for which there were from two to six firms with at least 50 percent of their sales in the industry (industries and firms are listed in the appendix). We chose six as an upper cutoff since the computer costs of running the tests for more than six firms were prohibitive. In some industries (e.g., 291, petroleum refining, where more than six firms met the 50 percent sales criterion), the industry was further subdivided into groups of firms with reasonably close product structure. These

---

[14] Schmalensee (1987) also concludes that intraindustry differences in profits across firms are more significant than interindustry differences (see especially p. 351).

Table 3.4. *Firm effects versus industry effects in profit adjustment equations*

Industries in which firm effects models accepted					Industries in which common industry effects models accepted					
Model I					*Model II*					
202	2031	2062	2063	2081	2012	264	2842	291-1	322	
2082	2083	221	265	283-2	331-2	331-3	341	357	363	
291-2	314	324-2	331-1	331-4	371-3	3721	3722			
335-2	335-3	366	3723		*Model III*					
Model V					204	207	324-1	358	382	
2061	283-1				*Model IV*					
Model VI					2011	2032	205	228	232	
None					251	262	282	2841	291-3	301
					329	331-5	333	335-1	351	353-1
					353-2	354	369	371-1	371-2	373
					386					

are designated, 291-1, 291-2, and so on. It was possible to construct 63 industry groups using these criteria.

Table 3.4 summarizes the results for testing for significant firm and industry effects on the profit adjustment equations using the methodology of Chapter 2, where the numbering of the different models corresponds to that used in Chapter 2. In Model IV a common adjustment process exists for all firms within an industry. No separate firm effects on the adjustment process groups leads to acceptance of this model.

The second most frequently accepted model is the firm effects Model I, with 19 industry groups leading to its acceptance. Overall, the number of industry groups for which one of the industry effects models is accepted (II, III, and IV) is exactly double the number for which a firm effects model is accepted (I, V, VI), 42 and 21, respectively.

One might expect that distinct firm adjustment patterns would be more common in differentiated product industries and common industry adjustment patterns in homogeneous product industries. A hint that this generalization is valid exists, but only a hint. Both pharmaceutical product groups, 283-1 and 283-2, lead to acceptance of a firm effect model. Pharmaceuticals are probably the most differentiated of all product groups. Eight of the 14 food and drink industries (two-digit industry 20) are also on the left side of Table 3.4. But so many anomalies exist (e.g., 291-2 on the left whereas 291-1 and 291-3 are on the right) that too much should not be made of this point. The only safe generalization one can make is that common industry patterns in the profit adjustment processes of firms exist in twice as many industry groups as do not.

IX   Explaining the speed of adjustment

Further insight into the characteristics of the adjustment processes of individual firms can be obtained by relating the speeds of adjustment for individual firms, the λ_i of the model of Section I, to firm and industry characteristics. In Section V, we estimated a rather complicated equation containing several interaction terms between market share and industry concentration and product differentiation. This equation was shown to equal the firm's profit rate. But $\hat{\lambda}$ is the speed of adjustment of short run rents to zero. There is no reason to expect it to be related to the same functional form as the profit rate. We did regress $\hat{\lambda}$ on the same set of variables, but a better fit was obtained by simply introducing the individual variables separately.[15]

Although most of the variables performed in explaining $\hat{\lambda}$ as they had in explaining $\hat{\pi}_p$, π_{50} entered with a negative and significant sign. The larger a firm's initial profits, the more quickly its short run rents seem to disappear. Given the strong relationship between π_{50} and $\hat{\pi}_p$, it is possible that it is the permanent rent component of π_{50} that is driving the negative correlation between $\hat{\lambda}$ and π_{50}; that is, firms with large permanent rents have short run rents of short duration.

But rents can be positive or negative. If the preceding conjecture is true, then one wonders whether the same relationship holds for negative permanent rents. That is, do firms with large, negative permanent rents also have relatively small $\hat{\lambda}$'s? To see whether they do, separate slopes were estimated for the π_{50} variable for firms with $\hat{\pi}_p > 0$ (π_{50}^+) and those with $\hat{\pi}_p < 0$ (π_{50}^-). The best fit equation was

$$\hat{\lambda} = 0.075 - 0.863m + 1.95m^2 + 1.14C_4 - 1.21C_4^2 + 0.022\text{ADV}$$
$$\phantom{\hat{\lambda} =}\ 0.75 \qquad 2.88 \qquad 4.02 \qquad 2.59 \qquad 2.60 \qquad 3.60$$

$$- 4.20\pi_{50}^+ + 3.01\pi_{50}^-, \qquad \bar{R}^2 = 0.378, \tag{3.13}$$
$$\ 11.47 \qquad 6.59$$

where π_{50} is measured as a deviation from the sample mean. Thus, (3.13) states that for those firms with positive permanent rents, an increase in initial profits (π_{50}^+) is associated with a decline in the persistence of short run rents, a decline in $\hat{\lambda}$. Similarly, for firms with negative permanent rents, the lower initial profitability, the *lower* $\hat{\lambda}$, that is, the less permanent the short run rents are. Thus, for both negative and positive permanent

---

[15] Each observation is weighted by $1/\sigma_\lambda$ to correct for heteroscedasticity.

rents, the greater the deviation of initial profits from the average in the direction of the permanent rents, the greater the tendency is that the time profile of profits resembles a horizontal line. The closer initial profits are to the average, the slower the adjustment process of short run rents over time.

The signs on concentration and industry advertising are the same as in the permanent rent equation. Market share also enters nonlinearly, but as a normal-U shape. Beyond a market share of 0.23 increases in market share increase the persistence of short run rents. A market share of 0.23 is roughly three times the sample average, however. For most firms, therefore, increases in market share bring about reductions in the persistence of short run rents. Given the strong positive effect on permanent rents of market share in conjunction with industry advertising and patenting, this result seems to resemble the π_{50} results. That is, higher market shares generally result in higher permanent rents *and* short run rents of shorter duration.

Stepwise regressions using $\hat{\lambda}$ as dependent variable and industry particiipation rates as independent variables resulted in 36 of the 141 industry vectors entering into the equation (0.25 probability criterion) and an $\bar{R}^2$ of 0.402. As with the $\hat{\pi}_p$ equations, the number of industries entering is precisely the number one expects when one uses a 0.25 criterion, and there are no significant differences across industries. But, 17 industry vectors enter when one uses a 0.05 criterion, more than double the expected number under the null hypothesis, so one can safely conclude that there do exist significant differences in the extent to which short run rents persist across industries.

X   Conclusions

In a dynamically competitive economy, firms should not earn substantial positive or negative long run rents, and short run deviations from normal returns should quickly disappear. We have found that the typical firm's profits do converge fairly quickly on its long run equilibrium rate, but these long run rates differ significantly across firms. Fifty percent of the firms in the sample had permanent rents significantly different from the average. Some 69 percent of the deviations in company profit rates in the three initial sample years appeared to persist indefinitely.

The model used to explain these permanent differences in profitability predicts a positive correlation between market share and profitability *if* differences in costs and product quality are significant across firms. That market share is positively related to profitability in the presence of high advertising and patent intensity implies that significant efficiency or perceived product quality differences exist. It is important to recognize that it is these differences across firms that cause the market share–profit rate relationship. Market share does not determine profits, but rather both market share and profitability are determined by the underlying quality-efficiency characteristics of firms in conjunction with industry attributes (Geroski, 1982).

Concentration was observed to have a negative association with firm profitability after a point and one that was stronger the more advertising intensive the industry. It was speculated that the implied increases in rivalrous behavior that accompany increased concentration were in the non-price modes of competition.

The persistent differences in profitability across firms that exist are partly obscured by the averaging effect of mergers. When one observes only aggregate company profit rates, the heavy merger activity over the past 30 years tends to create the false impression that profit rates converge on normal levels. Beyond their averaging effect, mergers appear to reduce the returns of the acquiring firms, a result consistent with other empirical evidence (Meeks, 1977; Mueller, 1980, ch. 9).

The estimates reported in this chapter are based on the histories of 551 companies from 1950 through 1972, before the first OPEC oil crisis, its negative impact on the U.S. economy, the inflation of the seventies, and the tremendous increase in import penetration since 1972. These profit profiles project the outcomes that might have been expected had the U.S. economy continued to perform in the seventies and eighties as it had in the fifties and sixties. Their relevance to predicting the performance of companies today remains on the agenda for future research. But independent of how that question is answered, these results do imply that during one of the most prosperous generations this country has ever seen, the forces of competition within the U.S. economy allowed significant differences in long run rents to persist.

Our efforts to determine whether the differences in projected profits and in the adjustment processes were explained by characteristics peculiar to individual firms or to their industries indicated that both were important. Firm characteristics appeared relatively more important in explaining the long run projected profit rates. However, industry characteristics were relatively more important in determining the adjustment process.

Appendix

Annual accounting data by firm are from Standard & Poor's COMPUSTAT tape and conform to its definitions. Where COMPUSTAT data were not available, data from *Moody's Industrial Manual* were substituted.

Variable definitions

$\pi_{it} =$ Firm i's profit rate in year t
  $= $(income $+$ interest)/total assets
$\hat{\pi}_{ip} = \hat{\alpha}_i/(1-\hat{\lambda}_i)$, from $\pi_{it} = \alpha_i + \lambda_i \pi_{it-1} + \mu_{it}$
$\pi_{i50} = (\Sigma^{52}_{t=50}\pi_{it})/3$

GAQ $=$ Growth by acquisition. Let AQ_{it} be i's assets acquired in year t, and K_{it-1} its assets at end of year $t-1$; then GAQ $= \Sigma^{72}_{t=50}(\text{AQ}_{it}/K_{it-1})$.

$C_4 =$ A projected four-firm concentration ratio. Projection made by assuming concentration follows the path $C_{4t} = a + b/t$. The coefficient a is then the projected concentration at $t = \infty$. Two measures of concentration were used to make the projections, the sales-weighted average C_4 for a firm in 1950 and in 1972. The 1972 figures were adjusted for imports and geographic differences in market definition as in Weiss (1981). Since the projected concentration places heavy weight on the 1972 figure, this figure was used to proxy C_4 when the 1950 figure was missing.

$m =$ Projected market share. This projection was made in the same way C_4 was projected. To adjust for imports and geographic differences in market definition, the 1972 market share figure was multiplied by the ratio of the 1972 Weiss-adjusted C_4 to the unadjusted C_4.

ADV $=$ Industry advertising-to-sales ratio. Sales-weighted average advertising-to-sales ratio based on 1963 Internal Revenue Service advertising and sales data. The year 1963 was chosen because it falls in the middle of the sample period.

PAT $=$ Industry patent-to-sales ratio. Sales-weighted average patent-to-sales ratio from period 1966–8 as reported in NSF (1977), with 1967 Census of Manufacturing sales as deflator. Years 1966–8 were used because they are earliest reported by NSF (1977).

$\bar{\beta} =$ Mean β estimated over five 5-year time intervals spanning 1949–73 using firm's own monthly returns regressed on return of market portfolio. When data were not available for some years, the $\bar{\beta}$ is based on those time periods for which data were available.

$\sigma_{\pi_p} =$ Standard error of $\hat{\pi}_p$:

$$\sigma_{\pi_p} = \left[\left(\frac{1}{1-\lambda}\right)^2 \sigma^2_\alpha + \left(\frac{\alpha}{(1-\lambda)^2}\right)^2 \sigma^2_\lambda + 2\frac{1}{1+\lambda}\frac{\alpha}{(1-\lambda)^2}\sigma_{\alpha\lambda}\right]^{1/2}$$

LG $=$ Logarithm of growth in sales; $\log(S_{72}/S_{50})$.

Firms and industries in adjustment model tests

Industry SIC code	Industry name	Company names
2011	Meat products	Swift, Hormel, Oscar Mayer, Rath Packing, Tobin Packing
2012		General Baking, Hygrade Food, United Brands
202	Dairy products	Arden Farms, Carnation, Fairmont Foods, Foremost Dairies, National Dairy
2031	Canned fruits and vegetables	California Packing, Green Giant, Libby, McNeil & Libby, Seabrook Farms, Stokely Van-Camp
2032	Canned soups and baby food	Campbell Soup, Gerber, H. J. Heinz
204	Grainmill products	International Milling, Kellogg, Pillsbury, Quaker Oats, Ralston Purina
205	Bakery products	American Bakeries, Interstate Bakeries, United Biscuit, National Biscuit
2061	Sugar products	Amalgamated Sugar, American Crystal Sugar, American Sugar, Great Western Sugar, Holly Sugar
2062	Confectionary products and chewing gum	Hershey, Peter Paul, Sucrest, Wrigley
2063	Sugar products	National Sugar, Savannah Sugar, Utah-Idaho Sugar
207	Fats and oil	Anderson, Clayton, Archer-Daniels-Midland, Central Soya, E. L. Bruce
2081	Beer	Armada, Carling, Falstaff, Heilman, Pabst
2082	Distilled liquors	Brown-Forman, Seagram, Glenmore, Heublin
2083	Soft drinks	Coca-Cola, Dr. Pepper, Pepsi Cola, Royal Crown
221	Weaving mills	Cannon Mills, Cone Mills, Lowenstein
228	Yarn and thread mills	Bates, American Thread, Standard-Coosa-Thatcher, Textiles, Inc.
232	Men's and boys' furnishings	Blue Bell, Oxford Industries, Phillips-Jones
251	Household furniture	Kroehler, Simmons, Bassett
262	Papermills	Consolidated Water Power & Paper, Great Northern, Sorg, Southland
264	Miscellaneous converted paper	Hudson, Kimberly-Clark, Scott
265	Paperboard containers	Greif Brothers, Container Corporation, Sonoco, Stone Container
282	Plastic materials	American Enlea, Celanese, Reichhold Chemicals, Rohm & Haas

Industry SIC code	Industry name	Company names
283-1	Drugs	Abbott, Eli Lilly, Miles, Pfizer, Smith-Kline-French, Upjohn
283-2	Drugs	Merck, Vick, Schering-Plough
2841	Cosmetics	Avon, Faberge, Helena Rubinstein, Noxell
2842	Soaps and cleaning products	Colgate-Palmolive, Gillette, Stanley Home, Lever Brothers
291-1	Petroleum refining	American Liberty Oil, Ashland Refineries, Atlantic Refineries, Cities Service, Continental Oil, Crown Central Petroleum
291-2	Petroleum refining	Tidewater, Gulf, Marathon, Socomy-Vacuum, South Penn, Quaker State
291-3	Petroleum refining	Shell, S. O. California, S. O. Industries, S. O. Ohio, Texaco, Union Oil
301	Tires and inner tubes	Armstrong Rubber, Mansfield Tire, Mohawk Rubber
314	Footwear, except rubber	Brown Shoe, International Shoe, McElwain
322	Glass, pressed or blown	Anchor Hocking, Corning, Owens-Illinois
324-1	Cement	Amcord, Kaiser Cement, Marquette
324-2	Cement	General Portland, Ideal, Lehigh Portland, Lone Star, Medusa Portland
329	Miscellaneous nonmetallic mineral products	Carborundum, General Refractories, Johns-Manville, Owens-Corning, Raybestos-Manhattan
331-1	Steel products	Allegheny Ludlum, Pittsburgh Screw, Armco Steel, Atlantic Steel, Bethlehem Steel, Bliss & Laughlin
331-2	Steel products	Carpenter Steel, Copperweld, Crane, Universal-Cyclops, Inland Steel, Interlake
331-3	Steel products	Kaiser-Frazer, Keystone Steel, LTV, Laclede, Lukens, McLouth
331-4	Steel products	National-Standard, National Steel, Northwestern, Penn-Dixie Cement, Barium Steel, Republic
331-5	Steel products	USS, Washburn, Wheeling, Youngstown
333	Primary nonferrous metals	American Smelting, Inspiration Colsolidated, Kennecott, St. Joseph Lead
335-1	Nonferrous rolled metals	Anaconda Copper, Phelps Dodge
335-2	Nonferrous rolled metals	Belden, Cerro, General Cable
335-3	Nonferrous rolled metals	Continental Copper, Copper Range, Revere

Industry SIC code	Industry name	Company names
341	Metal cans	Continental Can, Crown Cork, National Can
351	Engines and turbines	Briggs & Stratton, Cummins Engineering, Outboard Marine
353-1	Construction and industrial machinery	Bucyrus-Erie, Caterpillar, Clark Equipment, Halliburton, Joy
353-2	Construction and industrial machinery	Koehring, Northwest Engineering, Otis, Pettibone Mulliken, Reed Roller
354	Metalworking machinery	National Acme, Black & Decker, Skil
357	Office and computing machines	Burroughs, Minneapolis-Honeywell, IBM, National Cash Register, Pitney-Bowes, Victor Comptometer
358	Refrigeration and service machinery	Carrier, Copeland, Fedders, Tecumseh, Trane
363	Household appliances	Hoover, Maytag, National Union, Sunbeam, Whirlpool
366	Communications equipment	Chesapeake Corporation, Collins Radio, Harris-Seybold-Potter, Raytheon
369	Miscellaneous electrical equipment	Champion Spark Plug, Electric Storage Battery, Globe-Union
371-1	Motor vehicles and equipment	Noblitt-Sparks, Fruehauf, Kelsey-Hayes, Maremont
371-2	Motor vehicles and equipment	Chrysler, Dana, Weatherhead, White Motor
371-3	Motor vehicles and equipment	Monroe Auto, Pacific Car, Purolator, Signal Company, A. O. Smith, Trico
3721	Aircraft and parts	Avco, Beech, Cessna, Fairchild Industries, Rohr, United Technologies
3722	Aircraft and parts	Boeing, Lockheed, McDonnel Douglas
3723	Aircraft and parts	Grumman, Northrup
373	Ship and boat building	American Ship Building, National Automotive Fibres, Ogden, Todd
382	Measuring and control devices	Ranco, Robertshaw-Fulton, G. D. Searle
386	Photographic equipment	Kodak, Polaroid, Xerox

Notes: Names are typically the names as of 1950 (FTC, 1972). For more recent names, see Mueller (1986, appendixes).

CHAPTER 4

The persistence of profits in U.S. manufacturing industries

IOANNIS N. KESSIDES

In this chapter we develop and test a simple autoregressive model that describes the profits of industries over time. The model explicitly addresses the issue of incomplete adjustments of profitability and distinguishes long-run from short-run effects. The model is fit to census data on U.S. manufacturing industries over the period 1967–82. Industry-specific estimates of the speed of adjustment of the profit rate toward its long-run equilibrium level and hence measures of the degree of persistence in performance across the various industries are obtained. These estimates are then linked to structural characteristics that theory suggests might be pertinent in determining the rate at which the forces of competition erode excess returns. The results of the chapter provide support for the view that competition in an industry is rooted in its underlying economic structure. We find support for both the Chamberlinian hypothesis and the more recently advanced contestability conjecture that states that the performance of industries depends continuously on the degree to which they exhibit imperfect contestability.[1]

I   A partial adjustment model

Let π_{it} denote the profit rate of industry i at time t. We postulate that the level of π_{it} reflects industry-specific characteristics determining both the internal conditions of actual competition among the established firms in the industry and also the external conditions of potential competition from outside firms. Among the internal conditions we include brand loyalties, cost and informational asymmetries, demand inelasticities, and so on. Prominent among the industry characteristics that determine the competitive pressure exerted by potential entrants is the height of entry barriers. In addition to these microinfluences, observed industry profitability is also affected by changing macroeconomic conditions and may be partly influenced by factors that are purely random.

---

[1] See Scherer (1980) for an excellent exposition of the Chamberlinian hypothesis. The implications of contestability for performance are analyzed in Baumol, Panzar, and Willig (1982).

Some of these industry characteristics could be thought of as temporary or transitory. Others may be constant or changing so slowly over time that they can be assumed to be relatively permanent. Consider, for instance, the nature of entry conditions describing the advantages of established sellers over potential entrants. Among these advantages we traditionally include patent holdings, brand identification and customer loyalties, control of and favorable access to scarce resources, favorable access to distribution channels and financing, and the learning or experience curve. Clearly, some of these advantages are fairly impregnable and may be enjoyed over long periods of time. Such advantages are therefore permanent to the extent that they operate on the profit rate for several consecutive periods. Others may be more temporary.

It is our hypothesis that these advantages and characteristics are mainly reflected in the ability of incumbent firms to raise price above the competitive level without attracting new entry. One may then plausibly argue that the measured rate of profit π_{it} is composed of two parts: a long-run or permanent component π_{ip} reflecting the effects of factors that remain almost constant over time and a short-run or transitory component s_{it} reflecting the influence of short-run conditions. Thus, we write the following definitional equation:

$$\pi_{it} = \pi_{ip} + s_{it}. \tag{4.1}$$

The permanent component π_{ip} can itself be partitioned into two terms as

$$\pi_{ip} = c + r_i, \tag{4.2}$$

where c is the competitive rate of return (the return that would be earned by a perfectly competitive industry) and r_i is an industry-specific permanent rent. Traditionally, the competitive return is approximated by the yield on long-term government securities. The permanent rent r_i, on the other hand, is usually assumed to reflect the effective cost of entry into (or exit from) the industry and hence the level of supranormal profits that are sustainable during the period that entry conditions remain stationary.

We assume that competition continually works to eliminate rents (both the long- and short-run rents r_i and s_{it}) and drive the profit rate toward the competitive norm. Rates of return higher than the competitive norm stimulate the flow of investment into the industry either through new entry or through additional investment and expansion by existing competitors. The underlying structural features of an industry that determine the strength of its competitive forces also determine the rate at which this inflow of investment occurs and hence the rate at which rents are eroded. Implicit in the use of the terms "permanent" and "transitory" is the assumption that the erosion of r_i takes place on a long time scale, whereas that of s_{it}

is defined over a fast time scale. Let τ and $\tilde{t}$ denote the fast and slow time variables, respectively. If the time interval T during which we seek to examine the behavior of the profit rate is such that $\tau \ll T \sim O(\tilde{t})$, then it is appropriate during that period to focus on the variation of s_{it} alone. Assume further that because of data constraints, t is measured in years. If $\tau \ll t$, then we could assume that the transitory components in successive years are uncorrelated, that is, $\mathrm{corr}(s_{it}, s_{it+1}) = 0$. This would simply imply that the forces of competition work so fast that any short-run rents earned this year are independent of any rents that were earned last year. If, on the other hand, t and τ are of the same order, then a more reasonable assumption would be that $\mathrm{corr}(s_{it}, s_{it+1}) \neq 0$, that is, that short-run rents are intertemporally related. Let us further assume, for computational convenience, that s_{it} follows the first-order autoregressive process.

$$s_{it} = \lambda_i s_{it-1} + \epsilon_{it}, \tag{4.3}$$

where, for stationarity, $|\lambda_i| < 1$ and the ϵ_{it} are independently and identically distributed random variables with zero mean and finite variance.

Lagging equation (4.1) and using (4.2) and (4.3) leads to the quasi-first-difference transformation of equation (4.1),

$$\pi_{it} - \lambda_i \pi_{it-1} = (1 - \lambda_i)(c + r_i) + \epsilon_{it}, \tag{4.4}$$

which can be written in the autoregressive form

$$\pi_{it} = \alpha_i + \lambda_i \pi_{it-1} + \epsilon_{it}, \qquad i = 1, 2, \dots, N, \quad t = 1, 2, \dots, T, \tag{4.5}$$

where $\alpha_i = (1 - \lambda_i)(c + r_i) \equiv (1 - \lambda_i)\pi_{ip}$. As we have noted in the preceding, the ϵ_{it} are assumed to be uncorrelated over time. These disturbances capture the influence of random factors that could be common to many industries, especially those that are closely related. In that case, the disturbances in different industries will be correlated at a given point in time. That is,

$$\mathrm{cov}(\epsilon_{it}, \epsilon_{js}) = \begin{cases} \sigma_{ij} & \text{if } t = s, \\ 0 & \text{if } t \neq s. \end{cases} \tag{4.6}$$

The autoregressive structure of equation (4.5) represents a simple description of movements in the profit rate of industry i over time that allows incomplete adjustments to deviations of the profit rate from its long-run equilibrium level. The parameter $1 - \lambda_i$ measures the speed of adjustment and indicates how quickly the profit rate π_{it} approaches its long-run equilibrium level π_{ip}. When λ_i is large, short-run rents erode slowly and the profit rate adjusts slowly toward its permanent level – the observed profit rate in period t depends largely on its value in period $t - 1$ and very little on its permanent level. If, on the other hand, λ_i is small, short-run rents erode very rapidly. In that case, it can be assumed that the sampled industries are observed in long-run equilibrium except for purely random displacements.

II   Factors affecting the speed of adjustment

Implicit in the formulation of the partial adjustment model (4.5) is the assumption that the speed of adjustment is an industry-specific parameter. In this section we seek to identify those industry characteristics that theory suggests might be pertinent in the determination of λ.

The presence of excess profits in an industry signals profitable opportunities and serves to stimulate inflow of capital into the industry either through entry by outside firms or through additional investment by established competitors. As a result of such inflow, industry output expands and the rate of return is driven toward the competitive norm. The rate at which such inflow of investment occurs and the consequent rate at which excess returns are competed away depends on the industry's state of competition.

In this chapter we accept the proposition that oligopolists wish to collude to prevent the erosion of their excess profits as a reasonable description of the behavior of firms. In their effort to defend their excess returns, the incumbents are likely to adopt strategies that limit the degree of actual competition within their industry or strategies that inhibit new entry. However, although such strategies might be desirable, they are not necessarily always feasible. The types of strategies the incumbents adopt and the degree of their success depend on the incentives they face and the market form of the industry. This market form in turn is a function of the number and resources of the established competitors, the physical nature of the market, and the legal and informational environment of the industry. (See Shubik and Levitan, 1988.) Our basic conjecture is that these variables limit the strategies available to the incumbents in their attempts to both reduce actual competition within the industry and limit the competitive pressure exerted by potential entrants, that is, the feasibility of restrictive arrangements depends crucially upon the structural features of the industry. Thus, an industry's economic structure, by constraining the course of action adopted by the established sellers, will affect λ, the rate at which market forces bid away the industry's excess profits.

The number and size distribution of sellers is an important structural dimension that affects oligopolistic coordination. As the number of sellers increases, the oligopolists are increasingly apt to ignore the effect of their actions on their rivals and on price. Also, the likelihood of mavericks and the probability that any existing agreement will be broken off by a member pursuing an aggressive and independent pricing policy will be larger the greater the number of firms in the industry. Chamberlin asserted that when the number of firms is small, they are bound to recognize their mutual interdependence. Each firm would therefore refrain from under-taking any action that when countered, would leave all members of the industry worse off. It was further conjectured that successful tacit or ex-plicit collusion is more likely the smaller the number of firms and the more concentrated the industry. When an industry is dominated by one firm, for example, such a firm can exercise undisputed leadership, imposing discipline, punishing self-serving aggression, and coordinating behavior in the common interest. If, on the other hand, the competitors are rel-atively balanced in terms of size and resources, then their collusive ar-rangements are bound to be more unstable – actions that conflict with the group's interests are more likely since the threat of punishment from com-petitors of similar size, strength, and resources is less credible. We should also note that in an unconcentrated industry with a large number of sellers, the initiation of retaliatory measures against an entrant is subject to free-rider problems. In a concentrated industry, on the other hand, the for-tunes of the firms are strategically interlinked, and such sellers might find it easier to engage in collusive punitive actions against newcomers.

We therefore propose to test the Chamberlinian conjecture in the con-text of our dynamic partial adjustment model of profitability by testing the following two hypotheses:

Hypothesis 1: Excess returns are competed away more slowly in indus-tries with a small number of firms; thus,

$$\frac{\partial \lambda}{\partial N} < 0,$$

where N denotes the number of firms.

Hypothesis 2: Excess returns are competed away more slowly in indus-tries that are highly concentrated; thus,

$$\frac{\partial \lambda}{\partial C} > 0,$$

where C is a measure of industry concentration.

The identification of those industry characteristics that influence compet-itive conduct among the established sellers in a market is certainly an important component of any dynamic analysis of profitability. However, of equal (if not greater) importance are the effects of potential competition for the market as well as those conditions that might limit such potential rivalry. External conditions of potential competition from outside firms will also influence the choices of the firms inside the market, and competition for the market disciplines behavior almost as effectively as actual competition within the market.[2]

When an industry experiences a slow growth in demand for its product, the incompatibility of the positions firms seek to attain within the industry is enhanced. The struggle for market shares is likely to be more intense and volatile than in instances where rapid growth permits firms to improve their positions by just expanding at the same rate as the industry. Industries with slow growth are susceptible to breakdowns in pricing discipline, especially when their overhead costs are high and sluggish demand conditions do not permit full-capacity utilization. Under rapid growth conditions, entry by outside firms does not require capturing sales away from established sellers, and so such sellers will have less of an incentive to engage in aggressive postentry response. Thus, the potentially destabilizing effects of entry on any tacit or overt collusive arrangements that might exist within an industry will be less severe under rapid growth conditions.

Hypothesis 3: Excess profits will erode more rapidly in industries experiencing slow growth in that such slow growth intensifies the volatility of internal market share competition and enhances the destabilizing effects of entry; thus,

$$\frac{\partial \lambda}{\partial \text{GR}} > 0,$$

where Gr denotes the rate at which demand for the industry's product grows.

The ease with which outside firms can enter an industry is a structural characteristic that significantly affects competitive performance. Indeed, the ability of established firms to protect excess returns will be severely limited in instances where entry into their industry is easy and potential rivals are lurking in the wings. On the other hand, high structural entry barriers can diminish the rate at which entry responds to positive incumbent profits, and in that case excess returns will erode at a slow rate.

In his pioneering analysis of entry conditions, Bain identified economies of scale and absolute capital requirements as two major sources of barriers to entry. Economies of scale might deter entry because they force the entrant to come in either at a large scale and risk a strong retaliatory

---

[2] For the distinction between internal and external market conditions, see Shepherd (1985).

response from incumbents unwilling to accept large reductions in their market shares (which successful large-scale entry would render inevitable) or at a small scale and face a significant cost disadvantage relative to the existing competitors. The financial capital required for entry can also constitute a barrier to entry. If the absolute amount of capital required is large and entry represents a risky use of that capital, then banks and other financial institutions will be reluctant to provide the needed financing or may require very high interest rates. Thus, larger increments of capital sought by a potential entrant will probably come at a higher effective cost giving rise to advantages for the established sellers.

Hypothesis 4: Excess profits will erode slowly in industries with strong scale economies; thus,

$$\frac{\partial \lambda}{\partial \text{MES}} > 0,$$

where MES is a measure of the minimum efficient scale.

Hypothesis 5: Excess profits will erode slowly in industries with high absolute capital requirements; thus,

$$\frac{\partial \lambda}{\partial K} > 0,$$

where K represents the capital required for an MES firm.

In their analysis of contestability Baumol et al. (1982) have challenged the traditional notion that fixed costs constitute the prime impediment to entry. They effectively argue that what is crucial to the decision of entering a market is not the amount of capital required but the amount of this capital that is sunk – the share of entry investment that is composed of sunk capital, or alternatively what is termed as the "sunkenness" of such capital.

The irreversibility of the investment required to participate in the market efficiently gives rise to asymmetries in the strategic opportunities facing firms. When such asymmetries are exploited, entrenched positions of market power may result. Thus, irreversibility reinforces internal market power by raising exit costs and facilitating a credible commitment by the incumbent to defend its market position. In the theory of contestable markets, then, the role of sunk costs has been properly emphasized.[3] For the entrant, the act of entry requires either the conversion of liquid assets into frozen physical capital, only part of which is recoverable in the event

---

[3] On the role of sunk costs as an entry barrier, also see Caves and Porter (1977).

of failure, or the purchase of advertising units (for recognition) that are almost completely nonsalvageable. For the incumbent, on the other hand, who is already beyond the regime of potential failure (at least relative to the entrant), these commitments either have already been made (initial capital investment) or simply constitute a normal cost of doing business (advertising). Therefore, the need to sink a given amount of capital upon entering a market generates an asymmetry in the incremental cost and incremental risk faced by a potential entrant and an incumbent firm. The entrant's incremental cost includes the irrecoverable portion of the entry investment that is bygone to the incumbent. It is in this sense that sunk costs constitute an entry barrier. In addition, sunk costs enhance the entrant's vulnerability to retaliatory responses by the incumbent. Consequently, sunk costs lower the quasi-rents the entrant can expect to earn by committing resources to the market; they diminish the rate at which entry responds to positive incumbent profits; and like entry barriers, they impede the establishment of new firms. Through their effect on entry, sunk costs constrain structure and can influence that rate at which excess profits are competed away.

One of the important welfare characteristics of perfectly contestable markets is that such markets never offer more than a normal rate of profit. Potential entry or competition for the market by outside firms disciplines incumbent behavior and forces them to adopt socially efficient prices yielding only normal returns. Since entry is assumed to be perfectly free and exit absolutely costless, any excess profit would simply provide entrants with "hit-and-run" opportunities. Entrants who have nothing to lose would respond to any opportunity for excess profit, however transient it might be. Whereas in the short run, as in the case of competitive markets, excess profits may be present, we would expect such profits to be eliminated very rapidly.

We postulate that market performance depends continuously on the degree to which they exhibit imperfect contestability. We further conjecture that the smaller the share of investment that is composed of sunk capital, the more contestable that industry will be. Thus, we would expect the adjustment parameter λ to be larger the higher is the "sunkenness" of the capital employed. To evaluate the contestability conjecture we test:

Hypothesis 6: Excess profits will erode more slowly in industries where the share of sunk outlays that must be committed by entrants is large. Thus,

$$\frac{\partial \lambda}{\partial \text{SUNK}} > 0,$$

where SUNK is a measure of the share of the entry investment that is composed of sunk capital.

Increased product differentiation reduces the cross-price elasticity of demand between competing brands in a given market and also between the established brands and the new variants offered by entrants. The imperfect substitutability among competing sellers' products in differentiated industries slows down the transfer of customers between brands, thereby permitting firms to raise price (or to maintain an elevated price) without suffering rapid and significant erosion in their sales volume. Differentiation creates an entry barrier by forcing entrants to incur high selling costs or accept a lower price in order to overcome the goodwill assets of the incumbents.

In many differentiated markets, according to the *Advertising = Persuasion school,* innate differentiation is complemented by an artificial one induced through advertising. Such advertising increases brand loyalty, reduces the perceived number of product substitutes, and ultimately lowers the cross-price elasticity of demand. The implication of this view is that excess returns in heavily advertised industries will erode slowly because the operating firms in such industries are insulated from actual and potential competitors by loyal and persuaded customers. In contradiction to this, the *Advertising = Information school* maintains that advertising is an attention-getting device that provides information about the attributes and prices of products, thus reducing the search costs faced by consumers.[4] Advertising acts as a substitute for experience, adds to the perceived number of product substitutes, and is a means of overcoming consumer loyalty and inertia. This school seems to suggest that excess returns will erode faster in heavily advertised industries in that such industries are likely to exhibit high rates of brand switching and to contain well-informed and mobile consumers.

How much advertising is beneficially informative and hence competition enhancing and how much is merely persuasive and therefore inhibiting competition? No clear-cut answer can be given since in most real-world markets advertising probably exhibits both traits. These conflicting forces can balance either way. In addition, it is important to note that advertising adds to the sunk costs required for entry. (See Kessides, 1986.)

Hypothesis 7a (Advertising = Market Power school): Excess profits will erode more slowly the greater are industry advertising expenditures; thus,

$$\frac{\partial \lambda}{\partial(A/S)} > 0.$$

Hypothesis 7b (Advertising = Competition school): Excess profits will erode faster the greater are industry advertising expenditures; thus,

[4] For studies representing and supporting these two alternative views, see Comanor and Wilson (1979).

$$\frac{\partial \lambda}{\partial (A/S)} < 0$$

where A/S is the advertising intensity (advertising-to-sales ratio).

III   Data and estimation issues

The autoregressive equation (4.5) was fit to four-digit U.S. manufacturing industries over the period 1967–82. Industries that were defined or redefined for the 1972 census had data available only for the 1972–82 period and were subsequently eliminated from the sample. The exclusion of those industries may give rise to a sample selection bias; on the other hand, it will reduce the measurement problems arising from poorly defined industries and will also improve the precision of our autoregressive estimates. The final sample consists of 344 of the 448 four-digit industries.

In equation (4.5), π_{it} was measured as the ratio of value-added minus payroll to total sales. One may plausibly argue that capital markets serve to equalize risk-adjusted rates of return on investment, not on sales. Therefore, a more appropriate measure of π_{it} might be the ratio of operating income to total assets. However, we must note the difficulty of obtaining accurate asset figures. Indeed, at the four-digit level sales are measured much more accurately than assets. The price–cost margin can thus be measured precisely at the four-digit level, and it avoids most of the accounting difficulties of corporate profit margins. (See Strickland and Weiss, 1976.) Still, these are accounting rates of return on sales, and we must note that there has been considerable controversy over their usefulness.

Given the assumptions underlying the first-order autoregressive process of equation (4.3) that describes the movement of short-run rents over time, the parameters of equation (4.5) can be estimated by ordinary least squares. However, the contemporaneous covariance in (4.6) implies that possible gains in efficiency could be obtained by jointly considering all the equations in (4.5). To the extent that the contemporaneous correlation in (4.6) arises because of the presence of random factors that are common to closely related industries, we group the (four-digit) industries of our sample according to their three-digit classification (i.e., the hypothetical three-digit industry in which they belong). We then jointly estimate the equations in (4.5) within each group separately as a set of seemingly unrelated regressions. There were 80 such sets of disturbance-related equations.

Asymptotically efficient estimators of π_{ip}, the long-run profit rate of industry i, are obtained from this joint estimation. If $\hat{\alpha}_i$ and $\hat{\lambda}_i$ are the generalized least squares estimators of α_i and λ_i, then

$$\hat{\pi}_{ip} = \frac{\hat{\alpha}_i}{1 - \hat{\lambda}_i}.$$

The hypothesis that competition drives down the profit rate across industries toward the competitive norm can be tested by discriminating between

$$H_0: \frac{\alpha_i}{1 - \lambda_i} = \gamma \quad \text{and} \quad H_1: \frac{\alpha_i}{1 - \lambda_i} \neq \gamma \quad \text{for at least some } i.$$

The rejection of H_0 in favor of H_1 would imply that long-run profit rates differ significantly across industries and that the forces of competition have not eliminated long-run rents during the 16-year period analyzed in this study.

We next examine the relationship between the speed of adjustment and market structure. The specification implicit in this link is the following:

$$\lambda_i = Z_i \beta + v_i \tag{4.7}$$

where λ_i and β are vectors of unknown parameters, Z_i is a matrix of independent structural variables, and v_i is a vector of unobservable random variables with zero mean and variance σ_v^2. Because the true parameters λ_i are unobservable, they must be replaced by their estimates $\hat{\lambda}_i$ from (4.5). Thus, in the empirical analysis that follows we adopt a two-step procedure. In the first stage, we estimate the λ_i in (4.5) efficiently using joint generalized least squares techniques. In the second stage, we estimate (4.7) where λ_i is replaced by $\hat{\lambda}_i$ using again generalized least squares where an appropriate allowance is made for the possible presence of heteroscedasticity.[5] Since the main hypotheses of the chapter relate to structural factors that influence the rate of erosion of excess returns, in estimating equation (4.7), we restrict our sample only to industries whose profit rates, averaged over the first three years of the sample period, exceeded their long-run profits, that is, industries with positive initial short-run rents. There were 137 such industries.

Finally, one could argue that the structural factors determining the adjustment parameter λ_i will also influence the long-run profit π_{ip}. To test this conjecture, we estimate the equation

$$\pi_{ip} = Z_i \gamma + u_i \tag{4.8}$$

---

[5] On how to estimate (4.7) efficiently when λ_i is replaced by $\hat{\lambda}_i$, see Saxonhouse (1976, 1977). In this chapter we adopt the straightforward procedure of obtaining the adjustment parameter estimates $\hat{\lambda}_i$ and their sampling variances from the first-stage equation (4.5) and weighting each observation on all variables used in the second-stage equation (4.7) by the inverse of the estimated standard error of the dependent variable $\hat{\lambda}_i$. This weighting technique is equivalent to an application of generalized least squares where the true variance–covariance matrix is replaced by its estimate.

Table 4.1. *Profit adjustment equations: summary of joint generalized least squares estimates*

| Equation (4.5) | $\pi_{it} = \alpha_i + \lambda_i \pi_{it-1} + \epsilon_{it}$ | | $i = 1, 2, \ldots, 344$ | |
| | $\hat{\pi}_{ip} = \hat{\alpha}_i / (1 - \hat{\lambda}_i)$ | | $t = 1967, 1968, \ldots, 1982$ | |
	Mean	Mean standard error	Minimum	Maximum
$\hat{\pi}_{ip}$	0.279	0.133	−0.125	1.456
$\hat{\lambda}_i$	0.430	0.201	−0.548	1.147
$\bar{R}^2$	0.337	—	0.033	0.828
A	66 (82.5)			
B	180 (51.7)			
C	2 (0.58)			
D	5 (1.45)			

A = number of seemingly unrelated regression systems that are significant at the 5% level,

B = number of cases for which the value of $\hat{\lambda}$ is significantly positive at the 5% level,

C = number of cases for which the value of $\hat{\lambda}$ is significantly negative at the 5% level,

D = number of cases for which the value of $\hat{\lambda}$ violates the stationarity condition $|\lambda| < 1$.

where π_{ip} and γ are vectors of unknown parameters, Z_i is a matrix of independent structural variables, and the u_i are independently and identically distributed random variables with zero mean and variance σ_u^2. Since the true π_{ip} are unobservable, they must be replaced by $\hat{\pi}_{ip}$ – again a two-step procedure. In estimating (4.8), we employ the full sample.

IV   Empirical findings

Table 4.1 summarizes the results of the joint generalized least squares estimation of the profit adjustment equations (4.5) – where, as we indicated in the previous section, the 344 equations were combined into 80 systems of seemingly unrelated regressions. The computed values of the weighted R^2 statistic for each system indicate that the "fits" of the equations are reasonably good. Indeed, we find that 64 of the 80 estimated systems of disturbance-related regressions are significant at the 5 percent level. The slopes of these regression equations, which represent the estimate of the adjustment parameter λ, were significant for a large fraction of the industries in the sample and reveal a widely diverging partial adjustment structure.

For 164 of the 344 sampled industries, the values of the adjustment parameter estimator $\hat{\lambda}$ are not significantly different from zero, implying a very rapid (less than a year) profit rate adjustment. In those industries, short-run rents seem to move independently over time and such industries, therefore, can be assumed to be at their long-term equilibrium positions except for purely random displacements. The values of $\hat{\lambda}$ are negative in 29 cases, but of these only two are statistically significant at the 5 percent level. In addition, we should note that our estimates violate the stationarity condition $|\lambda_i| < 1$ in only five cases. The mean value of the 178 $\hat{\lambda}$'s that are found to be significantly positive is equal to 0.65, indicating, on average, a moderately slow erosion of short-run rents. By contrast, the mean value of the $\hat{\lambda}$'s that are positive but statistically insignificant is only 0.27, signifying a rapid erosion of short-run rents and a movement in the profit rate over time that is characterized by random displacements around the long-run equilibrium position.

The results of the generalized least squares estimation of equation (4.7), linking market structure and the speed of adjustment, are reported in Table 4.2.

Taking equations (a) and (b) first, we note that the number of firms N has a negative and statistically significant (at the 0.01 level) effect on the rate of profit adjustment λ, whereas the effect of concentration C is positive and significant (also at the 0.01 level). Thus, the smaller the number of firms and the more concentrated an industry is, the slower the rate at which the industry's excess returns are competed away (Hypotheses 1 and 2). This finding is consistent with the predictions of Chamberlinian theory.[6] The estimated coefficient of C implies that an increase of one percentage point in concentration would, on average, result in an increase of 0.37 percentage points in the adjustment parameter λ. Thus it appears that the effect of concentration is quantitatively important.

Equation (c) provides support for Hypothesis 3. We note that the effect of Gr is positive and significant (at the 0.01 level), indicating a slower erosion of excess returns in industries that experience rapid growth in demand for their products. This result is consistent with the conjecture that rapid growth mitigates the price-depressing effects of market share rivalry by limiting the volatility and intensity of such rivalry among the established competitors and by reducing the destabilizing effects of entry by new firms on existing industry arrangements.

---

[6] We should note that the *differential efficiency hypothesis* offers an alternative explanation of the positive correlation between concentration and the speed of adjustment.

Table 4.2. *Speed of adjustment and market structure*

Explanatory variables	Equation							
	(a)	(b)	(c)	(d)	(e)	(f)	(g)	(h)
Constant	0.769[a] (0.068)	0.325[a] (0.042)	0.410[a] (0.032)	0.467[a] (0.020)	0.249[a] (0.074)	0.249[a] (0.069)	0.372[a] (0.025)	0.218[a] (0.044)
$\log N_i$	−0.054[a] (0.012)							—
C_i		0.365[a] (0.086)						0.297[a] (0.074)
Gr_i			0.037[a] (0.012)					0.033[a] (0.011)
MES_i				1.105[b] (0.587)				—
$\log K_i$					0.044[a] (0.013)			—
$SUNK_i$						2.069[a] (0.576)		—
$(A/S)_i$							13.324[a] (2.186)	10.001[a] (2.001)
$(A/S)_i^2$							−101.583[a] (23.246)	−79.476[a] (20.695)
$\bar{R}^2$	0.124	0.116	0.065	0.023	0.073	0.112	0.260	0.375

Notes: Dependent variable: adjustment coefficient λ_i. Standard errors in parentheses. Number of observations is 137.
[a] Significant at the 0.01 level.
[b] Significant at the 0.10 level.

The results of equations (d) and (e) indicate a slower rate of erosion of excess returns in industries with large minimum efficient scale or high absolute capital requirements (Hypotheses 4 and 5). The effects of MES and K are positive and significant (at the 0.10 and 0.01 levels, respectively). These findings are consistent with the conventional wisdom that economies of scale deter entry and also that the need to invest large financial resources in order to compete in a market effectively creates an entry barrier.

Equation (f) supports the hypothesis that the performance of markets depends continuously on the degree to which they exhibit imperfect contestability. We find that the effect of SUNK is positive and significant (at the 0.01 level), indicating a slower rate of erosion of excess returns in industries where the share of investment that is composed of sunk capital is large (Hypothesis 6). This result is consistent with the conjecture that the smaller the share of sunk outlays, the more contestable the industry is, the more vulnerable the industry will be to hit-and-run incursions, and hence, the more rapid the elimination of excess profits.

Finally, equation (g) reveals a nonlinear (inverted-U) relationship between advertising intensity and the erosion rate of excess returns. To the extent that advertising is an indicator of product differentiation, higher levels of advertising intensity are associated with slower rates of erosion of positive rents, reflecting the monopolistic potential created by enhanced product differentiation. Indeed, the finding that over most of the sample advertising slows down such an erosion may be interpreted as supporting the *Advertising = Market Power* view. However, λ increases with A/S but at a decreasing rate. In fact, beyond a critical level of advertising intensity equal to 0.06, advertising seems to facilitate a faster erosion of excess profits. This result could signify the weakening of collusive arrangements as product differentiation becomes more prominent and the competitive pressure resulting from different sellers attempting through intensive advertising to concentrate demand upon their own brands increases.

Because of their collinearity, it becomes difficult to precisely identify the separate effects of the structural variables involved in this chapter when they are all introduced in the same equation. Thus, to test the various hypotheses in equations (a)–(g), we have entered these variables separately. In equation (h), on the other hand, where we enter concentration C, growth Gr, and advertising intensity A/S, these variables seem to account for 37.5 percent of the variance of the adjustment parameter λ, signifying a quantitatively important relationship.[7]

These data reject the hypothesis that within the sampled period, the forces of competition drive profit rates toward the competitive norm, thereby equalizing such rates across industries. Indeed, hypothesis H_0 is rejected in favor of H_1 at the 1 percent level.[8] Thus, long-run rents do not

---

[7] In addition, we obtained the following results:

(i) $\quad \lambda_i = 0.552 - 0.041 \log N_i + 0.036\, Gr_i + 10.418\,(A/S)_i - 77.033\,(A/S)_i^2,$
$\qquad (0.065)\quad (0.012)\qquad\quad (0.011)\qquad\quad (2.016)\qquad\qquad (21.155)\qquad \bar{R}^2 = 0.357$

(j) $\quad \lambda_i = 0.306 + 0.034\, Gr_i + 1.535\, MES_i + 10.805\,(A/S)_i - 83.149\,(A/S)_i^2,$
$\qquad (0.036)\quad (0.012)\qquad (0.614)\qquad\quad (2.073)\qquad\qquad (21.635)\qquad \bar{R}^2 = 0.319$

To give an example of the collinearity problem we also estimated:

(k) $\quad \lambda_i = 0.219 + 0.271\, C_i + 0.035\, Gr_i + 0.390\, MES_i + 9.920\,(A/S)_i$
$\qquad (0.045)\quad (0.087)\qquad (0.011)\qquad (0.696)\qquad\quad (2.013)$

$\qquad - 78.414\,(A/S)_i^2,$ $\qquad\qquad\qquad\qquad\qquad\qquad \bar{R}^2 = 0.371$
$\qquad (20.849)$

A comparison of equations (j) and (k) indicates that the introduction of C reduces the coefficient of MES to insignificance.

[8] To discriminate between H_0 and H_1, we estimate model (4.5) and its restricted version

$\qquad \pi_{it} = \gamma(1 - \lambda_i) + \lambda_i \pi_{it-1} + u_{it}$

Table 4.3. *Long-run profitability and market structure*

Explanatory variables	Equation		
	(i)	(ii)	(iii)
Constant	0.059^a	0.207^a	0.197^a
	(0.008)	(0.009)	(0.010)
π_i^0	0.786^a	—	—
	(0.031)		
C_i	—	0.053^a	—
		(0.015)	
Gr_i	—	0.009^a	0.008^a
		(0.002)	(0.002)
$\log K_i$	—	—	0.006^a
			(0.002)
$(A/S)_i$	—	1.230^a	1.285^a
		(0.202)	(0.203)
$\bar{R}^2$	0.661	0.251	0.248

Notes: Dependent variable: long-run profit π_{ip}. Standard errors in parentheses. Number of observations is 344.
^{a} Significant at the 0.01 level.

seem to have been completely dissipated during the 16-year period covered in this study.

We find that industries with relatively high (low) initial profit rates continue to earn high (low) profit rates even in the long run. Aside from the fact that hypothesis H_0 is rejected in favor of H_1, the persistence of differences in profitability across industries (during the 16-year period of this study) is also evidenced by the high rank-order correlation between initial-period profitability π_i^0 and long-run profitability π_{ip}. The estimated value of the Spearman coefficient is $\rho(\pi_i^0, \pi_{ip}) = .74$, which is significant at the 0.01 level. The tendency of industry profits to persist is also strongly confirmed by the results reported in Table 4.3. According to equation (i), 78.6 percent of initial-period profitability is projected to persist indefinitely.

Among the structural factors that influence the speed of adjustment, concentration, demand growth, capital requirements, and advertising also

and then we apply an F test. The computed value of the F-statistic is

$$F = \frac{(5.397 - 4.402)/344}{4.402/4472} = 2.94 > F_{344,4472}^{0.99} = 1.20.$$

seem to be important determinants of long-run profitability. According to equation (ii) in Table 4.3, the effects of C, Gr, and A/S are all positive and significant (at the 0.01) level. Differences in these variables across industries account for 25.1 percent of the variance of π_{ip}, indicating that the effects of these variables are both statistically significant and quantitatively important. Similarly, according to equation (iii), differences in demand growth, capital requirements, and advertising seem to account for 24.8 percent of the variance of long-run profitability, signifying again a quantitatively important relationship.

V   Summary

The results of this chapter reveal a widely diverging profit adjustment structure across the U.S. manufacturing industries and provide strong support for the hypothesis that the speed with which excess profits erode in an industry depends crucially upon its underlying economic structure.

We find that excess returns erode more slowly in industries with a small number of operating firms and high levels of concentration, experiencing rapid demand growth, and characterized by significant economies of scale, large absolute capital requirements, large sunk outlays, and high advertising expenditures. These results support both the Chamberlinian and contestability conjectures and are consistent with the entry barriers identified by Bain and his followers.

Our results establish a very strong pattern of persistence of industry profits over time. We detect a very strong rank-order correlation between long-run and initial-period profits in cross section. We also find that permanent profits differ significantly across industries and that such differences can be explained by differences in their underlying economic structure.

CHAPTER 5

The persistence of profitability in Canada

R. SHYAM KHEMANI AND DANIEL M. SHAPIRO

I   Introduction

The state of competition and pace of adjustment are frequent themes in public policy discussions regarding Canadian industry. Compared with other Western industrialized countries, Canadian industry tends to be highly concentrated, and domestic markets are generally small relative to efficient scale of production and subject to tariff protection. Over the past decade or so, however, the trends toward increased industry concentration have been less marked, tariffs have on average been reduced to half their pre-1970 levels, and import competition pressures have been exerted in a wide spectrum of markets (see Khemani, 1986). Negotiations for bilateral free trade between Canada and the United States are also currently under way.

In light of these developments, it is of some interest to examine the trend of corporate profits over time. To the extent that the competitive process is relatively fast, profits above or below the competitive norm should disappear (allowing for factors such as uncertainty, innovations, and changes in tastes). If, however, profits persist over time, they may be indicative of impediments in the competitive process such as barriers to entry and oligopolistic coordination of firm price–output policies.

In this chapter, we first measure the extent of persistence in long-run profits of large Canadian corporations over the period 1964–82. We then examine the determinants of these profits and the role played by entry and exit of firms in the adjustment process. Our conclusions are that the competitive process does work in pushing profit rates toward the competitive norm but it does not succeed in equalizing profit rates. There is

We wish to thank the members of the POP group, particularly Paul Geroski and Dennis Mueller, for valuable suggestions. John Cable, Paul Gorecki, and Lorne Switzer also provided helpful comments and assistance. Howard Nemiroff did an admirable job as research assistant. The financial support of the Bureau of Competition Policy, Ottawa, is gratefully acknowledged. Views expressed in this chapter are those of the authors and do not necessarily reflect the views of their institutional affiliations.

variation in the adjustment of profit rates depending on the initial profit position of the firm and across industries. The industry to which a firm is classified is found to be an important determinant of whether the firm has high or low long-run projected profits. Although the entry and exit of firms respond to profit incentives, their impact on the speed of adjustment is not found to be significant.

II   The model: measuring persistence

In this section we derive the equation that forms the basis for all studies in this volume. Our exposition follows Mueller (1986 and Chapter 3).

It is assumed that a firm i's return on capital in year t, π_{it}, may be decomposed as

$$\pi_{it} = c + r_i + s_{it}, \tag{5.1}$$

where c is a competitive return earned by all firms, r_i is a firm-specific permanent rent, and s_{it} is a transitory (short-run) rent with zero expected value.

The short-run rents s_{it} are assumed to be serially correlated and follow the first-order autoregressive process:

$$s_{it} = \lambda_i s_{it-1} + u_{it}, \tag{5.2}$$

where $0 < \lambda < 1$ to ensure convergence and u_{it} are distributed $N(0, \sigma^2)$. The substitution of (5.2) and (5.1) and some rearrangement yields

$$\pi_{it} = (1 - \lambda_i)(c + r_i) + \lambda_i \pi_{it-1} + u_{it}. \tag{5.3}$$

Equation (5.3) may be rewritten as a simple autoregressive equation:

$$\pi_{it} = \alpha_i + \lambda_i \pi_{it-1} + u_{it}, \tag{5.4}$$

which is the basic equation to be estimated. Letting $\hat{\alpha}_i$ and $\hat{\lambda}_i$ denote the estimated coefficients in (5.4), we derive an estimate of the long-run projected profits of firm i $(c + r_i)$ as

$$\hat{\pi}_{ip} = \frac{\hat{\alpha}_i}{1 - \hat{\lambda}_i}. \tag{5.5}$$

Evidently, if all firms were earning the competitive rate of return, then $\hat{\pi}_{ip} = c$ for all i and $r_i = 0$ for all i. Conversely, if $\hat{\pi}_{ip}$ is not equal across firms, then firms earn permanent rents, which are not eroded by competitive forces. This latter case would indicate that some firms earn returns above (or below) the competitive norm and that these returns are expected to persist indefinitely. In this sense one may refer to the persistence of long-run profits.

However, there is a second sense in which the term "persistence" may be employed, and this is measured by $\hat{\lambda}_i$. The term $1 - \hat{\lambda}_i$ provides a measure of the rate at which short-run rents are eroded and therefore is a measure of the speed of adjustment to the firm's long-run rate of profit. Therefore, the larger the value $\hat{\lambda}_i$ assumes, the slower is the rate at which short-run rents are eroded and short-run rents may be said to be more persistent.

In the succeeding sections we provide estimates of $\hat{\pi}_{ip}$ and $\hat{\lambda}_i$ for a sample of Canadian firms and analyze both long-run and short-run persistence.

III   The data

The data required for the estimation of equation (5.4) were obtained from Standard & Poor's Canadian COMPUSTAT tape. The COMPUSTAT tape provides times-series financial information on some 400 stock-exchange-quoted Canadian companies. Privately owned firms are not surveyed, and although this is true of many countries, it is particularly important in Canada since wholly owned subsidiaries of foreign companies are *not* included in the tape. No time-series data on such firms are publicly available, and these firms are therefore not represented in the sample.

The sample is restricted to firms in mining (including fossil fuels) and manufacturing. The decision to include mining firms was made because Canada's resource-intensive economy is such that many of its largest firms are found in this sector. Moreover, many of these firms are vertically integrated and do engage in some manufacturing activity. It is therefore not unusual for Canadian studies on firm-level profitability to include such firms (see, e.g., Caves et al. 1980, ch. 12 and Appendix A).

As of 1982, which is the last year for which data were available, there were 181 firms on the COMPUSTAT tape that were classified to mining and manufacturing. To illustrate the importance of wholly owned subsidiaries, we examined the *Financial Post* list of the largest 500 Canadian industrials in 1982. It was found that 88 firms in mining and manufacturing were wholly owned subsidiaries of foreign (primarily American) corporations. Since other research (Shapiro, 1980) has shown that wholly owned U.S. subsidiaries are the most profitable firms in Canada, our sample excludes firms that are potentially the most persistently profitable. It should be noted that these companies are to a large extent concentrated in a few industries, namely, food, chemicals and pharmaceuticals, electronics (including computers), rubber, and automobiles.

Of the 181 listed firms, continuous time-series data were not available for all firms. Two samples were employed, differing by the choice of initial year. The first sample was comprised of firms for which continuous data

Table 5.1. *Profile of surviving and nonsurviving firms*

	1964–82		1968–82	
	n	%	*n*	%
Surviving (1982)				
Continuous	129	71.3	161	88.9
Initiated after 1964 (1968)	25	13.8	8	4.5
Nonsurviving (1982)				
Acquired/merged	24	13.3	10	5.5
Liquidated	3	1.6	2	1.1
Total	181	100	181	100

existed for the period 1964–82 (129 firms); the second sample covered the period 1968–82 (161 firms). Table 5.1 provides a profile of the 181 firms.[1]

In addition to the bias created by omitting wholly owned subsidiaries, Table 5.1 suggests that the sample may also overrepresent continuing firms. Evidence provided by Baldwin and Gorecki (1983) for Canadian *manufacturing* firms beween 1970 and 1979 suggests that continuing firms represent 75 percent of the manufacturing census, as compared to our 89 percent over roughly the same period. Of the 161 continuing firms in the second sample, 97 were included in the Toronto Stock Exchange (TSE) 300 Index as of 1982. The TSE 300 index is used to represent trends in stock market activity. It is to be noted that the TSE 300 contains 182 firms in mining and manufacturing so that the 97 firms represent 53 percent of this part of the index.

Profitability was measured by profits plus interest payments divided by total assets, both net and gross of taxes. It was decided to employ two measures of profitability because of the nature of the sample. Tax regimes may differ between mining and manufacturing, and it is therefore important to account for this possibility by measuring profitability before – and after – taxes. The means and standard deviations for the time series are recorded in Table 5.2.

IV   Results: the degree of persistence

Equation (5.4) was estimated for each firm in each sample using the two measures of profitability. To allow for the effects of business cycles, each firm's annual rate of profit is expressed as the deviation from the sample

[1] The industrial composition of the sample is found in Table 5.5.

Table 5.2. *Means and standard deviations of time-series profit rates*

	Before tax		After tax	
	1964–82	1968–82	1964–82	1968–82
Number of firms (n)	129	161	129	161
Mean (m)	17.671	16.991	13.761	12.999
Standard deviation (s)	8.364	11.904	6.036	9.533
Coefficient of variation (v)	0.505	0.727	0.476	0.756
Correlation between m and s	−0.732	−0.754	−0.801	−0.851

Table 5.3. *Mean $\hat{\pi}_p$ and λ by subsample: profits defined after tax*

	1968–82, 161 firms			1964–82, 129 firms		
Subsample	π_0	$\hat{\pi}_p$	$\hat{\lambda}$	π_0	$\hat{\pi}_p$	$\hat{\lambda}$
1	0.1440994	0.0791197	0.3404535	0.1452143	0.0577394	0.3391697
2	0.0446035	0.0266929	0.2947784	0.038444	0.0141868	0.3362034
3	0.0103416	0.0183294	0.2036664	0.0045478	0.0072554	0.2272618
4	−0.0154159	−0.0001625	0.2329808	−0.0224102	0.0140764	0.3585247
5	−0.048846	−0.0120592	0.2520245	−0.0524078	−0.0024968	0.4507333
6	−0.1277406	−0.1080114	0.4650474	−0.1256459	−0.0638755	0.4795536
A		76 (47.2)			76 (58.9)	
B		33 (20.5)			39 (30.2)	
C		23 (14.3)			19 (14.7)	
D		83 (51.6)			59 (45.7)	
E		0 (0.0)			1 (0.8)	
F		0 (0.0)			0 (0.0)	
G		0.454			0.506	
H		0.876			0.883	

A = number of cases for which $\bar{R}^2 > 0.1$
B = number of cases for which $\hat{\pi}_p$ is significantly positive (10% level, two-tailed test)
C = number of cases for which $\hat{\pi}_p$ is significantly negative
D = number of cases for which $\hat{\lambda}$ is significantly positive (10% level, one-tailed test)
E = number of cases for which $\hat{\lambda}$ is significantly negative (10% level, two-tailed test)
F = number of cases for which $\hat{\lambda} > 1$
G = correlation coefficient between $\hat{\pi}_p$ and π_0
H = correlation coefficient between $\hat{\pi}_p$ and $\bar{\pi}$ (the average of the normalized profit rate for the sample period)
Note: Figures in parentheses are percentages.

mean for that year. This provided estimates of the projected long-run rate of profit ($\hat{\pi}_{ip}$) and the rate of adjustment ($\hat{\lambda}_i$) for each firm. The results are summarized in Tables 5.3 and 5.4. To examine the question of persistence, the sample was divided into six approximately equal-sized

Table 5.4. *Mean $\hat{\pi}_p$ and λ by subsample: profits defined before tax*

Subsample	1968–82, 161 firms			1964–82, 129 firms		
	π_0	$\hat{\pi}_p$	$\hat{\lambda}$	π_0	$\hat{\pi}_p$	$\hat{\lambda}$
1	0.197095	0.0967077	0.4593334	0.204456	0.0909097	0.4739509
2	0.0604335	0.0381147	0.3448213	0.0589569	−0.0014265	0.4084387
3	0.0143116	0.0212216	0.2650604	0.009195	0.0157466	0.3403951
4	−0.0257635	−0.0091263	0.2786551	−0.0325742	0.0003538	0.383614
5	−0.0703787	−0.0179383	0.3296068	−0.0820923	0.0056587	0.5603588
6	−0.1649487	−0.1166487	0.4687834	−0.1653497	−0.081046	0.4864179
A		72 (44.7)			35 (27.1)	
B		38 (23.6)			22 (17.1)	
C		28 (17.4)			22 (17.1)	
D		77 (47.8)			93 (72.1)	
E		0 (0.0)			0 (0.0)	
F		0 (0.0)			0 (0.0)	
G		0.402			0.514	
H		0.841			0.867	

Notes: Figures in parentheses are percentages. See Table 5.3 for definitions of *A–H*.

categories defined by the level of average profitability in the initial two years of the sample period (π_0). A comparison of π_0 and $\hat{\pi}_p$ across subgroups reveals the extent to which the ordering of the subgroups persists.

As an example, consider the 1968–82 sample where profits are defined after tax. The average profitability of the most successful firms in 1968 and 1969 was 14.4 percentage points above the mean for those years. The mean profit rate for all firms in this sample for the entire time period was 13.0 percent. The long-run rate of profit for these firms is projected to be 7.9 percentage points above this mean figure. The projected profits of the subgroup with the highest initial profits are higher than all other subgroups. Similarly, the least successful firms earned initial profits that were 12.8 percentage points below the mean and were projected to earn long-run profits that were 10.8 percentage points below the mean, which is lower than all other subgroups. In general, the ordering of the subgroups remains unchanged, with one exception being the 1964–82 sample, when profits are defined before tax. In all other cases it is true that firms that began the sample period in the most (least) profitable category were projected to earn long-run returns that maintained them in that category. In other words, the best (worst) performing firms at the beginning of the period are projected to remain the best (worst) performing firms into the future. In this sense, one can state that there are persistent differences in profitability among firms. This is also evident by examining the simple correlation coefficient between $\hat{\pi}_{ip}$ and π_0, which ranges from 0.40 to 0.51, thus confirming that, on average, high (low) initial rates of return are expected to persist. It is to be noted that although profits do persist, there is some adjustment toward the mean over time. The range in profitability between the highest and lowest subgroups is always reduced when comparing π_0 with $\hat{\pi}_p$. Thus, the competitive process does work in pushing profit rates toward the mean, but it does not succeed in equalizing profit rates. In general, these results and conclusions are similar to those reported for other countries. A direct comparison may be made by referring to Odagiri and Yamawaki (Chapter 10).

The projected long-run profit rates of each firm were also aggregated by broad industry categories, results of which are found in Table 5.5. In Canada, it would appear that the most persistently successful firms are found in the chemical, pulp and paper, petroleum refining, and food and beverage industries. The least successful firms are found in the textile and resource industries, particularly petroleum exploration. The Canadian results may therefore be sensitive to the fact that a significant percentage of the sample comes from the resource sector. Various tests for pooling, reported in the following paragraphs, suggest that the sample composition is not of critical importance.

The mean values of the adjustment parameter $\hat{\lambda}$ are also reported in Tables 5.3 and 5.4, by subgroup. The means for the entire sample ranged between 0.28 and 0.34. Recalling that lower values of $\hat{\lambda}$ imply a faster speed of adjustment, these values suggest that on average the speed of adjustment for Canadian firms was faster than for any other country over roughly comparable time periods (see Odagiri and Yamawaki, Chapter 10). Only Mueller (Chapter 3) reports a lower average value for $\hat{\lambda}$, but this was for the period 1950–72. In addition, the mean values are U-shaped across subgroups, indicating that the speed of adjustment was lowest for the most and least profitable firms. This result is not consistent with the notion that competition works to erode the profits of the most profitable firms or to speed up the convergence of low-profit firms to levels closer to the mean. It is apparently the case that firms with initial levels of profitability much above (below) the mean are slower to adjust to their long-run levels. For these firms, short-run or transitory profits above (below) the mean are more slowly dissipated. Thus for these firms profits can be said to persist in both of the senses defined in the preceding. They have larger projected permanent deviations from the normal return on assets, and the short-run deviations from these permanent profit levels erode more slowly than for the other firms.

To analyze the quantitative aspects of persistence more fully, a regression analysis was undertaken. The magnitude of long-run persistence was

Table 5.5. *Mean of $\hat{\pi}_p$ by industry*

	$\hat{\pi}_p$, 1964–82			$\hat{\pi}_p$, 1968–82		
	After tax	Before tax	N	After tax	Before tax	N
Food	0.0187186	0.0268874	19	0.0163111	0.0192315	20
Textiles and clothes	−0.0392729	−0.0692715	4	−0.0243406	−0.0521981	5
Pulp and paper	0.0108764	0.0072983	9	0.0161357	0.0142668	10
Chemicals (including pharmaceuticals)	0.0256769	0.0187941	4	0.0166636	0.0062899	6
Petroleum refining	0.0039668	0.0030976	9	0.0145529	0.0155094	9
Rubber products	−0.0067279	−0.0228875	1	0.0042326	−0.0088561	1
Cement products	0.0001943	−0.0132954	7	−0.0112359	−0.026054	10
Iron and steel	0.0088539	0.0021455	8	0.0102891	0.0038903	8
Nonferrous metals	−0.0011336	−0.0131605	1	0.0341085	0.0434602	2
Metal products	0.0192651	0.0321758	3	0.035339	0.0485533	7
Machinery and tools	NA	NA	0	−0.0107797	−0.0296608	2
Electrical equipment	−0.00456	−0.0038745	9	0.0131237	0.0162174	10
Cars and other	−0.0014852	0.0019622	4	0.0081348	0.004884	5
Wood products	0.0096576	−0.0021209	2	0.0087001	−0.0075961	3
Printing and publishing	0.0818404	0.1134254	8	0.094942	0.120375	9
Mines (excluding coal)	−0.0017908	0.0003493	25	−0.0593437	−0.0431953	34
Coal	−0.0732764	−0.105306	2	−0.0823599	−0.1165334	2
Petroleum exploration and development	−0.0201007	−0.0178038	14	−0.020636	−0.0212658	18

Note: NA, not available.

Table 5.6. *Magnitude of persistence*

	After tax			Before tax		
	1	2	3	1	2	3
Constant	0.008	0.012[a]	0.017[a]	0.003	0.009[a]	0.016[a]
	(0.006)	(0.003)	(0.004)	(0.004)	(0.004)	(0.006)
π_0	0.555[a]	0.532[a]	—	0.555[a]	0.526[a]	—
	(0.046)	(0.046)		(0.047)	(0.048)	
π_0^+	—	—	0.427[a]	—	—	0.406[a]
			(0.069)			(0.074)
π_0^-	—	—	0.702[a]	—	—	0.690[a]
			(0.094)			(0.092)
D_R	—	−0.016[a]	−0.014[a]	—	−0.023[a]	−0.020[a]
		(0.006)	(0.006)		(0.009)	(0.009)
$\bar{R}^2$	0.479	0.497	0.506	0.460	0.481	0.492

Notes: Figures in parentheses are standard errors; $n = 161$.
Dependent variable: $\hat{\pi}_p$ (weighted).

$$\pi_0^+ = \pi_0 \text{ for } \pi_0 > 0, \qquad D_R = \begin{cases} 1 & \text{if firm is in mining,} \\ 0 & \text{otherwise.} \end{cases}$$
$$\pi_0^- = \pi_0 \text{ for } \pi_0 < 0,$$

[a] Significant at 5%.

investigated by regressing $\hat{\pi}_p$ on π_0. The results are reported in Table 5.6. To conserve space, we report only the results for the 1968–82 sample; those obtained for 1964–82 are similar. Since the dependent variable is itself estimated, we weight each observation by the standard error of $\hat{\pi}_{ip}$ as suggested by Saxonhouse (1976). This procedure takes account of the fact that $\hat{\pi}_{ip}$ was not significantly different from zero in all cases by giving greater weight to observations with lower standard errors. The results in column 1 suggest that 55.5 percent of initial profit deviations from the sample mean are projected to persist indefinitely. This may be compared to Mueller's (Chapter 3) finding that 54.2 percent of profit differences persist in the U.S. sample (unadjusted for mergers). However, this does not represent the best-fit equation. Tests for common slopes and intercepts between manufacturing and mining (resource) industries revealed no slope differences but did indicate that the intercepts were different. Column 2 reports the results obtained by estimating the equation with a dummy variable for mining firms (D_R). These results indicate that firms in the resource sector were less profitable than those in manufacturing. The disparity was reduced using after-tax profits, suggesting that the tax

Table 5.7. *Magnitude of the speed of adjustment*

	After tax		Before tax	
	1	2	1	2
Constant	0.344^a	0.252^a	0.405^a	0.322^a
	(0.019)	(0.024)	(0.019)	(0.026)
π_0	−0.166	—	−0.041	—
	(0.157)		(0.115)	
π_0^+	—	0.597^a	—	0.434^a
		(0.204)		(0.156)
π_0^-	—	-1.766^a	—	-1.124^a
		(0.334)		(0.276)
$\bar{R}^2$	0.001	0.147	0.000	0.093

Notes: See footnote to Table 5.6; $n = 161$.
Dependent variable: $\hat{\lambda}$ (weighted).
[a] Significant at 5%.

system worked to the advantage of resource-based firms. However, it remains true that around 53 percent of initial profit differences persist. Finally, column 3 addresses the question of whether the degree of persistence differs according to whether initial profits were above or below the mean. For firms that began the sample period with above-average profits, between 41 and 43 percent of initial profit deviations are expected to persist; for firms that began with below-average profits, between 69 and 70 percent of the initial deviations are expected to persist. These results imply that the best performing firms are subject to competitive pressures that erode but do not eliminate their advantages. However, the worst performing firms are apparently under less pressure to improve.

A similar exercise was undertaken with regard to $\hat{\lambda}$. The results are reported in Table 5.7. As in the previous case, all observations are weighted by the standard error of the dependent variable ($\hat{\lambda}$). Tests for pooling revealed that neither the slope nor the intercept differed between manufacturing and mining firms. Column 1 reports the results of the simple regression of $\hat{\lambda}$ on π_0 and indicates no significant relationship. For the United States, Mueller (Chapter 3) found a negative and significant relationship. However, it is evident from Tables 5.3 and 5.4 that the relationship is nonlinear. We therefore estimated an equation, column 2, that allowed the rate of adjustment ($\hat{\lambda}$) to vary according to whether initial profits were above or below the mean. These results confirm the U-shaped pattern discussed in the preceding and indicate that the speed of adjustment was fastest the closer the firm was to the mean at the beginning of the period. The slowest adjustment speeds are found for firms that began the period further away from the mean. This is not what the competitive hypothesis would suggest. If all deviations from the mean are short-run rents, then one would find the opposite pattern. Therefore, these results also imply the existence of permanent rents.[2]

V The determinants of long-run profits

In the preceding section it was established that persistent differences in long-run profits exist. The purpose of this section is to examine the determinants of interfirm differences in $\hat{\pi}_p$. In classical industrial organization theory interfirm differences in profitability are explained by industry-specific variables such as concentration and the height of entry barriers. However, recent challenges to this view have argued that firm-specific advantages generating interfirm differences in efficiency will be more important than industry-specific factors in determining relative profitability. The empirical literature related to this debate has, for the most part, focused on the relative contribution of concentration and market share. In this volume, Mueller (Chapter 3) proposes a model in which concentration, market share, and advertising intensity interact to explain differences in long-run profits.

Our data did not allow us to pursue these lines of analysis. We have no firm-specific data on market share, nor on other relevant variables such as research and development and advertising. As a consequence, we have adopted a somewhat different empirical strategy. We first specify a simple descriptive model of the determinants of firm-level profitability in which the explanatory variables fall into the following categories: industry specific (grouped), firm specific, and size specific. We then subject this model to a series of hierarchically nested tests along the lines suggested by Schmalensee (1985) to determine which of these is most important in determining interfirm differences in long-run profits ($\hat{\pi}_p$).

Thus, we estimate

$$\hat{\pi}_{ip} = \alpha + B_I I + B_T T + B_C C + \gamma S_i + \epsilon_i,$$

where

[2] It may then be true, as Mueller (Chapter 3) suggests, that the speed of adjustment depends not only on π_0 but on π_p as well. For the United States, Mueller found this to be true. Therefore, for the United States the speed of adjustment depends both on where a firm starts (π_0) and where it is headed ($\hat{\pi}_p$). For Canada, we found no such relationship. The best-fit equation is that discussed in the text.

$\hat{\pi}_{ip}$ = estimated long-run profit rate of firm i

I = a vector of dummy variables indicating the industry to which i is classified (41 industries)

T = a vector of dummy variables indicating the diversification strategy of the firm (four categories)

C = a vector of dummy variables indicating whether the firm is a multinational corporation and its nationality (four categories)

S = a measure of firm size (the logarithm of sales averaged over the period)

$\alpha; B, \gamma$ = the estimated constant; coefficients

ϵ = an error term, assumed $N(0, \sigma^2)$

The rationale for this model is as follows. The industry dummy variables are included to capture the industry-specific factor noted in the preceding. The industry to which the firm is classified was taken from the COMPUSTAT tape; the classification is primarily at the four-digit (U.S.) Standard Industrial Classification (SIC) level, although there are exceptions. Since the data are collected at the firm level, many of the sample firms operate in more than one industry.

The T and C variables are included to capture firm-specific advantages in management and asset utilization. The T-vector indicates the diversification strategy of the firm. For this purpose, we have adopted the Wrigley (1970) classification: single product, dominant product, related product, unrelated product (conglomerate). The classification for each firm was obtained from Caves et al. (1980) and Lecraw and Thompson (1978). The T-vector is interpreted to reflect firm-specific advantages in decision making and asset utilization. The extent to which a firm diversifies may reflect the ability of management to detect and exploit more profitable investment opportunities outside its main line of business. In part, this depends on the ability of management to exploit potential economies of scope. However, to the extent that firms possess specific assets (core skills) that are underutilized and fungible, a transaction costs analysis (e.g., Teece, 1982) would suggest that some diversification (at least up to conglomerate diversification) is an optimal strategy. Thus, a firm's diversification strategy may reflect management's ability to effectively deploy its assets. If this is the case, then one would expect that related diversification should be a relatively profitable strategy and that unrelated diversification should be relatively unprofitable. It is also possible that diversification is motivated by the desire to maximize managerial objectives such as size or growth. In this case all diversification may reduce profitability.

The C-vector is also included to capture the existence of firm-specific advantages. The theory of the multinational corporation (MNC) as it has

Table 5.8. *F-Tests: after-tax profits*

Test	F	d.f.	Restriction	Test	F	d.f.	Restriction
1	3.52	(3, 114)	T	15	3.10^a	(40, 115)	I
2	1.65	(3, 114)	C	16	0.47	(3, 115)	C
3	2.73^a	(40, 114)	I	17	2.59^a	(40, 120)	I
4	10.52^a	(1, 114)	S	18	4.38	(1, 120)	S
5	1.55	(3, 117)	C	19	2.24	(3, 157)	T
6	2.64^a	(40, 117)	I	20	19.03^a	(1, 157)	S
7	7.76^a	(1, 117)	S	21	0.94	(3, 157)	C
8	3.46	(3, 117)	T	22	17.14^a	(1, 157)	S
9	2.76^a	(40, 117)	I	23	0.42	(3, 118)	C
10	7.01^a	(1, 117)	S	24	2.89^a	(40, 118)	I
11	1.92	(3, 154)	C	25	0.86	(3, 155)	T
12	3.22	(3, 154)	T	26	0.17	(3, 155)	C
13	24.56^a	(1, 154)	S	27	2.54	(3, 118)	T
14	2.56	(3, 155)	T	28	3.12^a	(40, 118)	I

Notes: The test number is that indicated in Figure 5.1. Significance indicates that the null hypothesis that the omitted set has no impact is rejected. The letter indicates the restriction tested.
[a] Significant at 1%.

evolved from Hymer (1976) suggests that becoming an MNC has, as a prerequisite, the possession of firm-specific assets that impart domestic market power (market share) and can be transferred internally at relatively no cost. Thus, one would expect that firms that are MNCs also possess unique firm-specific assets. The C-vector contains four categories: Canadian non-MNC, Canadian MNC, U.S. MNC, other MNC. The distinction of MNCs by nationality was based on previous evidence (Shapiro, 1980) suggesting that subsidiaries of U.S. firms in Canada are more profitable than the subsidiaries of non-U.S. firms. Canadian MNCs were classified by referring to Rugman and McIlveen (1985), Niosi (1985), and Litvak and Maule (1981). Non-Canadian MNCs are subsidiaries of foreign firms where the parent (assumed to be an MNC) owns 50 percent or more of the voting shares. The identities of these companies and their nationalities were obtained from the Statistics Canada publication *Inter-Corporate Ownership*. The sample composition by diversification and ownership categories is presented in Table 5.8.

Finally, we include a measure of firm size (sales) to represent the advantages (if any) associated with large-scale operations. These advantages may reside in access to capital, political influence resulting in subsidies, tariff protection and advantageous regulation, or efficiency gains. It is to be noted that alternative measures of size (assets) do not affect the results reported in what follows.

The model was estimated on the sample of 161 firms (1968–82) with $\hat{\pi}_{ip}$ as the dependent variable and measured both before and after taxes. As before, all observations were weighted by the standard error of $\hat{\pi}_{ip}$. The procedure was then to successively eliminate sets of variables and to test the validity of the inward restrictions. The procedure is illustrated in Figures 5.1 and 5.2, and Tables 5.9 and 5.10 present the F-test values. The results in the before- and after-taxes cases are virtually identical, so we focus on the latter. We began with the unrestricted model, which includes I, T, C, and S. Each was dropped sequentially and the inward restriction tested. The numbers along the arrowed lines in Figure 5.1 correspond to the F-tests in Table 5.9.[3] In all, 32 different tests were undertaken, including the null model, although Table 5.9 reports only the first 28. It can be seen that the null hypothesis that the industry effect (I) does not matter is rejected in all tests. Individually, I accounts for 32 percent of the variation in $\hat{\pi}_p$, whereas the full model accounts for 39 percent. Conversely, all restrictions involving the firm-specific variables T and C were accepted. The size restriction was rejected in all cases, except test 18, where it was tested against industry. Beginning with the unrestricted model, we therefore accept the restricted models $I+C+S$ and $I+T+S$ (tests 1 and 2). From these, we only accept the restricted model $I+S$ (tests 5 and 8). Tests 17 and 18 then indicate that we can accept the industry-only model. Finally, the industry-only model is accepted against the null model. We therefore conclude that only industry matters: Variations in long-run profitability are explained by industry affiliation.

These results are certainly contrary to much recent evidence in the industrial organization literature that suggests that firm effects (market share) are important. They are, however, consistent with Schmalensee's (1985) results and with recent evidence provided by Grant, Jammine, and Thomas (1986). The latter estimate a model similar to ours and conclude that product and multinational diversity are much less important than industry in explaining profitability differences among U.K. firms. Indeed, they find that diversity (product and multinational) accounts for only 1–2 percent of the variation, which is similar to the amounts in our $T+C$ equations.

---

[3] As noted by Mizon (1976), when one performs tests on nested models that require two or more inward tests, the required level of significance at the intermediate steps should follow $(1-\epsilon)^n = (1-\alpha)$, where α is the required level of significance for accepting the model as a whole, n is the number of models (not including the null model), and ϵ is the required level of significance for the intermediate steps. In our case, we set $\alpha = 0.05$ and $n = 4$ so that $\epsilon = 0.0127$. For simplicity we adopt the 1% level for the tests, but all results hold at 1.27%. It is to be noted that if we were to adopt the 5% criterion at each step, then based on the preceding formula, this would be equivalent to using a level of significance of 18.55% for the model as a whole.

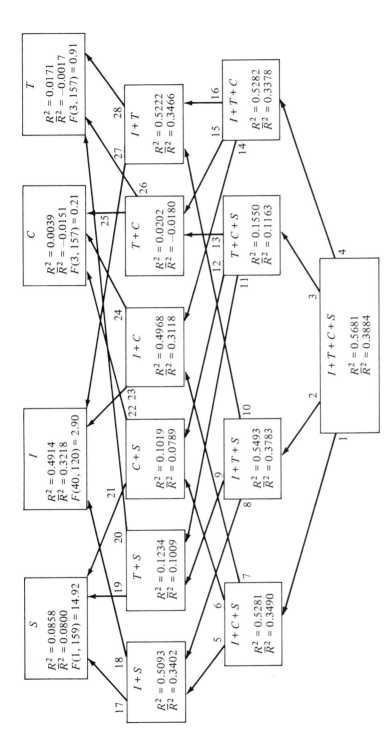

Figure 5.1. Flowchart of nested tests, after-tax profits. *Notes*: I = industry dummy variables (41); T = strategy dummy variables (4); C = control dummy variables (4); S = average size (ln sales).

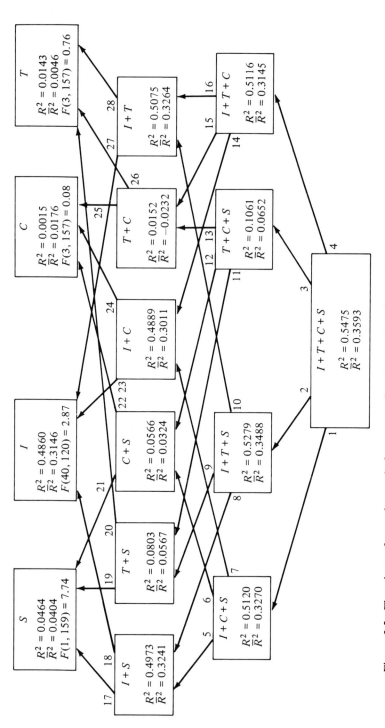

Figure 5.2. Flowchart of nested tests, before-tax profits. *Notes*: I = industry dummy variables (41); T = strategy dummy variables (4); C = control dummy variables (4); S = average size (ln sales).

Table 5.9. *F-Tests: before-tax profits*

Test	F	d.f.	Restriction	Test	F	d.f.	Restriction
1	2.98	(3, 114)	T	15	2.92^a	(40, 115)	I
2	1.65	(3, 114)	C	16	0.32	(3, 115)	C
3	2.78^a	(40, 114)	I	17	2.69^a	(40, 120)	I
4	9.04^a	(1, 114)	S	18	2.71	(1, 120)	S
5	1.18	(3, 117)	C	19	1.92	(3, 157)	T
6	2.73^a	(40, 117)	I	20	11.23^a	(1, 157)	S
7	5.55	(1, 117)	S	21	0.56	(3, 157)	C
8	2.52	(3, 117)	T	22	9.17^a	(1, 157)	S
9	2.77^a	(40, 117)	I	23	0.23	(3, 118)	C
10	5.06	(1, 117)	S	24	2.81^a	(40, 118)	I
11	1.48	(3, 154)	C	25	0.72	(3, 155)	T
12	2.84	(3, 154)	T	26	0.05	(3, 155)	C
13	15.66^a	(1, 154)	S	27	1.72	(3, 118)	T
14	1.78	(3, 155)	T	28	2.95^a	(40, 118)	I

Notes: The test number is that indicated in Figure 5.2. Significance indicates that the null hypothesis that the omitted set has no impact is rejected. The letter indicates the restriction tested.
[a] Significant at 1%.

Table 5.10. *Composition of the sample by diversification and nationality*

	n	%
Single product	49	30.4
Dominant product	46	28.6
Related product	44	27.3
Unrelated product	22	13.7
Total	161	100
Canadian non-MNC	114	70.8
Canadian MNC	16	9.9
U.S.	19	11.8
Other foreign	12	7.5
Total	161	100

However, it should be recognized that our methodology is such that firm effects may not have been given a fair chance. Our firm effects are measured by grouped effects, and it may well be the case that these are not sufficient to capture interfirm differences in efficiency. A continuous variable such as market share may have performed better in our tests. To further examine this possibility, we rely on the argument that π_0 (a continuous variable) captures both firm and industry effects. We therefore regressed $\hat{\pi}_{ip}$ on π_{i0} and the industry dummies (I) to ascertain whether π_{i0} has any explanatory power after controlling for industry effects. If so, this would point to the presence of firm effects. The results before and after taxes are similar and suggest that both firm and industry effects are present. For example, in the after-tax case the equation including both π_{i0} and I had an $\bar{R}^2$ of 0.531, whereas that for π_{i0} alone was 0.460 and for I alone 0.322. The F-test on the unrestricted versus the restricted equations indicated that each restriction is rejected at the 5 percent level. For the I restriction, $F(40, 120) = 1.66$, whereas for the π_{i0} restriction, $F(1, 159) = 54.97$. Again, we confirm the existence of industry effects, but in this case we cannot reject the presence of firm effects.

Finally, we compiled a list of firms with projected profits more than 50 percent above and below the mean. These firms, together with the industry to which they were classified, are listed in Table 5.11. Although the interpretation of such evidence is a matter of taste, we believe that two points emerge clearly. The first is that the classification is independent of the initial time period chosen. Thus, the table presents the results for the 1968–82 sample, but as is indicated, virtually all firms included in the 1964–82 sample would be classified in the same way. The same is true for before-tax profits (results not presented). The second point is that the industries to which highly profitable firms belong rarely appear on the low-profitability list, and vice versa. This would appear to confirm the previous result that industry is important. Beyond these two observations, it is difficult to draw general conclusions. The most profitable firms come from some highly concentrated industries (beer, newspaper, petroleum refining), but these differ in terms of product differentiation, technology intensiveness, and vertical integration. The least profitable firms come from some relatively unconcentrated industries (petroleum exploration, textiles), but these differ in terms of tariff protection and other government regulations.

Some specific aspects of the regression results warrant mention. The size term is positive and significant in all equations with a coefficient of around 0.01. Therefore a 1 percent increase in average size is associated with an increase in profitability (relative to the mean) of one percentage point. Given that the mean of $\hat{\pi}_p$ is close to zero, this may be considered sizable. The coefficients on the T and C terms depend somewhat on the equation considered. In the full (unrestricted) model, only the coefficient for Canadian MNCs was significant and positive. The coefficients for U.S. and other MNCs were positive but not significant (the standard being

Table 5.11. *Companies with projected profits 50% above and below the norm*

Above, 50 firms	SIC	Below, 25 firms	SIC
Canada Tungsten Mining[a]	1000	Consolidated Canadian Faraday[b]	1000
Craigmont Mines[a]	1021	La Luz Mines[b]	1021
Cominco[b]	1031	Discovery Mines[b]	1040
Pine Point Mines[b]	1031	Kerr Addison Mines[b]	1040
Westmin Resources[a]	1031	Campbell Resources[b]	1211
Campbell Red Lake Mines[b]	1040	McIntyre Mines[b]	1211
Dome Mines[b]	1040	Charter Oil[b]	1311
Giant Yellowknife Mines[b]	1040	McChip Resources[b]	1311
Sigma Mines[b]	1040	Numac Oil & Gas[b]	1311
Pan Canadian Petroleum[b]	1311	Scurry-Rainbow[c]	1311
Petrol Oil and Gas[b]	1311	Spooner Mines[a]	1311
Indusmin[a]	1499	Yellowknife Bear Resources[b]	1311
Standard Industries[b]	1499	Teck Corporation[b]	1311
Heritage Group[a]	2010	United Canso[a]	1311
Dover Industries[b]	2050	Brinco[b]	1381
B. C. Sugar Refining[b]	2063	Costain[a]	1520
Labatt[b]	2082	Canadian Foundation[a]	1520
Molson[b]	2082	Consolotex[b]	2200
Hiram Walker[b]	2085	Wabasso[b]	2200
Imasco[b]	2111	Rolland[b]	2649
Great Lakes Forest Products[b]	2600	Total Petroleum[b]	2911
Scott Paper[b]	2600	Algoma Steel[b]	3310
Southam[b]	2711	Slater Steel[b]	3499
Thompson Newspapers[a]	2711	Massey-Ferguson[b]	3520
Maclean-Hunter[b]	2721	Canadian General Electric[b]	3630
British American BankNote[b]	2750		
Lawson and Jones[b]	2750		
Photo Engravers & Electrotype[b]	2750		
Crain[b]	2761		
Moore[b]	2761		
DuPont[b]	2890		
C-I-L[b]	2890		
Husky Oil[b]	2911		
Imperial Oil[b]	2911		
Shell[b]	2911		
Stuart Oil and Gas[b]	2911		
Consumers Glass[b]	3221		
Vulcan Industrial Packaging[b]	3221		
Lake Ontario Cement[b]	3241		
St. Lawrence Cement[b]	3241		
Dofasco[b]	3310		
InterProvincial Steel & Pipe[b]	3310		
Kelsey-Hayes[b]	3320		
Phillips Cables[a]	3350		

Table 5.11 *(cont.)*

Above, 50 firms	SIC	Below, 25 firms	SIC
Atco[a]	3449		
Shaw Industries[a]	3449		
Mitchell[b]	3499		
Finning Tractor[a]	3520		
Federal Pioneer[b]	3610		
Magna International[a]	3670		

Notes: Profits are defined after tax for the 1968–82 sample (161 companies). Only firms with $\hat{\pi}_p$'s at least double their standard errors are included.
[a] Not in 1964–82 sample (15 cases).
[b] In the same category in 1964–82 sample (59 cases).
[c] In 1964–82 sample but not classified as either above or below the mean (1 case).

Canadian non-MNCs). The latter result probably reflects the bias in the sample arising from the omission of 100 percent foreign-owned subsidiaries. In a previous study Shapiro (1980) found that U.S.-controlled firms in Canada were significantly more profitable than all other firms and that their advantage increased with the percentage of shares owned by the parent. The diversification dummies indicate that relative to single-product firms, all other firms were less profitable. The coefficients on the dominant product, related product, and unrelated product terms were all negative; the first two were significant and the last was marginally significant ($t = 1.5$).

VI   The role of entry and exit

Resource mobility plays a prominent role in any discussion of the dynamics of the competitive process. When resources are freely mobile, then entry (exit) or the threat of entry should ensure that no firm will earn rents (positive or negative) in the long run. Moreover, the same process will ensure that short-run rents are quickly dissipated.

It has thus far been established that firms do earn long-run rents (positive and negative), and this implies that barriers to entry and exit do exist. Evidently, in stating the matter in this way, we adopt the Bainsian view of barriers to entry as any factor that impedes new competition. This does not imply rejection of the positions taken by Demsetz (1982) or von Weizäcker (1980). It is possible that a barrier to entry in the sense of Bain may be socially desirable, but this is not our concern in the present context.

In this section we examine the relationship between entry and exit and our estimates of the long-run rate of profit ($\hat{\pi}_p$) and the speed of adjustment ($\hat{\lambda}$). In broad terms we seek to explore the extent to which positive or negative long-run rents serve as a signal for entry and exit and the extent to which entry and exit hasten the dissipation of short-run rents. Specifically, we test the following hypotheses:

1. In the absence of entry barriers, any level of profitability above the competitive norm is expected to induce entry. Thus, in the absence of entry barriers, $\pi_p > 0$ should provide an incentive to entry. Our estimate $\hat{\pi}_p$, when it is positive, represents long-run profits that by definition cannot be competed away. Thus, $\hat{\pi}_p > 0$ should in fact measure the extent to which a firm is protected by barriers to entry, and when $\hat{\pi}_p$ is positive, it represents the minimum level of profitability required to induce entry. We therefore hypothesize that $\text{ENTRY} = f(\pi_t - \hat{\pi}_p)$ for $\pi_t > \hat{\pi}_p$ and $\hat{\pi}_p > 0$, where π_t is measured profits in time period t and where it is expected that entry is greater the greater is the difference between π_t and $\hat{\pi}_p$. A less restrictive version of the hypothesis would be that $\text{ENTRY} = f(\pi_t - \hat{\pi}_p)$ for $\hat{\pi}_p > 0$. In either case, this is a constrained version of the entry model suggested by Bain's analysis, as discussed by Geroski (Chapter 2) and as we have estimated it in previous studies (Khemani and Shapiro, 1986; Shapiro and Khemani, 1987). The constraint involves either the assumption that $(\pi_t - \hat{\pi}_p) > 0$ provides no incentive to entry when $\hat{\pi}_p < 0$ or this assumption plus that $(\pi_t - \hat{\pi}_p) < 0$ and $\hat{\pi}_p > 0$ also provides no incentive to entry.

2. When long-run profits are projected to be negative ($\hat{\pi}_p < 0$), not only will there be no incentive to entry, but there should be an incentive to exit. One might then interpret $\hat{\pi}_p < 0$ as an index of barriers to exit and formulate an exit model that is symmetrical to the entry model. Specifically, $\text{EXIT} = f(\pi_t - \hat{\pi}_p)$ for $\pi_t < \hat{\pi}_p$ and $\hat{\pi}_p < 0$. That is, exit occurs when observed profitability in time period t is less than the minimum level required to deter exit. Again, a less restrictive version of the preceding model would be for the equation to hold only for $\hat{\pi}_p < 0$. However, as we have noted elsewhere (Shapiro and Khemani, 1987), the treatment of entry and exit as symmetrical is problematical. In this study, these problems are exacerbated by the fact that the estimates of π_p are derived from observations on firms that did not exit even when $(\pi_t - \hat{\pi}_p) < 0$ for $\hat{\pi}_p < 0$. Given that some firms did not exit under these circumstances, it is likely that the determinants of exit are more complex than is suggested by our exit equation.

3. Whatever their determinants, one expects that entry and exit should hasten the adjustment of profits toward their long-run levels. To the extent that entry responds to the excess of short-run over permanent profits

when $\hat{\pi}_p > 0$, entry should be the primary source of adjustment in this case. Similarly, exit should serve that role when $\hat{\pi}_p < 0$. The hypothesis is therefore that $\hat{\lambda} = f(\text{ENTRY})$ when $(\pi_t - \hat{\pi}_p) > 0$ and $\hat{\pi}_p > 0$ (or at least when $\hat{\pi}_p > 0$) and $\hat{\lambda} = f(\text{EXIT})$ for $(\pi_t - \hat{\pi}_p) < 0$ and $\hat{\pi}_p < 0$ (or at least when $\hat{\pi}_p < 0$), where the predicted relationship is negative, since $1 - \hat{\lambda}$ is the speed of adjustment.

To test the first two hypotheses, the following equations were estimated:

$$\text{LENT} = \alpha_1 + \gamma_1(\pi_0 - \hat{\pi}_p)^R + \beta_1 \ln N + e_1$$

$$\text{LEXT} = \alpha_2 + \gamma_2(\pi_0 - \hat{\pi}_p)^R + \beta_2 \ln N + e_2$$

where LENT (LEXT) is the logarithm of the number of firms that entered (exited) the industry, $\ln N$ is the logarithm of the number of firms in the industry, π_0 and $\hat{\pi}_p$ are as defined previously, R indicates a restriction on π_0 and $\hat{\pi}_p$ (e.g., $\hat{\pi}_p > 0$), the α's, β's, and γ's are parameters to be estimated, and the e's are error terms.

The semilogarithmic specification is adopted for reasons discussed at length elsewhere (Khemani and Shapiro, 1986). The $\ln N$ term is included to control for differences in industry size. In general, it is expected that $\gamma_1 > 0$ and $\gamma_2 < 0$. Entry is measured by the number of de novo entrants (firms that did not previously exist) and exit by the number of firms that ceased operations entirely, in both cases at the four-digit industry level over the period 1972–6.

A number of issues arise from the manner in which entry and exit are measured. As emphasized by Geroski (Chapter 2), entry is a general concept referring to the creation of de novo firms, interindustry mobility, and intraindustry mobility. Moreover, entry may be actual or threatened. Our analysis focuses only on actual de novo entry. Similarly, problems exist with respect to exit, where, for example, plant closures (but not total exit) are not accounted for. Since the entry (exit) data are defined at the industry level whereas π_0 and $\hat{\pi}_p$ are measured at the firm level, estimation of the entry and exit equations at the firm level requires the assumption that entry (exit) to (from) the industry responds to the profitability of individual firms assigned to that industry. For entry, this assumption is not entirely implausible. Entrants may base their decisions on the performance of target incumbents. For exit, the assumption is rather less plausible since exit is less likely to be related to the performance of any other particular firm. However, to the extent that it is true that profitability is industry determined, firm-level profits may reflect conditions in the industry as a whole. In any event, we also aggregated firms into their relevant industries and estimated the equation at both the firm and industry level using the same industries as were employed in the previous section.[4] Finally, the period over which entry (exit) is measured requires some comment. Recalling that π_0 is the average rate of profit in 1968 and 1969, these equations would suggest that entry and exit be measured beginning in about 1970. In fact, the data we employ measure entry (exit) over the period 1972–6.[5]

The results are reported in Table 5.12. Tests for pooling revealed no differences between manufacturing and nonmanufacturing industries. It is to be noted at the outset that the high explanatory power of the equations is due primarily to the strong relationship between entry (exit) and the number of firms in the industry. We believe that this reflects the potential for displacement of small inefficient incumbents by small, more efficient entrants in industries with large numbers of firms as well as the deterrent effects of potential retaliation by incumbents in industries with small numbers of firms where it is easier both to detect entry and to coordinate responses to it. The first two columns of each entry (exit) equation present the results for the hypothesized relationship between $\pi_0 - \hat{\pi}_p$ and entry (exit). We also estimated various other equations and a representative of these (usually the best fit) is reported in the third column.[6]

The entry equations suggest that there is some positive response to the excess of measured profitability over projected long-run profitability, but the effect is weak. At both the firm and industry levels, neither of the coefficients in the first two columns are significant. However, there is some improvement as one moves to the less restricted form, implying that some entry occurs even when $\pi_0 < \hat{\pi}_p$. At the industry level, the coefficient on the $\pi_0 - \hat{\pi}_p$ terms for $\hat{\pi}_p > 0$ is nearly significant and no other specification proves superior. An example is provided in the third column. It would appear that when $\hat{\pi}_p > 0$, there is some incentive to enter based on profitability, whereas when $\hat{\pi}_p < 0$, any entry that occurs is related to exogenous factors. At the firm level, however, it was found that the most significant incentive to entry was π_0 alone, but only when $\hat{\pi}_p > 0$. Thus,

---

[4] Missing entry data reduced the number of industries from 41 to 38 and the number of firms from 161 to 136.

[5] Data for a more appropriate period (1970–9) have been collected by Baldwin and Gorecki (1983). However, their data do not include resource industries and are based on "long-form" census returns that include only larger entrants. The data we employ include resource industries and are based on "short-form" returns that measure entry in a more comprehensive way. Baldwin and Gorecki did make their data available to us, and it was found that their numbers were highly correlated with ours. Simple correlation coefficients (for entry, exit, and net entry) ranged from 0.83 to 0.89.

[6] These equations included ones using π_0 and $\hat{\pi}_p$ alone and others including $(\pi_0 - \hat{\pi}_p)$, each with a variety of restrictions. For example, the entry equations were run with $(\pi_0 - \pi_p)$ restricted by $(\pi_0 > \pi_p, \pi_p > 0)$, by $(\pi_0 > \hat{\pi}_p, \hat{\pi}_p > 0$ and $\pi_0 < \hat{\pi}_p, \hat{\pi}_p > 0)$, etc. Statements in the text reflect tests of these restrictions.

Table 5.12. *Entry, exit, and profitability, after-tax profits*

	LENT			LEXT		
Firm level ($n=136$)						
$(\pi_0-\hat\pi_p)^{++}$	1.217 (2.459)					
$(\pi_0-\hat\pi_p)^{--}$	—	—	—	−0.823 (3.043)		
$(\pi_0-\hat\pi_p)^{+}$	—	1.141 (1.153)				
$(\pi_0-\hat\pi_p)^{-}$	—	—	—	—	−0.614 (0.431)	
π_0^+	—	—	2.043^a (0.849)			
π_0^-	—	—	—	—	—	−0.767^b (0.435)
ln N	0.943^a (0.031)	0.943^a (0.031)	0.952^a (0.031)	0.915^a (0.032)	0.919^a (0.032)	0.918^a (0.032)
Constant	−1.502^a (0.155)	−1.488^a (0.152)	−1.594^a (0.155)	−1.171^a (0.159)	−1.188^a (0.158)	−1.209^a (0.159)
$\bar{R}^2$	0.871	0.872	0.878	0.855	0.857	0.860
Industry level ($n=38$)						
$(\pi_0-\hat\pi_p)^{++}$	5.973 (6.458)					
$(\pi_0-\hat\pi_p)^{--}$	—	—	—	−4.643 (2.965)		
$(\pi_0-\hat\pi_p)^{+}$	—	2.222 (1.458)	2.070 (1.487)			
$(\pi_0-\hat\pi_p)^{-}$	—	—	1.511 (3.418)	—	−1.536 (4.502)	
$\hat\pi_p^-$	—	—	—	—	—	−4.690^a (2.178)
ln N	0.949^a (0.060)	0.968^a (0.061)	0.965^a (0.061)	1.026^a (0.056)	1.010^a (0.057)	1.044^a (0.057)
Constant	−1.498^a (0.303)	−1.670^a (0.310)	−1.634^a (0.311)	−1.685^a (0.284)	−1.564^a (0.292)	−1.813^a (0.294)
$\bar{R}^2$	0.867	0.873	0.869	0.899	0.892	0.904

Notes: Numbers in parentheses are standard errors.

$$(\pi_0-\hat\pi_p)^{++}=(\pi_0-\hat\pi_p) \text{ when } \hat\pi_p>0 \text{ and } \pi_0>\hat\pi_p, 0 \text{ otherwise}$$
$$(\pi_0-\hat\pi_p)^{--}=(\pi_0-\hat\pi_p) \text{ when } \hat\pi_p<0 \text{ and } \pi_0<\hat\pi_p, 0 \text{ otherwise}$$
$$(\pi_0-\hat\pi_p)^{+}=(\pi_0-\hat\pi_p) \text{ when } \hat\pi_p>0, 0 \text{ otherwise}$$
$$(\pi_0-\hat\pi_p)^{-}=(\pi_0-\hat\pi_p) \text{ when } \hat\pi_p<0, 0 \text{ otherwise}$$
$$\pi_0^+=\pi_0 \text{ when } \hat\pi_p>0, 0 \text{ otherwise}$$
$$\hat\pi_p^-=\hat\pi_p \text{ when } \hat\pi_p<0, 0 \text{ otherwise}$$

^{a} Significant at 5%.
^{b} Significant at 10%.

firms with high initial levels of profitability and whose projected long-run rates of profit were above the average tended to attract entrants to their industry. Any entry that occurred in industries with firms having $\hat{\pi}_p < 0$ was not systematically related to the profitability of firms in these industries.

The exit results at both the firm and industry levels are similar in that we found no significant relationship between exit and $\pi_0 - \hat{\pi}_p$ when the latter was constrained according to the hypothesis. However, as in the entry case, we did find that exit was related to profitability. In the exit equations it is evident that exit responds to profitability signals when $\hat{\pi}_p < 0$. The lower (more negative) is $\hat{\pi}_p$, the greater is the observed amount of exit. Thus there is a systematic tendency for exit to occur where long-run profitability is highly negative. At the same time, when $\hat{\pi}_p > 0$, exit occurs but it is not systematically related to the profitability of existing firms.

We cannot claim that these results are strong, nor are they entirely consistent with our hypotheses. However, given the weaknesses of the data and the limitations of the research design, they do provide some useful insights into the dynamics of markets. It would appear that the measurement of long-run profitability and the distinction between firms (and industries) that are above and below the mean have some meaning. There is some evidence that entry responds to profitability signals when long-run profitability is above average. Moreover, there is weak support for the hypothesis that entry responds to the existence of short-run rents. On the other hand, below-average long-run profits are a signal to exit. It is true that barriers to exit must exist since we observe firms earning persistently below-average profits. Although some firms continue earning such profits, others in the same industry do exit. Similarly, the industry-level entry equation provides some evidence that barriers to entry exist when $\hat{\pi}_p > 0$.[7] The picture that emerges is therefore mixed. The competitive process does work in the sense that there is a tendency for resources to be allocated in response to market signals. However, the process is not perfect in that barriers to entry and exit impede the free movement of firms.

The third hypothesis to be tested is that entry and exit hasten the adjustment of profits to their long-run values. The preceding results suggest that entry should determine the speed of adjustment for $\hat{\pi}_p > 0$, whereas exit should do so when $\hat{\pi}_p < 0$. This hypothesis is tested by regressing $\hat{\lambda}$ on LENT$^+$ and LEXT$^-$, where LENT$^+$ = LENT if $\hat{\pi}_p > 0$ and LEXT$^-$ = LEXT if $\hat{\pi}_p < 0$. As noted in the preceding, there is entry (exit) when

---

[7] When net entry (LENT − LEXT) was used as the dependent variable, the coefficient on $(\pi_0 - \pi_p)^+$ was positive and significant in the firm-level equation and positive and nearly significant in the industry-level equation.

$\hat{\pi}_p < 0$ ($\hat{\pi}_p > 0$), and any effects of entry (exit) may be diluted by exit (entry). We therefore also estimate an equation with $(\text{LENT} - \text{LEXT})^+$ and $(\text{LEXT} - \text{LENT})^-$ as the explanatory variables, where the superscript plus and minus imply that $\hat{\pi}_p > 0$ and $\hat{\pi}_p < 0$, respectively. As in the previous case separate regressions were run at the firm and industry levels. All observations were weighted by the standard error of $\hat{\lambda}$. Since $1 - \hat{\lambda}$ measures the speed of adjustment, it is expected that the impact of entry (exit) on $\hat{\lambda}$ will be negative; that is, the greater is the amount of entry (exit), the more quickly will transitory rents be eroded (implying lower $\hat{\lambda}$). The term $\ln N$ is included in each equation to control for industry size. The impact of a single entrant on the speed of adjustment should be reduced when there are many firms in the industry.[8] However, $\ln N$ may also reflect the degree of competition in the industry, and higher concentration (small number of firms) may allow firms to maintain even short-run rents (see Odagiri and Yamawaki, Chapter 8). The equations are similar to those estimated by Kessides (Chapter 4).

The results are reported in Table 5.13.[9] There is no support for the hypothesis that the speed of adjustment is related to entry and exit. With one exception, the relevant coefficients are all positive, contrary to the maintained hypothesis, and in no case is the coefficient significant. The explanatory power of the equations is weak, and all attempts to improve it failed. Given the positive correlation between LENT and LEXT and $\ln N$, we estimated equations using the rate of entry (exit) as explanatory variables (ENTRY/N, EXIT/N). Following Odagiri and Yamawaki (Chapter 8), we added variables measuring import and export intensities, concentration ratios, and industry dummy variables (in the firm-level equation). None of these were significant in any equation. Indeed, the only variables that are consistently and significantly related to $\hat{\lambda}$ are π_0^+ and π_0^-, as described in Table 5.7. Moreover, when industry dummy variables were added to this equation, their collective significance was rejected. Thus, unlike Odagiri and Yamawaki (Chapter 8) and Kessides (Chapter 4), we can find no explanation for interfirm or interindustry differences in $\hat{\lambda}$ other than the initial level of profitability.

In spite of the fact that entry and exit do respond to profitability signals, we can find no evidence that they influence the speed of adjustment. There are a variety of possible explanations. We have previously suggested

[8] This assumes that the entrant is small, which is the case for these data. See Khemani and Shapiro (1986) and Baldwin and Gorecki (1983).

[9] Tests for pooling revealed no differences in slope or intercept between manufacturing and nonmanufacturing industries. We also estimated equations where the impact of entry was restricted to cases where $\pi_0 > \hat{\pi}_p$ and $\hat{\pi}_p > 0$ and the impact of exit was restricted to cases where $\pi_0 < \hat{\pi}_p$ and $\hat{\pi}_p < 0$. These did not produce results superior to those reported in the text.

Table 5.13. *Entry, exit, and the speed of adjustment, after-tax profits*

	Firm-level (n = 136)		Industry-level (n = 38)	
LENT $^+$	0.007 (0.014)	—	0.047 (0.043)	
LEXT $^-$	0.002 (0.013)	—	0.038 (0.042)	
(LENT − LEXT) $^+$	—	0.090 (0.097)	—	0.053 (0.118)
(LEXT − LENT) $^-$	—	0.021 (0.051)	—	−0.007 (0.055)
ln N	−0.048 (0.033)	0.011 (0.012)	−0.031 (0.041)	0.011 (0.016)
Constant	0.347^a (0.073)	0.261^a (0.060)	0.365^a (0.009)	0.218^a (0.086)
$\bar{R}^2$	0.004	−0.005	−0.032	0.068

Notes: Numbers in parentheses are standard errors.

$$\text{LENT}^+ = \text{LENT when } \hat{\pi}_p > 0, \ 0 \text{ otherwise}$$
$$\text{LEXT}^- = \text{LEXT when } \hat{\pi}_p < 0, \ 0 \text{ otherwise}$$
$$(\text{LENT} - \text{LEXT})^+ = (\text{LENT} - \text{LEXT}) \text{ when } \hat{\pi}_p > 0, \ 0 \text{ otherwise}$$
$$(\text{LEXT} - \text{LENT})^- = (\text{LEXT} - \text{LENT}) \text{ when } \hat{\pi}_p < 0, \ 0 \text{ otherwise}$$

^{a} Significant at 5%.

(Shapiro and Khemani, 1987) that exit (as measured here) is caused by entry and that the displacement effect is strong. In other words, small de novo entrants simply displace other small firms, and this turnover of small firms leaves industry structure and incumbent firms unaffected. It may well be the case that if entry (exit) had been defined to include entry (exit) by diversification or if intraindustry mobility had been included, then the results would have been different. However, it is also possible that the firm-level data cannot be explained by entry at the industry level and that our aggregation to the industry level is not accurate given the number of missing firms. The stronger results for similar equations reported by Kessides (Chapter 4) using industry data suggest that this might be the case. Finally, the time period for which entry is measured may be inappropriate.

VII   Conclusion

The preceding analyses of the long-run trend of corporate profits in Canadian industry suggest that the competitive process does push profits toward the competitive norm. The pattern of adjustment in these profits is similar to that of other countries analyzed in this volume. The speed of adjustment by which long-run projected profits converge in Canada is faster than Europe and Japan but less than that observed for the United States (see Odagiri and Yamawaki, Chapter 10, for further details). The process in Canada, however, does not equalize long-run projected profit rates, which tend to vary depending on the initial profitability of firms and across industries. Somewhat paradoxically, there is persistence in profits among firms with high initial profit levels and among firms with low initial profit levels. Although no generalizations can be made without further research, casual evidence suggests that high profits persist in industries characterized by factors such as product differentiation and technology or patents (pharmaceuticals, breweries, food, chemicals, petroleum refining), and low profits persist in industries subject to government support policies such as tariffs, quotas, and tax measures (textiles, steel, petroleum exploration and development).

Analyses of the determinants of long-run projected profit rates suggest that industry-specific factors are always significant determinants of interfirm differences. However, we cannot reject the presence of firm effects. Finally, the entry and exit of firms are found to respond to profit incentives but do not impact on the speed of adjustment by which profits converge toward the competitive norm. The observed convergence is likely due to interfirm competition among incumbents.

CHAPTER 6

The persistence of corporate profits in the Federal Republic of Germany

JOACHIM SCHWALBACH AND TALAT MAHMOOD

This chapter, on the persistence of corporate profits in Germany, is organized as follows: Section I presents the empirical model and describes the econometrics for the estimation of the parameters. Section II introduces the data sample, which consists of profit data from 299 German stock companies in the period 1961–82, and Section III provides empirical results. Section IV explains the differences in the explanation of profit rates between firms attributable to firm- and industry-specific factors. Section V provides empirical evidence about the degree of significance of selected firm-specific factors that explain permanent profit rates. Section VI draws some conclusions about firm profitability in Germany.

I   The empirical model

We begin our empirical analysis by assuming a profit convergence process as it is suggested in Chapter 2 and is specified as follows:

$$\pi_{it} = \alpha_i + \lambda_i \pi_{it-1} + \mu_{it} \quad \text{for all } i \text{ firms,} \tag{6.1}$$

where $\alpha_i = \pi_{ip}(1 - \lambda_i)$ and μ_{it} is the error term that reflects all other factors influencing the profit convergence process.[1] The term $1 - \lambda_i$ represents the speed of profit adjustment parameter. If $0 < 1 - \lambda_i < 1$, entry and intra-industry mobility drive profits down to the long-run equilibrium profit level π_{ip}, and the higher $1 - \lambda_i$ is, the faster will be that convergence. If $1 - \lambda_i = 1$, no entry and no intraindustry mobility occurs and profits persist over time ($\pi_{it} = \pi_{ip}$) at equilibrium levels.[2]

The research on German corporate profits was supported in part by the Deutsche Forschungsgemeinschaft, for whose help we are very grateful. We are also very grateful to Stefan Csutor, Carsten Grieger, Frank Hasenbein, Patrick Jerchel, Andreas Knaack, Klaus Ristau, and Olaf Seliger for their persistent effort in collecting and processing the data very competently. Last but not least, we are obliged to John Cable, Paul Geroski, Dennis Mueller, and Manfred Neumann for helpful comments.

[1] An alternative dynamic model can be found in Schwalbach, Grasshoff, and Mahmood (1988).

[2] For empirical evidence about the speed of entry into German industries, see Schwalbach (1987).

Beside the speed of profit adjustment, one is interested in the equilibrium profit level π_{ip} since entry and mobility might not necessarily lead to zero economic profits because of entry and mobility barriers. However, one expects that as more firms enter the industry or industry segments, the long-run divergence from competitive profit levels will decrease.

Simple linear regressions of equation (6.1) may yield biased estimates of the parameters if μ_{it} is autocorrelated. To test this, we apply a Lagrange multiplier test.[3] That is, the null hypothesis of serial dependence or the regression errors will be tested against pth-order autoregressive or moving average models by adding the first p lagged values of μ_t to the regression model as follows:

$$\pi_{it} = \lambda_i \pi_{it-1} + \sum_{j=1}^{p} \rho_j \mu_{it-j} + \epsilon_t,$$

where $|\rho_j| < 1$ and the ϵ_j are normally and independently distributed. If $\rho_j = 0$, the error term μ_{it} is serially independent. The significance of the estimated ρ_j coefficient will be tested by applying the conventional F-test to three alternative null hypotheses:

H_0: $\rho_1 = 0$.

H_0: $\rho_1 = \rho_2 = 0$.

H_0: $\rho_1 = \rho_2 = \rho_3 = 0$.

Furthermore, we have to examine whether the profit convergence process as it is specified in equation (6.1) is really of first-order autoregressive form, that is, that profits in period t depend only on profits in preperiod $t-1$. We therefore test econometrically whether current profits depend on profits in more than one preperiod and whether the profit convergence process can be of a different form, such as moving average or mixed form autoregressive–moving average. This sort of stochastic process, which assumes that a time series like $y_1, \ldots, y_T$ is generated by a set of jointly distributed random variables, that is, the set of data points $y_1, \ldots, y_T$, represents a particular outcome of the joint probability distribution function $p(y_1, \ldots, y_T)$.

For simplicity, we assume a convergence process of mixed form autoregressive–moving average (ARMA) of the pth order that can be written as follows:

$$\pi_{it} = \alpha_i + \phi_{i1} \pi_{it-1} + \cdots + \phi_{ip} \pi_{it-p} + \mu_{it} - \theta_{i1} \mu_{it-1} - \cdots - \theta_{ip} \mu_{it-p}. \qquad (6.2)$$

The ARMA(p, q) process differs from the autoregressive model in equation (6.1) by the higher lag structure and by additional stochastic variables

[3] For details see Breusch and Godfrey (1981) and Kmenta (1971).

μ_{it-j} $(j = 1, ..., p)$ that represent a "white noise" process and may be regarded as a series of shocks that drive the convergence process in addition to the stochastic variable μ_{it}. To interpret the parameter by ϕ_{ij} and θ_{ij} and to find the length of the time lag, we have to transform equation (6.2) into autoregressive form by successive substitutions. For an ARMA(1, 1) process, after transformation of equation (6.3), we derive

$$\pi_{it} = \alpha_i/1 - \theta_{i1} + (\phi_{i1} - \theta_{i1})\pi_{it-1} + \theta_{i1}(\phi_{i1} - \theta_{i1})\pi_{it-2}$$
$$+ \theta_{i1}^2(\phi_{i1} - \theta_{i1})\pi_{it-3} + \cdots + \theta_{i1}^{p-1}(\phi_{i1} - \theta_{i1})\pi_{it-p} + \mu_t. \qquad (6.3)$$

From equation (6.3) it follows that

$$w_p = \sum_{p=1}^{\infty} \theta_1^{p-1}(\phi_1 - \theta_1).$$

Here w_p becomes smaller as the time lag p increases if $|\theta_1| < 1$. If w_p becomes sufficiently small, we can truncate the AR approximation of ARMA(1, 1) and obtain the length of the lag structure of the profit convergence process.

II   Data sample and profit definitions

Until the end of 1985, German corporation laws required the annual publication of financial reports for companies with certain legal structures or size characteristics. Stock companies [Aktiengesellschaften (AGs)] and scrip companies [Kommanditgesellschaften auf Aktien (KGaAs)] generally had to publish their balance sheets and business reports regardless of their size. In contrast, companies with limited liability [Gesellschaft mit beschraenkter Haftung (GmbHs)] are required to disclose their financial information only if two of the following three criteria apply: The firm has total assets in excess of 15.5 million DM, its sales are higher than 32 million DM, or it has no more than 5,000 employees.[4] The overwhelming majority of GmbHs do not fulfill these criteria so that empirical company research has to be concentrated on stock companies (AGs).[5] The pool of stock companies from which we could choose for our empirical study is not large and has become smaller over time. In 1963, the number of AGs were 1,254, but by 1982 only 665 were left. The opposite trend is

---

[4] Since the beginning of 1986, the German corporation laws were adjusted to the corporation laws of the European Community with the result that all corporations of the type mentioned above are required to report about their financial situation. How detailed this report has to be depends on the size of the company. Most information has to be made available to the public by companies for which at least two out of the following three size characteristics apply: total assets in excess of 15.5 million DM, sales higher than 32 million DM, and more than 250 employees.

[5] In reality, scrip companies (KGaAs) play a very minor role.

found when one looks at the number of GmbHs, which increased from 16,395 to 60,893 during the same period. There are several causes for this development in the choice of legal structure. One cause was that the information disclosure requirements for the GmbHs were less stringent, and another was that the codetermination rights of employees in the GmbHs were not as expansive.

Another specific German phenomenon is that not all stock companies are quoted on the stock market. In 1982 only 475 out of 665 companies were actually quoted. Most of the 190 nonquoted companies are owned by families or a few individuals who are not interested in spreading the equity capital. Another reason that some stock companies do not use the stock market as an external capital market is that they have close links with banks and insurance companies. Representatives of these capital sources hold chairs on the supervisory board (Aufsichtsrat) and control substantial voting rights (Depotstimmrecht) in the annual general meeting (Hauptversammlung).

From the preceding discussion, it follows that only AGs are potential candidates for ex post company studies. We came up with a total of 299 companies for which there are continuous time series of published financial information from 1961 to 1982.[6] These 299 companies cover the whole spectrum of activities of the manufacturing sector. Only 214 of them were quoted on the stock market during the period studied.

Profit measures

We used the following four different measures of profits:

1. Nominal profit rate on total capital before tax, defined as profits available for dividends plus interest payments plus income payments divided by total assets.
2. Nominal profit rate on total capital after tax, defined as measure 1 but after tax.
3. Nominal profit rate on equity capital before tax, defined as profits available for dividends plus income tax payments divided by equity capital.
4. Market valuation ratio V as the ratio of market value (book value of debt plus market value of equity) to total assets.[7]

The reasons for using four profit measures are, on the one hand, that we are interested in the stability of the results of the adjustment process inde-

---

[6] We were not able to begin the time series before 1961 because, in 1959, major revisions of publication requirements were put into effect in the German corporate laws. For instance, until 1959, companies did not report total sales but instead reported only sales net of purchases of raw materials.

[7] The definition of V is applied according to Marris (1964, p. xviii).

pendent of the applied profit measure and, on the other hand, that we want to take into account the recent criticism on the use of accounting profit measures by comparing the results with a market valuation ratio. Instead of using Tobin's q, we applied Marris's V since it has the advantage of using the same denominator as for the accounting profit measures.

Table 6.1 displays means and standard deviations of the four profit measures between 1961 and 1982. The means show that there is a clear downward trend over time that was most severe for the profit rate on equity capital. The means also reflect the business cycle, as is most evident in the recession years 1967, 1971, and 1975. The time series of the standard deviations indicate that the profitability difference between companies diminished only slightly so that differences across firms persist over time, although it is not clear whether the same firms had high or low profit rates from year to year.

To eliminate business cycle and trend factors, the study group has chosen as its profit measure $\Delta\pi_{it}$, the absolute deviation from the total firm sample mean in each year,[8] that is,

$$\Delta\pi_{it} = \pi_{it} - \bar{\pi}_t \quad \text{for all } t,$$

where

$$\bar{\pi}_t = \sum_{i=1}^{N} \frac{\pi_{it}}{N} \quad \text{for all } t \quad (N = 299).$$

III   Empirical results

A   Specification test

The Lagrange multiplier test (for up to third-order autocorrelation) for serial independence of the regression errors in equation (6.1) was performed for the profit rate on equity capital before tax. Based on a 1 percent significance level, the test results suggested rejecting the null hypothesis of dependent errors for 290 firms. Since for only 3 percent of all firms we suspect that the empirical model is misspecified, we will leave all 299 firms in the sample.

B   Test of lag structure

The parameters of ϕ_1 and θ_1 in equation (6.2) were estimated for each firm. We relied on those parameters only where the value of the adjusted R^2 of the equation was positive, which was the case for 177 firms. The values of these parameters were used to calculate the coefficients in equation

---

[8] We also applied standard econometric techniques for trend elimination, such as differencing, and found that $\Delta\pi_{it}$ eliminated the trend fairly well.

Table 6.1. *Mean and standard deviation of rates of return of 299 German companies, 1961–82*

Year	Rate of return on total capital before tax		Rate of return on total capital after tax		Rate of return on equity capital before tax		Valuation ratio V ($N=214$)	
	Mean	Standard deviation	Mean	Standard deviation	Mean	Standard deviation	Mean	Standard deviation
1961	12.57	6.55	5.73	3.40	9.52	6.27	1.76	0.537
1962	12.18	6.41	5.63	2.95	9.20	5.95	1.40	0.390
1963	11.83	6.15	5.45	2.95	8.78	5.59	1.43	0.399
1964	11.99	5.92	5.69	2.83	8.99	5.52	1.44	0.388
1965	11.47	5.80	5.77	2.91	8.50	5.37	1.30	0.327
1966	10.08	6.12	5.44	3.92	7.03	5.70	1.17	0.267
1967	9.35	5.37	5.31	3.41	6.58	5.33	1.27	0.336
1968	9.65	5.79	4.99	3.24	6.83	5.45	1.32	0.355
1969	9.28	5.54	4.91	2.93	6.63	5.50	1.48	0.449
1970	9.04	5.28	5.03	3.09	5.67	5.11	1.30	0.392
1971	8.69	5.06	4.95	2.95	5.45	4.67	1.29	0.368
1972	8.52	5.38	4.57	2.97	5.69	5.02	1.49	0.440
1973	8.20	4.68	4.70	2.82	4.91	4.51	1.36	0.388
1974	8.22	5.14	4.78	3.41	4.35	4.87	1.24	0.293
1975	7.20	5.73	3.84	3.97	3.97	5.11	1.27	0.288
1976	7.72	5.16	4.23	3.43	4.92	5.03	1.15	0.269
1977	7.43	5.05	3.57	2.73	4.70	4.80	1.19	0.273
1978	7.30	5.35	3.42	2.87	4.73	4.88	1.24	0.299
1979	7.32	5.38	3.54	2.93	4.63	5.00	1.18	0.299
1980	7.53	4.92	4.30	2.87	4.09	4.78	1.14	0.270
1981	6.93	4.59	4.24	3.25	2.99	4.44	1.11	0.241
1982	6.40	5.36	3.81	3.85	2.64	4.99	1.15	0.283

(6.3) for each of the 177 firms with 22 time lags. The firm-specific lag structure was derived where the coefficient of the pth lag became smaller than the mean of all coefficients for all firms. For these 177 firms we found that 70 firms, or 40 percent, had a lag of first order; 86 firms, or 49 percent, had a lag structure that varied between 2 and 7; and for 15 firms the number of lags varied between 10 and 20. This test shows that the lag structure of the profit convergence process of first order as it is assumed in the empirical model in equation (6.1) is a rather strong assumption.

C   Regression results of the empirical model

The regression results of equation (6.1) for all four profit measures are summarized in Table 6.2. The total sample of firms was divided into six subgroups of about equal size according to the average firm's profit rate for the first two years of the time series. For each subgroup, Table 6.2 reports the means of the projected long-run profit rate $\hat{\pi}_{ip} = \hat{\alpha}_i/(1 - \hat{\lambda}_i)$ as the absolute deviation from the firm sample mean in column 1, the speed of profit convergence $(1 - \hat{\lambda}_i)$ in column 2, and the initial profit $\bar{\pi}_0$ in column 3. Comparing columns 1 and 3, one sees that the ordering of the subgroups persists over time for all profit measures, including the market valuation ratio. For example, firms in the subsample with the highest initial profit rates on total capital before tax earned, on average, profits that were 12 percentage points above the sample mean, and their long-run projected values were about 2 percentage points above the sample mean, the highest for all six groups. Despite persistent profits over time within the subgroups, the results in columns 1 and 3 also indicate that the magnitude of profit rate differences between the best and the worst performing firms in the sample declined over time. This can be seen by comparing standard deviations of $\hat{\pi}_{ip}$'s and $\bar{\pi}_0$'s across subgroups. In the initial period, the values of $\bar{\pi}_0$'s were higher in the first and last subgroups than elsewhere, whereas the standard deviation of the $\hat{\pi}_{ip}$'s were only slightly above average for the best and below average for the worst performing group. Thus, although we see some profit adjustment toward the mean profit rate, it remains clear that persistent differences of success across firms exist.[9]

Let us now turn to column 2, which shows the mean values of the speed of profit adjustment parameter $1 - \hat{\lambda}_i$. These are considerably larger than zero, which according to our empirical model suggests that entry into industries and mobility between industry segments caused the profit

---

[9] This is also evident by taking the simple correlation between projected and initial profits into account where coefficients of the various profit measures have values between 0.36 and 0.41.

Table 6.2. *Empirical results*

Profit measures	Subgroups	$\hat{\pi}_{ip}$ (1)	$1 - \hat{\lambda}_i$ (2)	$\bar{\pi}_0$ (3)
Total capital before tax, $N = 299$	1	2.323	0.376	12.162
	2	0.870	0.536	4.365
	3	0.578	0.665	0.359
	4	−0.289	0.558	−2.906
	5	−0.457	0.478	−5.104
	6	−2.803	0.479	−8.632
Total capital after tax, $N = 299$	1	0.480	0.483	4.574
	2	0.353	0.731	1.655
	3	0.466	0.666	0.186
	4	0.243	0.564	−0.851
	5	−0.361	0.610	−1.768
	6	−1.138	0.594	−3.705
Equity capital before tax, $N = 299$	1	2.169	0.386	10.288
	2	0.916	0.525	3.720
	3	0.792	0.551	0.374
	4	−0.216	0.612	−2.366
	5	−0.911	0.467	−4.519
	6	−2.324	0.473	−7.292
Valuation ratio V, $N = 214$	1	0.205	0.348	0.993
	2	0.098	0.444	0.348
	3	0.015	0.365	0.028
	4	−0.082	0.450	−0.225
	5	−0.092	0.400	−0.453
	6	−0.107	0.304	−0.731

convergence over time. The mean values are inverted-U-shaped across subgroups, which indicates that the speed of adjustment was slower for firms with the highest and the lowest initial profit rate. This suggests that the highly profitable firms were able to protect their dominant position fairly well; at the other extreme, the poorly performing firms generally converged very slowly to slightly higher levels. Notice that the size of the speed of adjustment parameter differs depending on which of the various profit measures are used. Among the accounting profit measure, $1 - \hat{\lambda}_i$ had lower mean values for the after-tax profit measure, whereas for the profit measure based on the market valuation ratio of corporate profits (Marris's V), $1 - \hat{\lambda}_i$ was higher and of about the same size in the different subgroups. This suggests that capital markets valued the adjustment of the stream of future income differently from that indicated by accounting profit rates.

Table 6.3. *Firm and industry differences*

Industries	Code	Number of firms	$\hat{\pi}_{ip}$	Standard deviation of $\hat{\pi}_{ip}$
Chemicals	200	32	0.891	1.249
Stone and clay	220	18	0.251	1.342
Iron and steel	230	13	−2.325	1.820
Machinery	242	41	−0.805	1.684
Electrical equipment	250	16	−0.322	1.993
Metal products	256	10	0.721	1.812
Textiles	275	35	−1.430	2.015
Food	280	13	4.150	2.118
Beer brewing	293	14	3.052	0.950

IV Firm-specific versus industry-specific effects explaining firm profit differences

How can persistent profit differences between firms be explained? Following classical industrial organization theory, one would argue that any kind of firm differences can be exclusively explained by industry differences. Since firms in the same industry are all alike, differences between firms arise due to common industry factors like different heights of entry barriers. Empirical literature exists that seems to support the dominance of industry effects in explaining industry and firm performance (see, e.g., Schmalensee, 1985). In contrast, a growing literature rejects the classical hypothesis and favors efficiency or market power differences between firms as the cause of different successes of firms (see, e.g., Demsetz, 1982; Mueller, 1986). This literature does not deny industry effects but claims that firm effects have more explanatory power.

We can use our empirical results to get some initial insight into the relative significance of firm and industry effects. For this purpose, we grouped the firms on the basis of a three-digit industry classification and calculated the average long-run profit projection ($\hat{\pi}_{ip}$) and the standard deviation for the individual firm's profit rate on equity capital. Table 6.3 reports the firm and industry differences for industry groups in which there are at least 10 firms. The results indicate considerable differences between firms and industries. Long-run profit projections are highest in the food and beer industries and moderately high in the chemicals, metal products, and stone/clay products industries.

Whether the observed industry differences were mainly caused by industrywide factors can be partly answered by examining variations in firm long-run profit rates. The last column in Table 6.3 shows that the highest variation occurred in the best and worst performing industries, food and textiles. Furthermore, the beer industry seems to have the lowest variation in long-run profit rates, and the remaining industries show about equal variation. This suggests that in some industries (like the beer industry) firms are protected by entry barriers, and low mobility barriers guarantee about equal profit rates throughout the industry. But in most industries, firm effects are at least equally as important as industry effects in determining the profits that individual firms enjoy.

For a deeper insight into the relative importance of firm and industry effects our analysis relies on two alternative models and different estimation methodologies: First, we apply the model and the estimation methodology suggested in Chapter 2. The model extends the basic empirical model [equation (6.1)] by firm- and industry-specific profit components as follows:

$$\pi_{it} = \alpha_i + \lambda_i(f_i \pi_{it-1}^F + d_i \pi_{it-1}^I) + \mu_{it} \tag{6.4}$$

where π^F and π^I are the firm- and industry-specific profit components of firm i, respectively; the π^F cannot be observed and therefore have to be calculated by $\pi^F = \pi_i - \pi^I$, whereas the π^I are the profits on average across all members of firm i's industry. Second, we extend the preceding model by taking into account the multiindustry character of firms. Thus equation (6.4) will be extended as follows:

$$\pi_{it} = \alpha_i + \lambda_i\left(f_i \pi_{it-1}^F + \sum_{j=1}^{N_i} d_{ij}\gamma_{ij} \pi_{ijt-1}^I\right) + \mu_{it}. \tag{6.5}$$

According to (6.5), firm i is operating in N industries with the share γ_{ij} ($\sum_{j=1}^{N} \gamma_{ij} = 1$). Therefore there are N_i industry effects for firm i. Because of the heterogeneous industry portfolios of firms, we assume no interdependence of firms so that the covariance between μ_{it} and μ_{kt} ($i \neq k$) is assumed to be zero.

A   Results on the firm versus single-industry effects analysis

Table 6.4 summarizes the results of the application of the methodology in Chapter 2. Firms are assigned to three-digit industries in which their main activities are concentrated. If there are more than six firms in a three-digit industry, one has to build subgroups of a maximum of six firms since the available econometric software (in our case the FRLM procedure in TSP 4.0) sets this as an upper limit. Table 6.4 illustrates that we had to build subgroups in all industries. The methodology leaves open the question of how subgroups should be built. The results in Table 6.4

Table 6.4. *Firm versus industry effects*

Industry code	Industry name	Number of subgroups	Number of firms	Acceptance of models					
				M1	M2	M3	M4	M5	M6
200	Chemicals/pharmaceuticals	7	32	2	1	—	2	2	
215	Rubber	2	7	1	—	—	1		
220	Stone and clay	5	19	—	1	—	4		
224	Ceramic	2	7	—	—	—	2		
230	Iron and steel	3	13	2	—	—	1		
232	NE metal[a]	3	9	—	—	—	3		
242	Machinery	9	41	1	5	—	3		
244	Automobiles	2	9	—	—	1	1		
246	Shipbuilding	2	7	2	—	—			
250	Electronic	3	16	—	—	—	3		
252	Feinmechanic and optic	2	7	—	1	—	1		
256	EBM products[b]	3	10	—	1	—	2		
275	Textiles	8	34	3	2	1	1	1	
280	Food	3	13	—	1	—	1	1	
293	Beer brewing	3	14	2	1				
	Totals			13	13	4	23	4	0

[a] Nonferrous metals.
[b] Tools and finished metal products.

are based on arbitrary assignments of firms to subgroups. The suggested econometric testing procedure in Chapter 2 enables us to find out which submodel best represents the structure of the subgroup of firms. There are six submodels under consideration, and submodels 1, 5, and 6 stress firm effects as the main force for the profit adjustment process. As we move from submodels 1 to 5 and then to 6, the firms in those subgroups are more and more heterogeneous and less and less sensitive to industry effects. On the other hand, submodels 2, 3, and 4 emphasize the notion that firms respond similarly to industry-specific forces. As one moves from submodel 2 to submodel 4, the common response will be stronger. Table 6.4 illustrates that for most subgroups submodel 4 has been statistically accepted and that these subgroups are assigned to all industries except the shipbuilding and beer industries. For a considerable number of subgroups, submodel 2 and to a lesser extent submodel 3 have to be accepted, which indicates that together with the result of submodel 4 about 70 percent of all firms respond similarly to industry effects. The remaining firms' profit adjustment process is less sensitive to industrywide factors. Since for these firms only submodels 1 and 5 have been accepted, there is no statistically significant effect, implying that some firms respond solely to firm-specific forces. The firm effects seem to be most important in only a few industries, in particular in the chemicals/pharmaceutical, iron/ steel, shipbuilding, textile, food, and beer industries.

The results in Table 6.4 show quite clearly that in basically all industries firm as well as industry effects are important, but to different degrees. Consequently, there seems to be a structure within industries to which firms adjust differently. The degree of heterogeneity of the industry is, however, very sensitive to the method of building subgroups within industries, which we discovered by experimenting with the composition of subgroups. Most interestingly, we found the following results. Based on the theory of mobility barriers and strategic grouping (Caves and Porter, 1977), we grouped the firms within an industry according to size, measured in terms of sales. The results show quite consistently for nearly all industries that firm size and firm-specific effects are closely related; that is, the larger the firm, the stronger are the firm effects and consequently the less important are the industry effects.

B   *Results on the firm versus multiple industry effects analysis*

An alternative method for analyzing the significance of firm and industry effects is the application of the model specified in equation (6.5). According to this model, there are several industry effects that may drive a firm's profit convergence process. The information of the industry portfolio of each firm was taken from the diversification study by Schwalbach (1988), and the data on the profit time series for these industries were gathered from the *Statistical Yearbook* (*Statistisches Jahrbuch*) for various years. Simple ordinary least squares (OLS) estimations were performed for each firm i.

Table 6.5 summarizes the significance of the various industry effects next to the firm effects. The industries in which firm i is operating are ranked according to the firm's sales share or importance for the firm's business activities at the three-digit industry level. There were at most seven industries in which any firm operates simultaneously, whereas most firms operate in one to three industries. The results in Table 6.5 show that firms respond to several industry forces and not necessarily according to the ranking of industries with decreasing intensity. It therefore puts in question the general belief that only the major industry is of relevance in analyzing the importance of industry factors. As shown in Table 6.5, in half of the cases the firms respond more strongly to effects of the second-ranked industry than to the major industry.

Table 6.5 also illustrates that firm effects are strong overall. They are particularly weak in, for example, the petroleum refining, NE (nonferrous)

Table 6.5. *Significance of firm and multiple industry effects*

Industry code	Firm effect[a]	Industry effects by industry[a]						
		1	2	3	4	5	6	7
200	52% (48/25) $R^2 = 0.47$	56% (48/27)	34% (38/13)	17% (23/4)	25% (12/9)	66% (6/4)	0% (2/0)	0% (1/0)
205	25% (4/1) $R^2 = 0.48$	25% (4/1)	66% (3/2)	0% (1/0)				
215	50% (8/4) $R^2 = 0.41$	37% (8/3)	42% (7/3)	0% (4/0)	100% (1/1)	0% (1/0)		
220	39% (23/9) $R^2 = 0.43$	65% (23/15)	37% (8/3)	0% (1/0)				
230	46% (13/6) $R^2 = 0.33$	38% (13/5)	54% (11/6)	40% (5/2)	66% (3/2)	66% (3/2)	50% (2/1)	
232	12% (8/1) $R^2 = 0.39$	25% (8/2)	33% (6/2)	0% (3/0)	100% (1/1)			
242	35% (51/18) $R^2 = 0.30$	39% (51/20)	25% (40/10)	31% (16/5)	25% (8/2)	0% (3/0)	0% (1/0)	
250	52% (21/11) $R^2 = 0.28$	42% (21/9)	15% (13/2)	0% (8/0)	0% (2/0)	100% (1/1)		
264/5	66% (6/4) $R^2 = 0.17$	16% (6/1)	50% (2/1)					
275/6	57% (38/22) $R^2 = 0.24$	50% (38/19)	0% (2/0)					
280	59% (42/25) $R^2 = 0.46$	47% (42/20)	56% (16/9)	0% (1/0)	100% (1/1)	0% (1/0)		

Notes: Percentages represent significant estimates within the industry. Numbers in parentheses represent total number of firms in the industry per number of firms with significant effects. Average R^2 values are for significant equations.

[a] Selected at 10% level of significance, two-tailed test.

metal, and car industries, in which industry effects are weak as well. These industries seem to be particularly sensitive to other forces (e.g., macro-economic). It is also worth noting that the importance of firm effects seems to be independent of the extent of firm diversification.

V   Explanation of permanent profit levels by firm-specific factors

It can be deduced from the results in Section IV that there are (1) permanent profit differences, (2) different speed-of-adjustment processes toward the permanent profit level, and (3) firm-specific as well as multiple industry-specific effects explaining these differences. In this section we specify the effects of permanent profit differences in greater detail to derive their empirical significance. In this context it will prove useful to select the familiar structural variables in industrial economics research that explain profit differences between firms. Among them are firm-specific factors on which we want to restrict our analysis due to the lack of complete industry-specific information. Table 6.6 summarizes the firm-specific factors and gives coefficient values as a result of OLS regressions. The table reports on the case in which the dependent variable is the permanent profit rate on equity capital before tax. Regressions performed on the other three profit measures showed similar results and are therefore not reported here. In Table 6.6, most explanatory variables show the theoretically expected sign, but not all are statistically significant. The strongest association was found between financial risk and permanent profits. Financial risk is measured by the debt–equity capital ratio averaged over the time period 1961–82. According to the results, successful firms must have made use of the positive leverage effect, which means that if the difference between the profit rate on invested capital and the interest rate on debt capital remains positive over time, higher leverage may improve profitability or it may offset a decrease in profitability. In contrast to this association, the result with respect to the business risk variable turned out to be the opposite of what the risk premium hypothesis suggests. Business risk is measured by the standard deviation of the profit rate on total capital over the sample period and reflects the probability distribution of outcomes of the firm's operating decisions. The result indicates that successful firms managed their entire investment portfolios better by also devoting resources to risk-reducing means of entry and mobility barriers.[10]

The results in Table 6.6 further show that multimarket dominance is associated with high profit rates, but the relationship is not statistically

---

[10] This result is shared by studies that applied the same measure of business risk. See, e.g., Albach (1987), Bowman (1980), and Schwalbach (1988) for a more detailed analysis.

Table 6.6. *Regression results*

Independent variables	Coefficients
Business risk	-0.134^a
	(-3.13)
Financial risk (leverage effect)	0.016^a
	(7.43)
Multimarket dominance	0.003
	(1.40)
Extent of diversification	-0.0003^b
	(-1.92)
Growth	0.004^a
	(2.75)
Size	0.0007
	(0.79)
Advertising–sales relationship	0.048^a
	(2.45)
R&D success (number of patents)	0.0007
	(1.09)
Capital intensity	-0.0007^a
	(-2.92)
R^2	0.288
F	11.317
N	262

Note: Dependent variable: projected long-run profit rate on equity capital before tax. Numbers in parentheses are t-values.
[a] Significant at the 1% level, one-tailed test.
[b] Significant at the 5% level, one-tailed test.

significant.[11] Market dominant firms therefore have some control over the effectiveness of competitive strategies in at least one market. The results furthermore indicate that the presence in multiple markets does not improve profitability. Although it has been shown that diversification is an effective strategy in reducing firms' overall risk, as our result shows, it does not contribute to higher profitability. However, this does not mean

[11] Since market dominance is measured by a dummy variable, the results might have been stronger if we would have been able to calculate a time series of a weighted multiple market share. Information on market shares over time was not available for all firms and all markets. We also did not want to take the market share of one market and correlate it with the permanent firm profit rate, knowing that firms are diversified and their multiple market shares change over time.

that only specialized firms are the most successful firms. There are highly diversified firms in the group of firms with the highest permanent profit rates. But these highly diversified and successful firms are able to realize scope economies better than other diversified firms.

The results in Table 6.6 also suggest that a positive firm growth rate has a favorable and significant impact on the rate of return. Furthermore, firm size is associated with higher profit rates, but the coefficient is small and insignificant. We also found a strong relationship between the advertising–sales relationship and profitability, suggesting that the more profitable firms are those with higher investments in product differentiation. If we compare this result with the negative impact of diversification on profitability, one can stress that a market extension strategy via product differentiation seems to be more profitable than spreading the activities over several markets. Table 6.6 also shows that research-and-development (R&D) intensive firms (measured by number of patents) can expect a positive payoff, but one has to keep in mind that the association is not statistically significant. Somewhat surprising is the result that most successful firms are not those that have the highest capital–output ratio. However, the same result has been found by other studies as well and has been explained by the fact that in capital-intensive industries excess profit rates are competed away more vigorously. In addition, one may argue that exit barriers are high in capital-intensive industries, which forces each firm to invest in the latest technology immediately after it becomes available to remain at the cost-efficient frontier. Since all firms have to behave in the same way, competition will not lead to above average profit rates.

VI   Concluding remarks

Many studies in Germany have shown that corporate profit rates showed a clear downward trend over the period 1961–82.[12] These studies also indicated that profit rate differences between firms diminished only slightly. Our study provided empirical evidence for time-independent profit differences and slow profit convergence, particularly by the best and worst performing firms in the sample. This suggests that the most successful firms were able to protect their high profit rates over time, whereas the least successful firms made little progress in improving their profit situations. The permanent profit differences were also stable across the accounting and market valuation measures, whereas the speed of profit adjustment was not stable. Capital markets therefore expect more stability in firm performance than accounting information suggests.

---

[12] See, e.g., Albach (1985). For a complete reference list see Schwalbach (1988).

In the course of the study, it was also shown that profit differences could be explained by firm- and industry-specific effects. Firm effects seem to be related to firm size and mobility barriers; that is, the larger the firm, the stronger the firm effects and the higher the mobility barriers. Consequently, industry effects are less important for larger firms. On the other hand, there might be multiple industry effects depending on the extent of multimarket activities of firms. The results show, contrary to what mainstream industrial organization studies suggest, that the industry effects are not necessarily most pronounced in the firm's major industry. This result might have far-reaching implications for further empirical studies since it suggests that explaining firms' multimarket profit rates by single-market variables like market share, concentration, and so on might lead to biased results.

In explaining permanent profit differences, the study concentrated on firm effects only and showed that firm risk components and means of product differentiation contributed most to the stability of permanent profits. The selected firm-specific effects together explained 28.8% percent of profit variance, leaving more than 70 percent to other effects, for example, industry effects and other stochastic effects. The recipe of how successful firms in Germany are operated is therefore only partly provided. The other part remains for future research.

CHAPTER 7

The persistence of profits in France

FREDERIC YVES JENNY AND ANDRÉ-PAUL WEBER

The sample consists of all firms for which data were available over the entire period under review (1965–82). These included all firms listed on the stock exchange or subject to the legal obligation to publish financial statements. Although the number of firms subject to this legal obligation in 1965 was close to a thousand, a number of them were merged, liquidated, or transformed into holding companies during the period under review. Some were also not legally obligated to publish data in every year. Thus, our sample consists of 450 firms (see Table 7.1).

The profit rate variable is defined as follows: (profit before taxes + interest payments)/total assets. Although it would have been preferable to use after tax profits, the amount of taxes paid by the firms was not available. One should note that in previous structure performance studies in France, the same profit rate definition was used and the econometric results were consistent with those of other countries and what standard theories predict.

The average profit rates of the 450 firms in the sample and the dispersion of profit rates varied over time, as can be seen from Table 7.2. The 18-year interval can be subdivided into four periods: profit stability from 1965 through 1968; high average profit rates from 1969 through 1973, which was one of sustained growth in France; a period of profit rate instability (1974–80) reflecting adjustment to the oil crisis; and a decline in profits in 1981 and 1982, possibly due to the measures taken by the socialist government that came into power in 1981 but also to stiffening competition among firms in a period of declining growth.

To remove the impact of economywide fluctuations in profit rates over time, normalized profit rates for each firm were calculated using the following definition:

$$\pi_{it} = P_{it} - \bar{P}_t$$

where P_{it} is firm i's before tax profit rate in year t, and

$$\bar{P}_t = \sum_{i=1}^{450} \frac{P_{it}}{450}.$$

Table 7.1. *Summary of firms eliminated from sample*

Number of firms in the initial population (1965)	976
Number of firms that disappeared through mergers	273
Number of firms liquidated	38
Number of firms transformed into holding companies	68
Number of firms for which the data were incomplete	147
Remaining firms in the sample	450

Table 7.2. *Profit rates: mean and standard deviation between 1965 and 1982, 450 firms*

Year	Mean	Standard deviation
1965	6.46	5.64
1966	6.45	6.32
1967	6.30	5.77
1968	6.21	5.70
1969	7.29	5.40
1970	6.99	5.85
1971	6.82	5.43
1972	7.50	5.50
1973	7.70	5.78
1974	8.50	15.45
1975	6.37	7.18
1976	6.73	7.23
1977	7.18	15.18
1978	6.52	5.83
1979	6.87	6.20
1980	7.09	6.90
1981	6.44	7.31
1982	5.52	8.88

We estimate the same equation estimated in the other studies:

$$\pi_{it} = \alpha_i + \lambda_i \pi_{it-1} + \mu_{it}. \tag{7.1}$$

From this equation we determine the long run profit rate of a firm,

$$\hat{\pi}_{ip} = \frac{\hat{\alpha}_i}{1 - \hat{\lambda}_i},$$

Table 7.3. *Long run profit projections, $\hat{\lambda}_i$'s, and initial profit rates for six subgroups of firms*

Subgroup	$\hat{\pi}_{ip}$	$\hat{\lambda}_i$	$\bar{\pi}_{i0}$
1	6.40	0.543	8.50
2	1.72	0.392	2.90
3	−0.06	0.330	−0.20
4	−1.35	0.244	−1.50
5	−1.64	0.322	−3.30
6	−3.29	0.368	−6.60

A. Number of cases for which $R^2 > 0.1$ — 223 (49.6%)

B. Number of cases for which the estimated long run profit rate is significantly positive (10% level, two-tailed test) — 251 (56%)

C. Number of cases for which the estimated long run profit is significantly negative (10% level, two-tailed test) — 152 (33%)

D. Number of cases for which the slowness of adjustment is significantly positive (10% level, two-tailed test) — 204 (45.3%)

E. Number of cases for which the slowness of adjustment is significantly negative (10% level, two-tailed test) — 5 (1%)

F. Number of cases in which the estimated slowness of adjustment is larger than 1 — 5

G. Correlation coefficient between the estimated long run profit and the initial profit rate — 0.359

H. Correlation coefficient between the estimated long run profit rate and the average of the normalized profit rate for the entire period — 0.789

Note: Firms ranked by subgroup in declining order based on initial profit rates.

and the speed of adjustment to this long run profit rate $(1 - \lambda_i)$. Equation (7.1) was estimated using ordinary least squares.

In Table 7.3, the mean long run profit rates and $\hat{\lambda}_i$ estimates are presented for six subsamples of 75 companies each. The subsamples were formed on the basis of the mean profit rates for the firms in the first two years of the sample period (1965 and 1966). Thus, subsample 1 presents the average parameter estimates for the 75 firms with the highest mean profit rates in the first two years; subsample 2 presents results for the firms ranked 76–150 on the basis of their average profits over 1965 and and 1966, and so on. The third column reports the mean initial profit rates (π_{i0}) for each subsample. When $\hat{\lambda}_i > 1.0$, the long run profit rate of the firm is not projected to converge on a finite number. We estimated five $\hat{\lambda}$'s greater than 1.0. These five values were all set equal to 0.95 in the calculations for Table 7.3.

As Table 7.3 indicates, the ordering of subsamples by initial profit rates is identical to that of the estimated long run profit rates. Firms with profit rates initially above the average tended to have long run projected profits above the average. For example, firms in the highest initial profit subgroup had profit rates in 1965–6 averaging 8.5 percentage points more than the mean for the entire sample (6.45). They are projected to earn 6.40 percentage points more than the average firm. Similarly, firms in the lowest initial profit group had 1965–6 profits averaging 6.60 *less* than the mean profit rate of 6.45 and are projected to have long run profit rates some 3.29 percentage points below the mean.

The correlation between average profit rates over the entire period and expected profit rates in the long run is quite strong (the correlation coefficient between these two variables is equal to 0.789). The R^2's for the estimated equations are greater than 0.1 for nearly half the firms in the sample. The proportion of firms for which the estimated long run profit is significantly different from zero is roughly 0.90, and 45 percent of the $\hat{\lambda}$'s are significantly different from zero. Thus, the simple autoregressive equation used to predict long run profitability seems to fit the data fairly well.

The first two subgroups of firms have both higher long run projected profit rates ($\hat{\pi}_p$) *and* $\hat{\lambda}$'s. Thus, these firms not only converge on profit rates that are above the sample mean but also tend to converge more slowly than the other firms in the sample.

In contrast, the pressure to return to a normal rate of return seems more intense on underachievers. Their long run projected profit rates are 50 percent higher than their initial profit rates (-3.29 v. -6.60), and their speed of adjustment is higher ($1 - \hat{\lambda} = 1 - 0.368 = 0.632$ v. $1 - 0.543 = 0.457$ for the highest initial profit group).

These results suggest that both firms earning supranormal profits and firms earning subnormal profits in any one period tend to continue to do so in the long run. Market forces seem to do a less than perfect job forcing underachievers to improve their performance to avoid disappearing from the market and at the same time do not dissipate the "monopoly" profits of those earning above normal returns. These results are all the more striking in that during the sixties and seventies, with the gradual opening of French markets to international competition in Europe, one

Table 7.4. *Mean expected long run profit rates by sector of activity (295 firms for the period 1965–82, stable cases only)*

Sector	Number of firms	Average expected long run profit
Food	49	0.06
Textile and clothing	15	−2.18
Paper and pulp	16	−0.08
Chemicals	30	1.56
Pharmaceuticals	8	12.52
Petroleum refining	9	5.04
Rubber products	2	−2.70
Cement, stone, ceramics, glass	22	2.44
Iron and steel	13	−0.82
Nonferrous metal	8	−1.41
Metal products	23	0.49
Machinery and tools	31	0.25
Electrical equipment	34	0.05
Shipbuilding	2	−2.95
Cars and other transportation equipment	34	0.05
Precision instrumentation	3	−0.73

would have expected a faster and more vigorous disciplining of firms. What this suggests then is that a commonly held view according to which competition policy is useless, since no firm can permanently enjoy monopoly rents, may not be accurate and that competition policy may indeed complement usefully the market forces both in speeding up the adjustment and in making it more thorough.

The respective importance of firm specific and industry specific effects on the estimated difference in long run profit rates could not be fully analyzed because of insufficient data. However, we present in what follows the official classification of 295 firms in the sample according to the general sector of activity to which they belong (Table 7.4). We computed the average expected long run profit for the firms of each sector. When looking at the table, one should keep in mind that the classification of a firm in a sector is done on the basis of the fact that it has more employees working in this sector than in any other sector. Thus, for example, if a diversified firm manufactures two products (say, *A* and *B*) and has more employees working in the production of *A* than it has in the production of *B*, the whole firm will be assigned to the *A* sector.

This table suggests that industry differences are possibly important, as traditional industrial organization theory would suggest. Indeed, the pharmaceutical and the petroleum refining industries, two industries characterized over most of the period under study by high concentration and barriers to entry, show very high expected long term profits. It is worth mentioning that the estimated long run profits for the pharmaceutical firms are also very high in Japan and in the United States. Also, one should remember that during most of the period under study the refining of petroleum was not only concentrated (there were only four major refiners) but also subject to severe entry barriers as the government closely monitored entry into the field and controlled the import of refined products.

Similarly, the cement, stone, ceramic, and glass sector exhibits high long run estimated profits. One has to remember that because the firms in the general sample are all large firms, the firms of the sample belonging to this sector are mostly cement manufacturers and glass makers. The cement industry, although not particularly concentrated at the national level, is quite concentrated if one takes into account that transportation costs make it uneconomical to haul cement long distances. The glass manufacturing sector is very concentrated and exhibits high barriers to entry.

At the lower end of the scale, one finds the textile and clothing sector, which at the end of the sixties and the beginning of the seventies had low concentration and in which firms exhibited low economies of scale and were facing intense competition from Southeast Asian products. Each of the two shipbuilding firms in this industry also exhibited large negative projected long run profits. This sector was concentrated at the national level but was faced with stiff international competition.

Of course, these results are extremely tentative and do not preclude the possibility that firm specific factors such as market shares might be an important determinant of long run projected profit rates, a hypothesis we were not able to test.

CHAPTER 8

The persistence of profits in Japan

HIROYUKI ODAGIRI AND HIDEKI YAMAWAKI

This chapter reports the results of our study on the persistence of profits in Japan. It is separated into five sections. Section I discusses the movement of average profitability during a sample period, 1964–82. Section II presents our estimation results on the persistent differences in profit rates among Japanese firms. Section III examines the influences of market share and market concentration on the projected long-run profit rate and on the speed of adjustment toward this long-run rate. The results indicate that the long-run profit rate is more strongly affected by market share whereas the adjustment speed is more strongly affected by concentration. This suggests that the adjustment speed is more strongly influenced by industry or market characteristics. To examine this possibility further, we seek in Section IV the determinants of the adjustment speed at the industry level by assigning each firm into one of the 42 three-digit industries and calculating the industrial average of the adjustment speed. The adjustment speed is compared in a sample of matched U.S. and Japanese industries. Section V summarizes our findings.

I Average profit rates during 1964–82

Table 8.1 shows the movement of profit rates in Japan during the period of our inquiry, 1964–82. In the first three columns are the profit rates reported in the Corporation Enterprise Survey (Ministry of Finance) and in the fourth column is the average profit rate of 376 firms in our sample (to be discussed in detail in the next section). All the profit rates are defined as the ratio of after-tax profits inclusive of interest payments to total assets. The choice of after-tax rates versus before-tax rates makes little difference because the correlation coefficients between the two exceed 0.9. Profits are defined as inclusive of interest payments because total assets include those financed by debt.

We thank Dennis C. Mueller and Takeo Nakao for helpful comments.

Table 8.1. *Profit rates in Japan: 1964–82*

Year	Sector				
	All sectors (all sizes)[a] (1)	Manufacturing (all sizes)[a] (2)	Manufacturing (big firms)[a] (3)	Manufacturing (average of 376 firms)[b] (4)	Nonfinancial (average of 848 firms)[c] (5)
1964	5.95	6.59	6.42	6.82	—
1965	5.77	6.27	6.16	6.62	—
1966	6.10	6.95	6.99	7.44	5.5
1967	6.31	7.42	7.34	7.74	5.8
1968	6.37	7.46	7.17	7.65	5.7
1969	6.60	7.66	7.41	7.75	5.6
1970	6.35	7.24	6.96	7.21	5.2
1971	5.77	6.19	5.97	5.89	4.9
1972	5.71	6.36	6.21	5.96	4.1
1973	6.32	7.45	7.02	7.24	1.6
1974	6.12	6.75	6.17	6.09	0.4
1975	4.91	4.70	4.36	4.33	2.4
1976	5.43	5.87	5.76	5.28	2.3
1977	5.11	5.60	5.41	4.83	2.3
1978	4.94	5.52	5.32	5.33	2.5
1979	5.16	6.31	6.23	6.21	1.8
1980	5.86	6.72	6.82	6.56	2.4
1981	5.15	5.82	5.76	5.64	3.4
1982	4.81	5.36	5.53	5.03	—
Mean	5.72	6.43	6.26	6.30	3.49[d]
Standard deviation	0.57	0.82	0.80	1.05	1.75[d]
Correlation with	1				
(2)	0.95	1			
(3)	0.89	0.98	1		
(4)	0.91	0.96	0.97	1	
(5)	0.51[d]	0.48[d]	0.54[d]	0.60[d]	1[d]
PI	0.57	0.52	0.38	0.35	0.08[d]
GPI	0.55	0.64	0.70	0.71	0.69[d]

Notes:

Big firms = firms with paid-in capital of a billion yen or more

PI = trend-free production index in mining and manufacturing (trend has been eliminated by fitting an exponential curve)

PGI = the rate of increase of production index in mining and manufacturing from the
previous year

Sample: 1964–82 unless state otherwise.

[a] *Source:* Corporation Enterprise Survey.

[b] *Source:* Our sample.

[c] *Source:* Wagasuki et al. (1984).

[d] Sample: 1966–81.

The values of total assets used to compute these profit rates are all in book value, that is, they are usually evaluated at acquisition costs. To examine if their reevaluation at current prices results in significant differences in the profit rate movement, we present in the fifth column the real profit rate estimated by Wakasugi, Nishina, Kon-ya, and Tsuchiya (1984) for the period 1966–81. Except for the revaluation of total assets, the quoted rate [$ROC_W(AT)$ in their Table 9-2] uses basically the same definition as ours.

The table also shows the means and standard deviations. Manufacturing appears to have been earning a somewhat higher profit rate than other sectors on average. There is no indication that big firms are earning more than smaller firms.

The correlation coefficient matrix in the table clearly indicates a very strong correlation between any pair of the four nominal profit rates. Most importantly for our study, it suggests that the 376 firms in our sample can be regarded as representative of the entire manufacturing sector in Japan.

The correlation is somewhat weaker with real profit rates, though still significant at the conventional 5 percent level. The table reveals that the mean is lower and the standard deviation is higher for the real rate than for the nominal rate. This owes mostly to the high inflation rate in 1973 and 1974 immediately after the first oil crisis, which caused a sharp increase in the current value of assets and a sharp drop in real profit rates. In comparison, the decrease in nominal profit rates, which occurred with a one-year lag in 1974–5, was more modest.

The last two rows in Table 8.1 show the correlation coefficients between the profit rates and the trend-free level of the production index or the annual growth rate of the production index.[1] Since the coefficient is significantly different from zero at the 5 percent level if it is greater than 0.46 and at the 10 percent level if greater than 0.39, we find that the profit rates are all significantly positively correlated with production growth. That is, there is a significant tendency for profit rates to be higher when production is expanding.

In sum, the average profit rate of our sample is highly correlated with the profit rate of the entire economy or all of manufacturing, and any one of these profit rates tends to fluctuate in parallel with general business conditions.

---

[1] Alternatively, one may wish to compare the correlations with the level of gross national product (GNP). Unfortunately, due to the shift of the national accounting system into SNA during the period, GNP cannot be obtained in a continuous manner for the period 1964–82.

II   Persistence of profits

Our sample consists of 376 manufacturing firms that satisfy the following requirements: (i) the firm was listed in the First Section of the Tokyo Stock Exchange in 1964; (ii) its financial statement is publicly available for the period 1964–82 (this requires that it has to be listed in at least one of the eight stock exchanges in Japan throughout the period); and (iii) it experienced no large-scale mergers during 1964–82. The sample is more comprehensive than in our previous study (Odagiri and Yamawaki, 1986); for the difference, see Odagiri and Yamawaki (1985).

The period of study is accounting years (April to March of the following year) 1964–82. Thus we have 19 observations for each firm. The choice of the starting year, 1964, was dictated by the change in accounting rules in 1963. The data were obtained from the NEEDS data tape (Tokyo: Nihon Keizai Shimbun Sha) after adjustments were made to correct for the differences in accounting periods across firms.

As discussed earlier, the profit rate $P_i(t)$ of the ith firm in year t is defined as the after-tax profits inclusive of interest payments divided by total assets. Since this rate, as shown in the previous section, fluctuates with the business cycles, it is desirable to eliminate this factor to focus on the profit rate differences among firms. Hence, we define

$$\Pi_{it} = P_{it} - \bar{P}_t, \quad \text{where} \quad \bar{P}_t = \sum_{i=1}^{376} \frac{P_{it}}{376}. \tag{8.1}$$

Alternatively, one may normalize in ratio form as $\Pi_{it} = (P_{it} - \bar{P}_t)/\bar{P}_t$. Odagiri and Yamawaki (1985) have shown that the results are not sensitive to the choice of normalization method: Hence, we confine the present analysis to Π_{it} as defined in (8.1).

Following the discussion in Odagiri and Yamawaki (1986) and Chapter 2 of this book by Geroski, we employ the following autoregressive (or partial-adjustment) model to examine the persistence of profits:

$$\Pi_{it} = \alpha_i + \lambda_i \Pi_{it-1} + \mu_{it} \tag{8.2}$$

where α_i and λ_i are constants specific to firm i and μ_{it} is an error term assumed to be independently and identically distributed; $\hat{\Pi}_{ip} = \hat{\alpha}_i/(1 - \hat{\lambda}_i)$ gives the estimate of the long-run profit rate and $1 - \hat{\lambda}_i$ gives the estimate of the speed of adjustment, where $\hat{\alpha}_i$ and $\hat{\lambda}_i$ are the ordinary least squares (OLS) estimates of (8.2).

In Table 8.2, all the companies were grouped into six subsamples in the order of the initial profit rate Π_{i0}, which is the average of the profit rates in the first two years, 1964 and 1965. The averages of the estimated long-run profit rates $\hat{\Pi}_p$, the estimated slowness of convergence $\hat{\lambda}$, and

Table 8.2. *Estimated persistence of profits*

Subsample	$\hat{\Pi}_p$	$\hat{\lambda}$	Π_0
1	0.7369	0.6325	3.4095
2	0.2824	0.4579	1.1582
3	0.1476	0.4563	0.4219
4	−0.1913	0.3917	−0.2445
5	−0.6326	0.4447	−1.1735
6	−0.7571	0.4053	−3.5742
A		250 (66.5)	
B		62 (16.5)	
C		56 (14.9)	
D		285 (75.8)	
E		1 (0.3)	
F		1	
G		0.3046	
H		0.8687	
I		0.1571	

Notes:

A = number of cases for which $\bar{R}^2 > 0.1$

B = number of cases for which $\hat{\Pi}_p$ is significantly positive (10% level, two-tailed test)

C = number of cases for which $\hat{\Pi}_p$ is significantly negative (10% level, two-tailed test)

D = number of cases for which $\hat{\lambda}$ is significantly positive (10% level, one-tailed test)

E = number of cases for which $\hat{\lambda}$ is significantly negative (10% level, one-tailed test)

F = number of cases where $\hat{\lambda} > 1$ ($\hat{\lambda}$ set equal to 0.95 in this case)

G = correlation coefficient between $\hat{\Pi}_p$ and Π_0

H = correlation coefficient between $\hat{\Pi}_p$ and $\bar{\Pi}$ (the average of the normalized profit rate for the entire period)

I = correlation coefficient between $\hat{\Pi}_p$ and $\hat{\lambda}$

Numbers in parentheses are percentages.

the initial profit rates Π_0 were calculated for each group and are shown in the table. Since the profit rate is predicted to explode in the long run when $\hat{\lambda} > 1$ (there was no case of $\hat{\lambda} < -1$), such cases were assumed to have 0.95 as the true value of λ.

Table 8.2 clearly indicates that the ordering of $\hat{\Pi}_p$ across the six subsamples agrees with that of the initial profit rate Π_0. Thus a firm earning a higher-than-average profit rate in the initial two sample years is expected to earn a higher-than-average profit rate in the long run. Since the average unnormalized initial profit rate (the average over all firms of the profit rates in 1964 and 1965) was 6.72 percent (see Table 8.1), Table 8.2 implies that the first subsample, on average, had the initial profit rate of 10.1 (3.4 + 6.7) and is expected to earn the long-run profit rate equal to the long-run average profit rate plus 0.7369. If we approximate the long-run average profit rate by the average profit rate over the entire period, 1964–82, which was 6.3 percent (see Table 8.1), the estimated average long-run profit rate for the first subsample is about 7.0 percent. Similarly for the last sixth subsample it is 5.54 percent.

That the company with a relatively high (low) initial profit rate is expected to earn a relatively high (low) profit rate even in the long run suggests the persistence of supra- (sub-) normal profits. This tendency is also confirmed by the significantly positive correlation between $\hat{\Pi}_p$ and the initial profit rate (row G) or between $\hat{\Pi}_p$ and the profit rate averaged over the entire period (row H). That the correlation is stronger with the entire average rate than with the initial rate is not surprising because the estimation was made using the profit rates of the entire period. But the high correlation between $\hat{\Pi}_p$ and the average profit rate suggests that the factors affecting the average profit rate should also affect $\hat{\Pi}_p$. Therefore, the influences of market structure on profitability confirmed for profit rates averaged over time in the literature[2] are also expected to be present on our estimate of the long-run profit rate. This conjecture will be confirmed in the following sections.

Rows A to E of Table 8.2 give the measures of the fit of the model. The value of $\bar{R}^2$ is greater than 0.1 for two-thirds of the firms, the proportion of companies with $\hat{\Pi}_p$ being significantly different from zero is about 30 percent, and the proportion of $\hat{\lambda}$ being significantly positive is about three-quarters. Thus the model seems to have significantly explained the variation over time of profit rates for a majority of the companies.

The last row in Table 8.2 indicates that $\hat{\Pi}_p$ and $\hat{\lambda}$ are significantly positively correlated at the 5 percent level. This suggests that a firm with an above-average profit rate is slower to adjust to short-run disequilibrium gains or losses. Because such a firm, on average, decreases its profit rate over time (for $\hat{\Pi}_p < \Pi_0$ in the first subsample), this larger $\hat{\lambda}$ implies its ability to earn short-run excess profits for a longer duration. The persistence of above-normal profits in the long run, we may say, is associated with more persistent short-run rents as well.

III   The determinants of persistent profits at the firm level

Now that we have confirmed the persistence of profit differences across firms, the next question to ask, naturally, is what makes certain firms more

---

[2] See Uekusa (1982) for a survey of the Japanese results.

Table 8.3. *Effects of market structure on $\hat{\Pi}_p$ and $\hat{\lambda}$*

Constant	CR	MS	RINV	ADV	GIND	$\bar{R}^2$	Sample size
Dependent variable $= \hat{\Pi}_p$							
-1.729^a	0.018^b	—	—	0.190^a	0.015	0.126	100
(-2.760)	(2.489)			(3.034)	(0.431)		
-1.730^a	—	0.038^a	—	0.115	0.042	0.168	88
(-3.282)		(3.468)		(1.650)	(1.189)		
-2.105^a	0.010	0.029^b	—	0.119^c	0.033	0.168	88
(-3.277)	(1.020)	(2.057)		(1.703)	(0.912)		
-1.693^a	—	—	1.229^b	0.152^b	0.042	0.104	88
(-2.766)			(2.284)	(2.141)	(1.138)		
-2.967^a	0.022^a	—	1.174^b	0.129^c	0.027	0.177	88
(-4.050)	(2.904)		(2.276)	(1.890)	(0.753)		
Dependent variable $= \hat{\lambda}$							
0.358^a	0.003^a	—	—	0.021^a	-0.009^b	0.164	100
(4.579)	(3.618)			(2.683)	(-2.012)		
0.465^a	—	0.004^b	—	0.011	-0.006	0.079	88
(6.644)		(2.391)		(1.208)	(-1.180)		
0.339^a	0.003^a	0.001	—	0.012	-0.009^c	0.142	88
(4.119)	(2.673)	(0.248)		(1.396)	(-1.823)		
0.590^a	—	—	-0.055	0.018^c	-0.007	0.023	88
(7.318)			(-0.776)	(1.921)	(1.401)		
0.383^a	0.004^a	—	-0.064	0.014	-0.009^b	0.151	88
(4.077)	(3.687)		(-0.966)	(1.629)	(-2.021)		

Note: Numbers in parentheses are *t*-values.
[a] Significant at 1% level, two-tailed test.
[b] Significant at 5% level, two-tailed test.
[c] Significant at 10% level, two-tailed test.

profitable (and/or more slowly adjusting short-run disequilibrium rents). Needless to say, this question should be of particular interest to those concerned with industrial organization and antitrust policies. In this section, we investigate the impact of market structure, in particular, market concentration and market share, on firm profitability.

Table 8.3 gives the cross-sectional estimation results to explain $\hat{\Pi}_p$ and $\hat{\lambda}$. The independent variables are as follows:

CR = four-firm concentration ratio in 1964 (Source: Japan Fair
    Trade Commission, *Nihon no Sangyo Shuchu*, 1969)
MS = market share in 1964 (Source: *Toyo Keizai Tokei Geppo*)

RINV = the inverse of rank in the share of industry in 1964 (Source: *Toyo Keizai Tokei Geppo*)

ADV = purchased industry advertising divided by the industry domestic products in 1965 (Source: *Input–Output Table*)

GIND = the rate of growth in industry shipments in 1964–82 (Source: Ministry of International Trade and Industry, *Census of Manufactures*)

Because of the lack of well-organized concentration or market share data in Japan, the variables for some of the firms were measured from different data sources or for different years [see Odagiri (1987) for details]. The number of sample firms is 100 for regressions without MS or RINV and 88 for regressions with MS or RINV. That is, 276 of the original 376 firms had to be eliminated because of the lack of CR or MS data or because of substantial diversification. Each firm was matched to a certain industry (at about the three- to four-digit level), and the values in this industry were used for the preceding independent variables.

In the OLS estimation results in Table 8.3, several findings are noteworthy.[3] First, the market structure variables exert significant influences on the projected long-run profit rate ($\hat{\Pi}_p$). More specifically, the more concentrated the market, the larger the market share, or the higher the rank, the greater is the profit rate the firm is projected to earn in the long run. Note that the market structure variables are measured in 1964 whereas $\hat{\Pi}_p$ has been estimated using the 1964–82 time series of the profit rate. Hence, the reverse causality of profitability affecting market structure (Adelman and Stangle, 1985) is extremely unlikely. Also note that the positive correlation between profitability and concentration (or market share) is not a short-run disequilibrium phenomenon as argued by Brozen (1970).

Second, MS explains profit differences better than CR, suggesting that intraindustry differences among firms are important and, thereby, sug-

---

[3] Because the dependent variables $\hat{\Pi}_p$ and $\hat{\lambda}$ are themselves estimated parameters, the validity of using the OLS technique needs to be examined. We believe its validity on two grounds. First, we reestimated the equations by means of least squares weighted with the inverse of the standard errors of $\hat{\Pi}_p$ or $\hat{\lambda}$, following the discussion by Saxonhouse (1976). This implies that an observation with a larger standard error (i.e., less confidence in its estimate) should have a smaller influence on the cross-sectional estimation of the structure-performance relation. This methodology was adopted by Mueller (1986) in his American study of the determinants of $\hat{\Pi}_p$. We found that the weighting does not cause important changes in the results. Second, we repeated the regressions using the initial profit rate (averaged over 1964–5) and the average profit rate (averaged over 1964–82) as alternative dependent variables. These are highly correlated with $\hat{\Pi}_p$, and the (unweighted) regression results were quite similar to the (unweighted) regression results for $\hat{\Pi}_p$ shown in Table 8.3. These two facts are interpreted as implying that the unweighted OLS results in Table 8.3 are reasonably accurate descriptions of the true structure–performance relation. See Odagiri (1987) for details.

gesting the crucial importance of using the firm data. The same is not true for $\hat{\lambda}$, which is explained better by CR. The speed of erosion of excessive profits appears not to be as dependent on firm characteristics as on industry characteristics.

Third, when both CR and MS are used as explanatory variables in the $\hat{\Pi}_p$ equation, CR loses significance whereas MS is still significant. It was found that the simple correlation coefficient (r) between CR and MS is high, 0.619; no doubt, therefore, multicollinearity is present. To circumvent this problem, RINV was used as a proxy variable for market share. It is significantly correlated with MS ($r = 0.573$) and yet virtually uncorrelated with CR ($r = 0.040$); hence, multicollinearity is unlikely.

The estimation result with RINV is also in Table 8.3. As expected, both CR and RINV become significant in the equation for $\hat{\Pi}_p$, suggesting that the leading firm in a concentrated industry tends to be most profitable. This makes sense because a large CR and a large RINV together are likely to be associated with a large MS, and MS has been found to exert a significant influence on $\hat{\Pi}_p$. The fact that $\bar{R}^2$ increases only slightly when CR and RINV are used in place of MS may indicate that MS alone is sufficient to depict the market structure. In the $\hat{\lambda}$ equation, CR is significant but RINV is not, suggesting again the importance of industry characteristics in explaining $\hat{\lambda}$.

Fourth, the effects of industry advertising intensity, ADV, are always positive and in many cases significant. Hence the projected long-run profit rate is estimated to be higher and the adjustment to random shocks is slower for the firms in advertising-intensive industries. In Chapter 3, Mueller advocates the use of an interaction term between market share and industry advertising intensity. His model [equation (3.12)], estimated with the Japanese data, is as follows (a, b, and c denote significance levels; see the note in Table 8.3):

$$\hat{\Pi}_p = -2.180^a + 0.037^b \text{MS} + 0.016 \text{ CR}(1-\text{MS})$$
$$(-2.977) \quad (2.485) \qquad (1.358)$$

$$+ 0.362^b \text{ADV} \cdot \text{MS} + 0.030 \text{ GIND}, \qquad \bar{R}^2 = 0.190,$$
$$(2.264) \qquad\qquad (0.833)$$

$$\hat{\lambda} = 0.304^a + 0.0032^c \text{MS} + 0.0041^a \text{CR}(1-\text{MS})$$
$$(3.199) \quad (1.983) \qquad (2.729)$$

$$+ 0.034 \text{ ADV} \cdot \text{MS} - 0.0084^c \text{GIND}, \qquad \bar{R}^2 = 0.143,$$
$$(1.633) \qquad\qquad (1.812)$$

Compared to the results in Table 8.3, we find that the use of multiplicative terms resulted in an improvement in the $\hat{\Pi}_p$ equation but hardly in the $\hat{\lambda}$ equation. The positive significant effect of ADV $\cdot$ MS suggests, in

Mueller's interpretation, that product differentiation caused by advertising makes the demand curve of an oligopolistic firm less influenced by rival firms' outputs. This agrees with his American result. The coefficient on $CR(1-MS)$ is positive but insignificant in the $\hat{\Pi}_p$ equation similar to the American result (see Chapter 3, Table 3.3). This suggests that the negative effect of $1-MS$ (namely, the share of the rest of the firm) on $\hat{\Pi}_p$ or $\hat{\lambda}$ is stronger in more concentrated industries.

We also found that when the company advertising-to-sales ratio is used in place of ADV, the effects of advertising are insignificant and often negative (Odagiri, 1987). Two explanations appear appropriate for this difference. One is the inaccuracy of the company advertising data: Not all the firms reported them (thus the sample size is reduced to 78), and the definition of advertising may differ from firm to firm. The other is the importance of industry-specific characteristics, say, general product characteristics, rather than firm-specific characteristics in determining the extent of product differentiation.

Fifth and last, the rate of growth of industry shipments GIND has a positive but insignificant effect on $\hat{\Pi}_p$ and a negative effect on $\hat{\lambda}$. That $\hat{\lambda}$ is smaller in a growing industry seems reasonable because growth will induce entry thereby eroding the disequilibrium gains of incumbent firms more rapidly.

These results, particularly the positive effects on profitability of both concentration and market share (or inverted rank), agree with Shepherd's (1972) study of the U.S. company data but not with Ravenscraft's (1983) study of the U.S. line-of-business data. Whether this difference is the result of different observation units, different periods, or different countries cannot be determined.

For the speed of adjustment $(1-\hat{\lambda})$, the important finding was that unlike the projected profit rate $(\hat{\Pi}_p)$, it is more influenced by industry characteristics such as CR than firm characteristics such as MS. Hence, it is desirable to discuss its determinants more in detail using the industry-level variables. This we will undertake in the next section.

IV   The determinants of the speed of profit adjustment at the industry level

This section seeks to identify the determinants of the speed of profit adjustment. To identify the distinctive national characteristics of Japan, the speed of adjustment is compared in a sample of matched Japanese and U.S. industries so that common industry-specific factors that affect the profile of profits *over time* in the two countries are controlled for. These would be technical or structural traits of the industry and factors that shape the industry-specific pattern of the product life cycle or industry evolution. The latter may include product characteristics and the technological opportunities of the industry. Suppose a true structural model to explain intertemporal characteristics of profits is given by[4]

$$Y_J = a_J + X_J b_J + Zc + e_J \qquad \text{for Japan} \qquad (8.3)$$

and

$$Y_{US} = a_{US} + X_{US} b_{US} + Zc + e_{US} \quad \text{for the United States,} \qquad (8.4)$$

where Y is the vector of the dependent variable, X is the matrix of observed explanatory variables that vary between the two countries, Z is the matrix of unobserved exogenous variables that are common to the two countries, a is the vector of constants, b and c are the vectors of coefficients, and e is the vector of random disturbances. We assume that the unobserved variables Z represent the technological factors that are specific to the industry but common to the two countries. Our concern here is to obtain unbiased estimates of the coefficients for X_J and X_{US}, factors that depend on particular conditions in the Japanese and U.S. economies.

The variables Z are unobserved, so that their influence on Y is expressed by the equation error $v_i = Zc + e_i$, where i stands for the country. Since there is no a priori guarantee that the observed explanatory variables X and the unobserved industry characteristics Z are uncorrelated, the regression estimates of the coefficients b will be biased. Another econometric problem in estimating (8.3) and (8.4) independently arises if the errors are correlated across the two countries, that is, $\text{COV}(v_J, v_{US}) \neq 0$. The correlation of the errors can occur because the common unobserved industry characteristics Z represent the disturbances.

One can improve the regression estimates by taking differences of equations (8.3) and (8.4) and eliminating the industry-specific factors Z that are common to the two countries. Thus, our equation, which controls for the industry characteristics, becomes

$$Y_J - Y_{US} = (a_J - a_{US}) + X_J b_J - X_{US} b_{US} + (e_J - e_{US}). \qquad (8.5)$$

Equation (8.5) is an alternative specification to equation (8.3) or (8.4). We are particularly interested in asking the question whether the parameters of the structural equations are equal in magnitude between Japan and the United States.

From the sample of the 376 Japanese firms described in Section II, we further selected 278 firms for which a three-digit primary industry could be selected with some confidence. The U.S. sample used in the analysis

---

[4] For a detailed discussion on the comparative research design, see Caves, Porter, and Spence (1980, pp. 24–27, 29–31). See also Yamawaki (1987).

Table 8.4. *Determinants of the speed of profit adjustment at the industry level* ($N = 42$)

		Mean	
Symbol	Variable	United States	Japan
$\gamma = 1 - \hat{\lambda}$	Speed of adjustment of short-run profits	0.5267 (0.1690)	0.5139 (0.1557)
EXPORT	Exports/total shipments	0.0688 (0.0618)	0.1156 (0.1222)
IMPORT	Imports/(total shipments − exports + imports)	0.0687 (0.0656)	0.0837 (0.0767)
NTB	Nontariff barrier index	0.9966 (2.0440)	0.9899 (2.4837)
CR4	Four-firm producer concentration ratio	0.4301 (0.1693)	0.5890 (0.2177)
ADV[a]	Purchased advertising/total output	0.0185 (0.0296)	0.0101 (0.0143)
RDE	Scientists and engineers/total employment	0.0135 (0.0121)	0.0180 (0.0116)
GROWTH	Change in shipments 1967–77/shipments 1967	1.4391 (0.6382)	2.9753 (1.7067)
KL[b]	Gross fixed assets/total employment	32.9299 (33.9435)	27.7050 (37.8263)

Note: Numbers in parentheses are standard deviations.
[a] Same as ADV in Section III.
[b] In units of 1,000 U.S. dollars.

consists of 212 firms for which complete time-series data are available for 1964–80 and a counterpart U.S. industry is selected. Thus, each of the 278 Japanese firms and the 212 U.S. firms was assigned to one of the 42 three-digit industries matched between Japan and the United States.

The variables included in the analysis to explain the speed of adjustment of short-run rents are listed in Table 8.4. The choice of the years of observation for the variables is mainly governed by the years for which comparable data are available in both the United States and Japan within the 1964–82 period. When it was not feasible to secure average observations for periods within 1964–82, we selected the midpoint years within the period whenever possible.[5]

---

[5] Details are given in an appendix available from the authors. See also Yamawaki (1987).

The dependent variable is the difference in the speed of adjustment between Japan and the United States, $\gamma_J - \gamma_{US}$, where $\gamma_J = (1 - \hat{\lambda}_J)$ and $\gamma_{US} = (1 - \hat{\lambda}_{US})$. The speed of adjustment for each industry is defined as the mean value of $1 - \hat{\lambda}_i$ for those companies assigned in the industry. We first estimated equation (8.5) imposing no restrictions on coefficients (not reported) and tested the null hypothesis that the regression coefficients of paired structural variables are equal in magnitude but opposite in sign between Japan and the United States, that is, $b_{Ji} = -b_{USi}$. In a two-tailed test, the null hypothesis was accepted at the 10 percent level of significance for ADV, RDE, and NTB, but it was rejected for other variables. The null hypothesis was rejected even at the 1 percent level of significance for IMPORT, GROWTH, and KL. This result implies that the impact of ADV, RDE, and NTB on the speed of profit adjustment is statistically equal between Japan and the United States, but the impact of IMPORT, GROWTH, and KL is different between the two countries.

To improve the efficiency of the estimates, we reestimated the equation imposing the restrictions on the coefficients for which the null hypothesis was accepted. Equation 1 in Table 8.5 is a regression equation with the restriction on the coefficients for NTB, ADV, and RDE. The coefficients for these variables are to be equal in magnitude between Japan and the United States. Equation 2 in Table 8.5 imposes further restrictions on the coefficients of EXPORT and CR4 for which the null hypothesis was rejected at the 10 percent level of significance. The basic results in equation 1 remain unchanged except for the significance of the coefficient on EXPORT.

In equation 1 in Table 8.5, JADV–USADV and JRDE–USRDE are highly significant and are positively related to $\gamma_J - \gamma_{US}$. An increase in ADV or RDE in Japan relative to the United States increases the speed of profit adjustment in Japan relative to the United States. This implies that product differentiation through advertising and R&D activity accelerate the profit adjustment process and yield a quick erosion of short-run rents.[6] It appears that in both countries advertising and R&D activity create a market environment in which firms find it more difficult to maintain their market positions over time.[7]

---

[6] This finding on the effect of advertising may appear inconsistent with the finding in Section III. In Section III we found that industry advertising intensity is positively related to the slowness of adjustment, $\hat{\lambda}$, at the firm level. We also found, in an unreported equation, that the speed of adjustment, γ ($= 1 - \hat{\lambda}$), at the industry level is significantly and negatively related to JADV, which is consistent with the result in Section III. However, here we found JADV is positively related to γ_J within the framework of the United States–Japan comparison. That is, $\gamma_J - \gamma_{US}$ was found to be positively related to JADV when we include USADV in the equation. This reversal of sign might be due to the procedure taken here to eliminate industry-specific factors common to both countries. More discussion will be made on this point in the concluding section.

[7] It may also be true that advertising and R&D activities smooth out business cycle conditions, thus yielding a larger estimate of the speed of profit adjustment.

Table 8.5. *Regression equations explaining the difference in the estimates of γ between United States and Japan (with restriction on coefficients)*

Independent variable	Equation 1	Equation 2
JNTB–USNTB	−0.039 (−1.62)	−0.035 (−1.49)
JADV–USADV	7.188 (4.13)*	6.192 (3.58)*
JRDE–USRDE	14.014 (3.86)*	10.567 (3.09)*
JEXPORT–USEXPORT	—	−0.332 (−1.10)
JCR4–USCR4	—	−0.327 (−1.79)***
USEXPORT	1.034 (1.95)***	—
USIMPORT	−1.402 (−2.35)**	−1.149 (−1.86)***
USCR4	0.746 (2.86)*	—
USGROWTH	−0.203 (−3.08)*	−0.132 (−2.17)**
USKL	−0.001 (−0.62)	−0.001 (−0.38)
JEXPORT	−0.130 (−0.38)	—
JIMPORT	−0.629 (−1.04)	−0.129 (−0.22)
JCR4	−0.342 (−1.89)***	—
JGROWTH	−0.025 (−1.31)	−0.022 (−1.10)
JKL	0.006 (3.14)*	0.004 (2.31)**
Constant	0.206 (1.68)	0.319 (2.69)**
$\bar{R}^2$	0.489	0.435
F (degrees of freedom)	4.02 (13, 28)	3.87 (11, 30)

Notes: The dependent variable is $\gamma_J - \gamma_{US}$. *t*-values are in parentheses. Asterisks indicate levels of significance in two-tailed tests: * = 1%, ** = 5%, *** = 10%.

Seller concentration has a negative effect on the speed of profit adjustment in both countries. This confirms the previous findings in Section III of this chapter. The coefficient of CR4 tends to be larger for the United States than for Japan. The significant relation of CR4 to the speed of profit adjustment gives some support for the hypothesis that high concentration leads to a slower profit adjustment and thus the persistence of short-run rents. The difference in CR4 between Japan and the United States, JCR4 − USCR4, is also significant and has a negative sign in equation 2 in Table 8.5.

Imports are a significant competitive force particularly for the United States. USIMPORT is significant and has a negative sign, whereas JIMPORT is not significant. Confronted with import competition, the U.S. producers find it more difficult to maintain short-run rents. This asymmetry of the impact of import competition between the United States and Japan may be reflecting the rising importance of import competition in the U.S. economy through the 1970s. During the period, import share increased by more than 20 percent in 31 U.S. industries among the 42 industries in our data base, whereas it increased by more than 20 percent in 14 Japanese industries.[8]

On the other hand, the presence of export opportunities may have offset the competitive force of imports in the United States. USEXPORT has a significant positive sign, but JEXPORT is not significant. Exports thus lead to a slow adjustment of short-run profits in the United States, implying a U.S. comparative advantage in foreign markets in the 1964–80 period.

Industry growth is significant again only for the United States. USGROWTH is related positively to the speed of profit adjustment, but JGROWTH is not significant.[9] The Japanese economy experienced rapid macroeconomic growth through the 1960s and the early 1970s compared to that of the U.S. economy. Rapid macroeconomic growth presumably made the intertemporal profile of firms' profits less susceptible to industry-

---

[8] For the changing importance of foreign competition in U.S. manufacturing industries and its effect on price–cost margins, see Domowitz, Hubbard, and Petersen (1986).

[9] Although JGROWTH is not statistically significant, it has a negative coefficient that is inconsistent with our finding in Section III where the rate of industry growth (GIND) has a positive relation to the speed of adjustment $(1 - \hat{\lambda})$ at the firm level. In an unreported equation that explains γ_J at the industry level only by the Japanese variables, the sign of JGROWTH remains negative. Thus, the contradiction of the sign on the growth variable between the results in Sections III and IV is not caused by the application of the United States–Japan comparative analysis. However, whether this is the result of different observation periods for the two growth variables (JGROWTH for 1967-77, GIND for 1964-82), different observation units, or different samples is not clear.

specific growth. It seems that the importance of rapid aggregate growth in Japan dominated the effect of industry-specific growth.[10]

Finally, capital intensity, which indicates high-fixed-costs industries, is a significant determinant of the speed of profit adjustment for Japan but not for the United States. JKL is highly significant and has a positive sign, whereas USKL is insignificant.[11] This implies that in high-capital-intensive industries in Japan, short-run profits erode quickly. The difference in the impact of capital intensity between the United States and Japan appears to be explained again by the difference in economic and institutional environments between the two countries. Public policy toward industry in Japan, particularly during the 1960s and the early 1970s, differed in essence from that in the United States. Fearful of excess capacity and ensuing price competition, the Ministry of International Trade and Industry (MITI) promoted seller coordination on price and the construction of new capacity through administrative guidance in a number of capital-intensive industries, including steel, petroleum refining, petrochemical, paper and pulp, and synthetic fibers. Contrary to expectations, the efforts of MITI to regulate investment have created more excess capacity than there would have been without the intervention of MITI.[12] This resulted in deeper price cutting and thus stiff price competition in recession periods in industries with high overhead costs. To the extent that this is true, pricing discipline in high-capital-intensive industries was more fragile in Japan.[13]

We have identified distinctive national similarities as well as differences in relating market structure to the speed of profit adjustment. It appears that the specific national differences observed here could be explained by the underlying differences in economic and institutional environment between Japan and the United States.

V   Summary

This chapter has reported the major results of our study on the persistence of profits in Japan employing time-series data of 376 major Japanese

---

[10] Domowitz, Hubbard, and Petersen (1986) observe that for U.S. manufacturing industries aggregate demand as well as industry-specific demand explain intertemporal variations in price–cost margins.

[11] For some evidence on the negative effect of capital intensity on profitability in the United States, see Scott and Pascoe (1986).

[12] For a detailed argument on this thesis, see Imai (1980, pp. 208–20) and Yamawaki (1988).

[13] A time-series analysis by Yamawaki (1984) gives some evidence on the relation between investment competition, excess capacity, and ensuing pricing competition in the Japanese steel industry over the 1957–75 period. Scherer (1980, ch. 7) suggests that industries with high fixed costs are particularly susceptible to breakdowns in oligopolistic pricing discipline. High capital intensity therefore tends to depress profits, reflecting more fragile pricing disciplines.

manufacturing corporations for 1964–82. It found, first, that a company with a relatively high (low) profit rate is expected to earn a relatively high (low) profit rate in the long run. This finding suggests the persistence of supra- (sub-) normal profits.

Second, we found that the persistence of profit differences across firms is associated with market structure. The more concentrated the industry, the larger the market share, or the higher the rank of the firm in the industry, the greater the profit rate that the firm is projected to earn in the long run. Between concentration and market share, the latter was found to explain long-run profit differences better, which clearly indicates the superiority of using the firm-level data over the industrial data in the profit-market structure study. In contrast, the speed of profit adjustment was found to be more influenced by industry characteristics such as concentration (negatively and significantly) than firm characteristics such as market share (positively but insignificantly).

Finally, we identified the determinants of the speed of profit adjustment at the industry level by using a comparative research design. The analysis found that the speed of profit adjustment increases with advertising and R&D intensity equally in Japan and the United States. On the other hand, seller concentration decreases the speed of profit adjustment in both countries. The regression result suggested that the effect of imports, industry growth, and capital intensity on the profit adjustment process is particularly different between Japan and the United States.

In conclusion, the results for Japan imply that the long-run profit rate is positively associated with market share, in agreement with both the traditional market power hypothesis and the Demsetzian (1973) efficiency hypothesis. The speed of profit adjustment is negatively related to market concentration, which presumably suggests that entry barriers are higher in more concentrated industries. The effects of advertising intensity are particularly noteworthy. We found that the long-run profit rate tends to be higher in an advertising-intensive industry and that this effect is stronger for a firm with a higher market share. This may suggest that, as in the traditional view, the profit-raising effect of market share is enhanced by the entry barriers and product differentiation caused by advertising or, as in the Demsetzian view, corporate strategies are more important for success in an industry where the product can be easily differentiated. Taking Japan alone, the speed of profit adjustment, we found, was negatively related to industrial advertising intensity, which seems to suggest the entry-barrier-raising effect of advertising. However, our Japan–United States comparative study revealed that the Japan–United States difference in the speed of adjustment is positively related to the difference in advertising intensity. That is, when the influences of industry-specific factors (say, product characteristics and technological environment) that are common to the two countries are eliminated, advertising is observed to quicken the erosion of short-run excess rents. One explanation may be the fierce nonprice competition created by advertising, whereas another may be the use of advertising as a means of entry (see Hirschey, 1981; Lynk, 1981). Our results suggest that these have had the effect of speeding up the process of profit adjustment and yet have not been strong enough to eliminate all the excess profits in the long run. More generally speaking, the speed of profit adjustment and the extent of profit adjustment are two different indicators of market performance and are influenced by different factors. In confirming this simple and yet unrecognized fact, the methodology used here must be valuable.

CHAPTER 9

The persistence of profits in the United Kingdom

JOHN CUBBIN AND PAUL A. GEROSKI

I   Introduction

That the recent performance of the U.K. economy has been poor is beyond dispute. One diagnosis of this state of affairs asserts that the cause of the problem arises from the fact that U.K. markets are, in general, rather uncompetitive. There are two steps to the argument. The first asserts that strong and vigorous competitive processes stimulate the kinds of innovativeness and general dynamism that generate rapid economic growth and development. Entry and fringe firm activity, it is argued, encourage the generation and diffusion of new products and techniques and provide the kind of pressure needed to keep all industry members alert, efficient, and flexible. The second strand of the argument asserts that the competitive process in the United Kingdom is, in fact, quite weak. Relatively low rates of innovation and productivity increases, sluggish price responses to cost and demand changes, and a poor balance of trade in medium and high technology products are all taken to point to a lack of dynamism. Further, U.K. industries are highly concentrated, and high gross entry flows in the United Kingdom appear to produce little more than high gross exit flows. That the two sets of facts are associated is suggested by studies that indicate that highly concentrated, low entry industries may be less innovative and less price flexible than others (e.g., Encaoua and Geroski, 1986; Geroski, 1987). Although not conclusive, the overall argument has at least prima facie appeal.

Are industries in the United Kingdom competitive enough to ensure satisfactory rates of innovation and growth? To answer this, one must define the adjective "competitive" and then measure how extensive the

Although we benefited from the participation of Dick Allard in the early stages of this project and from Dennis Mueller and other members of the Persistence of Profits team throughout, the usual disclaimer applies. Participants at the Persistence of Profits Conference also made numerous useful suggestions, and Dennis Mueller provided useful comments on the penultimate draft. Financial assistance from the Office of Fair Trading and the IIM is gratefully acknowledged.

force of competition is in various industries. Although apparently prosaic, there is, in fact, a major decision to be made when undertaking this measurement exercise. The problem is whether one can rely on observables like market concentration or observed entry flows to reflect the pressures that rivalry generates. Although they are relatively easy to observe, the problem with such structural indicators is that firms are affected not only by actual competition, but also by potential competition. Since the response made by an incumbent to a potential entrant may be such as to discourage it from entering, any measure of "competition" based on the number, the relative size, or changes in the number of existing firms is likely to understate the true force of competition from all agents, actual and potential. Thus, the extent of competition in a market may be as difficult to measure as are many of the effects it is thought to bring.

In this chapter, we hope to cast some light on the extent of competition in U.K. markets. For our purposes, a competitive market is one where entry and imitative behavior – actual and potential – are sufficiently strong to keep profits near the "norm." Although both are useful (if noisy) signals of "competitiveness," there are several reasons for concentrating more on the speed of the process of convergence than on steady state levels of profits. On the one hand, long run economic profits are difficult to measure, and long run profits different from zero (or from some other norm) can be difficult to interpret. Further, long run steady states are of largely academic interest unless it can be shown that divergences from them are infrequent and temporary. By contrast, it is difficult to see how even systematic biases in the measurement of profits across firms or industries can distort a pattern of deviations from the norm over time for a specific firm or industry. Further, it may even be the case that phenomena like entry and exit are more directly and accurately reflected in the character of disequilibrium dynamics than in equilibrium steady states. Hence, there is at least a case to be made for examining competition as a process whose force is reflected in the dynamics of profitability, and that is our goal. Much as we would hope to associate competitiveness in this sense with the poor recent performance of the U.K. economy, we shall have to content ourselves here merely with charting its strength.

The plan is as follows. Section II outlines a simple, firm specific model of profitability that can be used to make inferences about the strengths of unobserved and unobservable competitive forces like entry, imitation, and so on. Section III describes the results of applying this model to a sample of U.K. firms for the period 1948–77. Since firms in the same industry ought to share certain common dynamics, examining the extent to which apparent rivals appear to enjoy a similar profitability experience provides a method of assessing the strength of industrywide competitive forces. In this spirit, the model of Section II is extended in Section IV to distinguish firm specific from industrywide effects, and empirical results for this second model are presented in Section V. A summary and set of conclusions appear in Section VI.

II A firm specific model of profits[1]

High profits relative to the norm encourage a variety of responses from actual and potential competitors that have the effect of bidding away excess returns, propelling profits back toward the norm. Whereas one would like to measure the aggregate of these responses – "entry" for short – to use as an index of competitiveness, the responses are often difficult to observe in practice and sometimes are quite unobservable in principle. A natural and convenient alternative method is to measure their force by looking at their cause and consequence, namely, profits relative to the norm. If entry operates as a proportional control mechanism in markets, it follows that one can measure the extent of entry by examining how quickly a given divergence of profits from the norm is eliminated. In particular, the size of systematic changes in excess profitability at different points in time ought to be positively correlated to the size of entry flows. Our goal in this section is to produce an empirically operational model to exploit this insight.

Since it is systematic movements in profits that are important, it is natural to commence by partitioning all of the forces that induce changes in observed profits into one of two general types: entry $E(t)$ and all other factors, $\mu(t)$, which are orthogonal to $E(t)$ by construction. We shall refer to this second set of factors as "luck" to emphasize their unpredictability. The difference between $E(t)$ and $\mu(t)$ lies in the fact that the former systematically respond to profits (the only observable variable in the model) and the latter do not. The cause and consequence of entry is a certain level of profits relative to the norm, one that varies systematically over time. Letting $\pi(t)$ be firm i's profits at time t and $\pi_p(t)$ be the norm toward which i's profits tend, $\rho(t) \equiv \pi(t) - \pi_p(t)$ is defined as the level of "excess profits" enjoyed by firm i. The model of the competitive process that follows links $\rho(t)$ to $E(t)$ in such a way that movements in the observed values of the former can be used to proxy the latter when it cannot be directly observed.

The effects of entry on profits can make themselves felt in any number of ways. Entry may alter collusive pricing patterns, spark a predatory

---

[1] The arguments of this section are drawn from Chapter 2 of this volume, and some initial results for the United Kingdom can be found in Geroski and Jacquemin (1988).

price response by incumbents, or lead to some form of strategic entry preventing behavior that dissipates profits. Although these various responses will have different effects on market structure and nonprice behavior, their net effect on profits is likely to take the form

$$\Delta\rho(t) = \gamma_0 E(t) + \gamma_1 \rho(t-1) + \mu(t), \tag{9.1}$$

where $\gamma_0 < 0$, $\gamma_1 < 0$, and $\Delta\rho(t) \equiv \rho(t) - \rho(t-1)$. Here γ_0 describes the effect of entry on $\rho(t)$ and varies inversely with the level of entry barriers protecting firm i. That $\gamma_1 \neq 0$ ensures that steady state values of $\rho(t)$ remain finite since otherwise $\Delta\rho(t)$ would follow a random walk at equilibrium. Luck is not predictable by any observable in the system, and so it is natural to characterize it as a normally distributed, i.i.d. stochastic process with mean θ_0 and variance σ_μ^2. Since $E(t) = 0$ and the expected value of $\Delta\rho(t) = 0$ at equilibrium, θ_0 is the permanent deviation of $\pi_i(t)$ from the norm enjoyed by firm i. At equilibrium, all fluctuations in profits relative to the norm are random and so are unpredictable. These variations in profits at equilibrium represent the inherent risk that firm i's earnings stream presents, and this observation suggests that σ_μ^2 might be thought of as a measure of risk that is at least superior to the variance of $\rho_i(t)$ itself.

The consequence of nonzero excess returns is entry. Whereas entry decisions are likely to be rather complicated and will depend on numerous factors, for our purposes it is only necessary to concentrate on the relation between entry and the one observable of the system, profits. Let ρ^* be the long run equilibrium value $\rho(t)$ (i.e., that value at which all entry is zero). Clearly $\rho^* = -\theta_0/\gamma_1$. Since positive excess profits can be expected to attract entry [$E(t) > 0$] and low profits to induce "exit" [$E(t) < 0$] with at least a short lag, it seems natural to write

$$E(t) = \phi[\rho(t-1) - \rho^*] + \epsilon(t), \tag{9.2}$$

where $\phi > 0$. The parameter ϕ measures the amount of entry attracted by a unit increase in excess profits (i.e., those profits that can be bid away). It reflects the number of potential "entrants," their alertness, and the heights of various barriers that weaken their ability to penetrate into the market and challenge firm i. By construction, $\epsilon(t)$ is orthogonal to excess returns. It is the exogenous flow of entry or exit that would occur even if $\rho(t-1) = \rho^*$. Since it is not predictable, we take it to be a normally distributed, i.i.d. random variable with zero mean (i.e., only excess profits are expected to induce entry) and variance σ_ϵ^2.

The parameters ϕ, σ_ϵ^2, γ_0, γ_1, and σ_μ^2 in equations (9.1) and (9.2) are not estimable since entry $E(t)$ is a latent variable. However, one can use the structure of the model to generate an equation expressed wholly in terms of observables that describes the net effect of the forces that non-zero excess returns set in motion. Combining (9.1) and (9.2), the time path followed by excess profits is

$$\rho(t) = \alpha + \lambda\rho(t-1) + v(t),\tag{9.3}$$

where $\alpha = (\theta_0 - \gamma_0\phi\rho^*)$, $\lambda \equiv (\gamma_0\phi + \gamma_1 + 1)$, and $v(t)$ is a zero-mean white noise stochastic process with variance $\sigma_v^2 = \gamma_0\sigma_\epsilon^2 + \sigma_\mu^2$.

The goal of this exercise is to measure the state of competition facing firm i. The long run steady state value of $\pi(t)$ for firm i is $[\pi_p(t) + \alpha(1-\lambda)]$. Clearly profits converge to the norm if $\alpha = 0$. If, in addition, $\pi_p(t)$ approximately equals the opportunity cost of capital, then $\pi(t)$ can be said to converge to a *long run competitive equilibrium* if $\alpha = 0$. However, both the difficulty of measuring the opportunity cost of capital as well as the question of how much time is required for convergence directs attention to λ. Here, λ is larger the less entry is attracted by excess profits and the less effect entry subsequently has on excess profits. Thus, the larger is λ, the slower is the decay of any divergence in profits from the norm, and so the weaker is competition.[2]

III Application of the firm specific model to U.K. data

The raw data for estimating equation (9.3) were derived from the Department of Trade and Industry (DTI)/Cambridge University U.K. Quoted Companies Databank for 1948–77, which provides a set of accounts for medium and large companies on which some standardization has been carried out by the compilers. Besides accounting information, the databank also includes miscellaneous items such as employment and sales (after 1968), type of ownership, acquisitions, and a three-digit industrial classification corresponding to the principal activity of the company. Highly diversified companies were unusual in the United Kingdom for this period, and most of those were classified to a category including financial holding companies that was excluded from our analysis.

As always, the presence of mergers creates problems in tracking companies over periods as long as 30 years. In the work to be discussed in Section V, we traced all the amalgamations contributing directly or indirectly to the companies surviving in 1977 and created "pseudocompanies" by amalgamating (for the period prior to the merger) the assets, profits, and so on, of companies that *eventually* merged into one. This enabled us to deal (albeit in a somewhat crude way) with the problem of disappearing companies on the one hand and externally growing companies on

---

[2] A natural way to measure the strength of competition in this sense is in terms of the half-life of any $\rho(t) \neq 0$. If $\alpha = 0$, the half-life of $\rho(t)$ in (9.3) is $T^* = \log\frac{1}{2}/\log\lambda$.

the other. However, for the purposes of facilitating international comparisons of the output from estimating equation (9.3), we have used a sample of 243 firms present throughout the entire period in the results to be reported immediately following (the general tenor of the results was the same for both samples). Of the companies in the data bank, these are the ones left after deletions due to the effects of merger, changing criteria for inclusion in the data bank, new entrants to the data bank, and exits due to bankruptcy (roughly in that order of importance). Profits were collected net of tax payments; assets were book values based on historic cost of purchase less depreciation. The assets of acquired companies were entered at their acquisition cost rather than net book value, although this can be expected to induce some dilution of profit rates.

Table 9.1 summarizes the results of the estimation of equation (9.3) for the entire sample of 243 and for the sample split into three roughly equal-sized groups according to assets in 1951. For the full sample, 9.2% percent of the α coefficients were significant, as compared with an expected value of 5 percent under the null hypothesis that profits show no long term permanent deviation from the norm [Geroski and Jacquemin (1988) report a much higher figure for a subsample of this group of firms]. There was, however, some variation in the pattern of α according to size. The smallest size category of firms produced both the highest proportion of significant coefficients and the highest mean value of α; both of these declined monotonically with initial size. The λ coefficients tended to be both positive and significant, with values of about 0.50 for every subsample (there is some reason to believe that these figures may understate the true values of λ).[3] Thus, some degree of year-to-year persistence is observed in the vast majority of cases, even though long term departures from the norm are a minority phenomenon. Since λ appears to be an increasing function of size, smaller firms tend to adjust somewhat more quickly to their permanent profit rates. Turning finally to the level of long term excess profitability, $\alpha/(1-\lambda)$, it is apparent that this is slightly asymmetrically distributed around zero with a positive mean and a maximum value greater (in absolute terms) than the minimum value. This asymmetry, however, is concentrated in the smallest initial size category; for the larger companies, persistently *negative* adjusted profitability is slightly more common than positive. The bottom part of Table 9.1 shows much the same information for firms ranked by initial profitability.

---

[3] See, e.g., Johnston (1972, p. 305). A statistical model $x(t) = \beta x(t-1) + \mu(t)$ produces an estimate of β, $E\{\beta\}$, which depends on the number of observations used. Thus, $E\{\beta\} = \beta(1-2/T) < \beta$, where T is the number of observations. For $t = 26$, $E\{\beta\} = (0.923)\beta$, so that an 8% upward correction of the estimates might be appropriate.

Table 9.1. *Summary of results of estimating equation (9.3),*
$\rho_{it} = \alpha + \lambda\rho(t-1)$

Sample	Statistic	Mean	Minimum	Maximum
Full sample:	α	0.118	−4.05	8.97
% significant values of $\alpha = 9.21\%$;	$t(\alpha)$	−0.025	−4.06	4.19
mean assets per firm were £5,625,950;	λ	0.482	−0.213	0.941
$N = 239$	$t(\lambda)$	2.92	−0.715	8.776
	R^2	0.253	0.00	0.747
	$\alpha/(1-\lambda)$	0.255	−8.59	11.878
Smallest one-third of sample:	α	0.746	−3.23	8.97
% significant values of $\alpha = 13.75\%$;	$t(\alpha)$	0.576	−2.19	4.05
mean assets per firm were £427,875;	λ	0.463	−0.109	0.881
$N = 80$	$t(\lambda)$	2.78	−0.558	6.15
	R^2	0.283	0.00	0.593
	$\alpha/(1-\lambda)$	1.415	−6.64	11.88
Middle one-third of sample:	α	−0.0715	−4.05	4.88
% significant values of $\alpha = 5\%$;	$t(\alpha)$	−0.143	−3.49	4.19
mean assets per firm were £1,378,625;	λ	0.483	−0.21	0.931
$N = 80$	$t(\lambda)$	2.920	−0.75	8.62
	R^2	0.253	0.001	0.741
	$\alpha/(1-\lambda)$	−0.002	−8.592	4.692
Largest one-third of sample:	α	−0.324	−3.87	2.69
% significant values of $\alpha = 8.8\%$;	$t(\alpha)$	−0.515	−4.06	3.36
mean assets per firm were £15,190,911;	λ	0.501	−0.11	0.94
$N = 79$	$t(\lambda)$	3.077	−0.56	8.77
	R^2	0.268	0.00	0.748
	$\alpha/(1+\lambda)$	−0.657	−6.70	5.31

Summary of results ranked by initial profit rate

Hexile	Mean π initial profit	Mean λ	Mean π_p
1	4.37	0.55	−0.67
2	6.52	0.47	−1.05
3	8.17	0.46	−0.58
4	10.14	0.45	−0.14
5	12.41	0.45	0.90
6	17.66	0.57	1.91

Notes: Although the original sample was 243, 4 observations were excluded where $\lambda > 0.95$. In this range small errors in λ produce large errors in $\alpha/(1-\lambda)$, and it was decided to exclude such cases from further analysis. $t(\alpha)$ gives the average t value of the estimated coefficient α, and similarly with $t(\lambda)$.

A useful way to describe the output of these 243 estimated values of α and λ across firms is to correlate them with various observable firm and industry characteristics [inspecting deviations of $\pi(t)$ from the norm automatically adjusts for effects of the general economic environment]. As may perhaps be expected, the main limitations on this type of analysis spring from considerations of data availability. One complication that we experienced was the system of industrial classification employed in the company data bank. Although nominally at the three-digit level, the so-called subgroups did not always correspond to an equivalent SIC Minimum List Heading (MLH) for the 1968 Census of Production (which formed the basis of our industry data). This meant that a mapping of subgroup into the MLH had to be used in order to connect industry data to companies, and the incompleteness of this mapping meant that just over half the data points were lost. Further, previous experience showed that attempts to go outside the original company data bank to collect extra data on the individual companies were likely to result in a further severe curtailment of the sample size, and so we restricted ourselves to items that could be deduced from the company data bank. The full set of variables used is shown on Table 9.2, and is as inclusive as possible given our constraints. For each variable, three specifications were adopted: (i) "industry" variables only; (ii) "company" variables only; and (iii) industry and company variables.

Consider first the regressions describing correlations between λ and the company and industry variables. None of the former is significantly related to the estimated value of this coefficient despite expectations that, for example, size would have a stabilizing influence or capital intensity a destabilizing effect on the time path of profits. Similarly, there is no indication that market share (or relative size) cushions companies against such fluctuations. On the other hand, two of the industry variables do show significant associations with λ: Advertising intensity, known to be associated with fluctuating market shares, seems also to create instability in profitability, and high import intensity has a similar effect. Neither of these appears to be offset by any stabilizing effect that might be thought to be associated with high concentration.

Two versions of the equations describing variations in α are presented in Table 9.2. Lines 4–6 show the results of an unweighted regression procedure, whereas in lines 7–9 the observations are weighted according to the inverse of the standard error of the dependent variable.[4] The main

---

[4] Both α and λ are estimated parameters, and using them as dependent variables induces heteroscedasticity. The weighting procedure follows Saxonhouse (1977). The weighted regressions for λ have been suppressed as they are virtually identical to the results reported in Table 9.2. No attempt was made to take explicit account of the limited variation in λ;

effect of this procedure is to considerably reduce the significance level of the five-firm concentration ratio. Looking at the results for the weighted regressions, the only industry variable of significance is the export–sales ratio, although this too loses its significance when the company variables are introduced. The most important of these latter appears to be the growth variable. The positive correlation observed is consistent with a large literature showing a positive relationship between profitability and growth. As with the export–sales ratio, however, the direction of causation is not wholly clear. Successful firms are most likely to be successful in exporting, but this does not imply that exporting is the key to success. Similarly, in a world of salaried management, one might expect to observe growth maximization subject to a profit constraint, which will lead to the observed positive relationship.

The only other variables even approaching significance in the α regressions are the number of acquisitions and "market share." These are both interesting variables in the light of the growth maximization hypothesis. The range of the acquisition variable varies between 0 and 30, and as one might expect this to have a diminishing effect, an alternative version of this variable, $\log(ACQ + 1)$, was tried. This too was significant at the 5 percent level. Both this negative coefficient and the negative coefficient on market share suggest the pursuit of expansion to the range of diminishing returns, which is again consistent with the managerial growth hypothesis. There is no support for the hypothesis that foreign-owned firms behave differently or that diversification has any effect on a firm's ability to earn long term excess profits. Our measure of market share is a rather crude one, and alternative interpretations of these variables are possible. The simplest explanation would be that firms pursuing a high market share strategy do so at the expense of long run profits. Alternately, it could be argued that the ratio of total company i sales to total sales by all companies in company i's principal market is operating as a measure of diversification. In an extreme case where company shares in each market were constant, our market share measure is an index of the number of markets in which a particular company is operating. If this interpretation is accepted, this provides further support to the managerial hypothesis that implies diversification occurs for reasons other than profit maximization.

The lack of robustness of the coefficient on concentration is a familiar finding. Those with a strong prior belief in the importance of the effects of advertising (in line 9) or import competition [equation (9.7)] may find some small comfort in these results. Finally, lines 10–12 of Table 9.2 show

appropriate logit or probit coefficients can be recovered following the procedure suggested by Amemiya (1981).

Table 9.2. *Regressions explaining the estimated parameters of equation (9.3)*

	Industry variables							Company variables						$\bar{R}^2$
	Constant	SF	CON	DV	AS	EXS	IS	ASSETS	MS	ACQ	PROD	GROW	CAPINT	
(1)	0.58 (6.35)	−2.3E−3 (−1.02)	5.6E−4 (0.53)	1.5E−3 (0.36)	−9.01 (−2.24)	0.32 (0.87)	−0.59 (−3.22)	—	—	—	—	—	—	0.082
(2)	0.43 (4.81)	—	—	—	—	—	—	4.8E−8 (0.35)	5.4E−6 (0.12)	−1.9E−3 (−1.18)	7.8E−6 (0.46)	0.11 (1.08)	1.7E−3 (0.56)	−0.023
(3)	0.52 (4.43)	−2.0E−3 (−0.82)	3.3E−4 (0.27)	4.2E−3 (0.87)	−7.88 (−1.84)	0.12 (0.28)	−0.54 (−2.80)	8.0E−8 (0.57)	−2.5E−5 (−0.52)	−1.2E−3 (−0.72)	7.7E−7 (0.05)	7.2E−2 (0.66)	2.1E−3 (0.65)	0.044
(4)	−0.86 (−1.30)	−1.9E−2 (−1.13)	1.5E−2 (1.89)	−1.0E−3 (−0.03)	2.62 (0.09)	6.43 (2.32)	−1.65 (−1.31)	—	—	—	—	—	—	0.06
(5)	−2.21 (−4.04)	—	—	—	—	—	—	3.7E−7 (0.43)	−4.6E−4 (−1.59)	−1.5E−2 (−1.35)	−0.9E−5 (−0.86)	3.54 (5.52)	−1.0E−2 (−0.53)	0.22
(6)	−2.93 (−4.00)	−2.2E−2 (−1.35)	1.5E−2 (1.93)	1.6E−2 (0.53)	16.82 (0.65)	4.23 (1.58)	−1.15 (−0.99)	5.7E−7 (0.65)	−5.9E−4 (−1.97)	−1.1E−2 (−0.99)	−1.4E−4 (−1.35)	3.10 (4.73)	−2.6E−2 (−1.21)	0.25
(7)	−0.26 (−0.51)	−4.7E−3 (−0.56)	2.3E−3 (0.39)	−1.7E−2 (−0.81)	13.67 (0.62)	5.81 (2.77)	−1.72 (−1.59)	—	—	—	—	—	—	0.05
(8)	−2.76 (−4.39)	—	—	—	—	—	—	2.3E−7 (0.49)	−3.1E−4 (−1.78)	−1.1E−2 (−1.66)	5.2E−5 (−0.63)	3.79 (4.99)	−4.0E−3 (−0.28)	0.20
(9)	−3.25 (−4.25)	−4.2E−3 (−0.33)	4.8E−3 (0.77)	6.8E−3 (0.28)	34.2 (1.60)	2.90 (1.35)	−0.86 (−0.84)	4.4E−7 (0.87)	−3.6E−4 (−1.83)	−1.1E−2 (−1.63)	−6.4E−5 (−0.78)	3.62 (4.69)	−9.0E−3 (−0.57)	0.23
(10)	−0.06 (−0.06)	−6.2E−3 (−0.23)	6.6E−4 (0.05)	−2.8E−2 (−0.63)	24.39 (0.53)	10.06 (2.34)	−3.42 (−1.57)	—	—	—	—	—	—	0.03

	(1)	(2)	(3)	(4)	(5)	(6)	(7)	(8)	(9)	(10)	(11)	(12)	(13)	(14)
(11)	−5.15	—	—	—	—	—	—	$1.9E-7$	$-6.1E-4$	$-1.6E-2$	$-1.6E-4$	7.06	$1.7E-2$	0.18
	(−4.07)							(0.20)	(−1.72)	(−1.23)	(−0.96)	(4.62)	(0.60)	
(12)	−5.91	$-1.9E-3$	$2.8E-3$	$3.3E-2$	62.49	3.65	−1.62	$7.3E-7$	$-7.3E-4$	$1.9E-2$	$-1.6E-4$	6.88	$1.8E-2$	0.20
	(−3.79)	(−0.07)	(0.22)	(0.67)	(1.39)	(0.82)	(−0.78)	(0.70)	(−1.83)	(−1.38)	(−0.96)	(4.39)	(0.57)	

Notes: Dependent variables: Equations (9.1)–(9.3): λ_1; equations (9.4)–(9.6): α; equations (9.7)–(9.9): α is weighted to generate heteroscedastic consistent estimates; and equations (9.10)–(9.12): $\alpha/(1-\lambda)$ weighted as in (9.7)–(9.9) by the standard error of α. *Industry variables:* SF = % of industry accounted for by foreign-owned firms; CON = five-firm industry concentration ratio; DV = diversification index; AS = advertising intensity; EXS = export intensity; and IS = import intensity. The source for all but the last two was the 1968 Census of Production; imports and exports are available from the Business Monitor. *Company variables:* ASSETS = assets in 1973, in thousands; MS = market share = company sales (1973)/industry sales (1968) at three-digits (MLH); ACQ = number of acquisitions, 1951–73; PROD = productivity increase (rate of change of scales/employee) 1968–73; GROW = (assets 1973 − assets 1951)/assets 1973; CAPINT = assets/employee, 1973. Numbers in parentheses are *t*-statistics.

Source: DTI/Cambridge U.K. Quoted Companies Databank.

the estimated equations describing variations in the long run profit rate, $\pi_p = \alpha/(1-\lambda)$.[5] Although the coefficients are generally bigger (reflecting the magnifying effect of the $1/1-\lambda$ term), the overall pattern of results is remarkably similar to lines 7–9, with growth playing the dominant "explanatory" role.

To summarize, these results describing the variation in α and λ across firms provide little support for the view that the long run rate of profit earned by companies is determined primarily by industry characteristics, at least in the United Kingdom. The relatively large size of λ suggests a "competitive" process that is weak enough to allow considerable discretion to managers in making strategic choices and opens up the possibility that rivals in the same industry will exhibit different profit streams over time. The role of industry characteristics appears to lie primarily in the adjustment process or, seen from another angle, in the short run stability of profitability.[6] The long run rate of return seems, if anything, to be determined by company characteristics (including, presumably, many that we have been unable to measure), suggesting that company specific factors may be more important in determining a company's success in the long run than industrywide factors. Clearly, the absence of strong industrywide competitive forces is likely to imply the existence of a substantial amount of organizational slack/X-inefficiency.

IV   A model with firm specific and industrywide effects[7]

Our results thus far point to an apparent importance of company specific factors and raise the question of whether (or to what extent) the profit experiences of particular firms is similar to that of rivals in the same industry.

[5] Since the long run profit rate involves the ratio of two estimated variables, there is no simple formula for the heteroscedasticity adjustment. Accordingly, the same weighting system was used as for lines 7–9.

[6] The relative weakness of the effects of concentration and market share are typical of British results using different methodologies and stand in marked contrast to typical U.S. findings. One possible explanation for this may lie in the difference in antitrust and competition policies in the two countries and in the different traditions of executive remuneration in the two countries. A consequence of stricter antitrust is that, in the United States, high market share may be more likely to be the outcome of successful internal expansion and therefore may include a respectable element of differential efficiency. Once a dominant position has been achieved, senior executives have incentives generated by profit-related compensation to maximize profits rather than growth. By contrast, the weak anti-merger and strongly size-related remuneration systems in the United Kingdom seem likely to create a bias toward high market share created through merger (with no necessary differential efficiency implications) plus strong incentives to strive for size at the expense of profits. Thus we have the phenomenon of large, not very efficient but dominant firms that use excess profits to finance further growth.

[7] The material in the following two sections is drawn from Cubbin and Geroski (1987).

If all firms in an industry had identical cost functions and if the good in question was homogeneous, then all firms would enjoy similar profits, and entry would affect each to the same extent. In this situation, the profits at any time t of one firm i could be used to predict the profits of some rival j at t. Conversely, to the extent that mobility barriers (e.g., Caves and Porter, 1977) impede the diffusion of competitive forces throughout an industry, both temporary and persistent profitability differences may arise between firms. In this alternative situation, the knowledge of i's profits at t may not convey much information about j's profits if i and j are in widely different strategic groups. This weakened inability to predict is, in the limit as mobility barriers rise, consistent with the view that only company (or, perhaps, strategic group) specific factors matter in determining profitability.

Our results thus far suggest that long run profitability differences between firms may arise largely from company specific factors but that industry factors seem to affect differences in the speed with which profits adjust to divergences from their long run equilibrium values. This result is consistent with the view that entry has at least an important short run effect on most industry members and gives rise to the possibility that at least short run changes in the profits of firm i at t can be used to predict short run changes in those of some rival j. Given the representation of profitability in equation (9.3), the ability to predict the value of $\rho(t)$ for firm j from the observation of $\rho(t)$ for i depends on whether α and λ are common to the two firms and on the extent to which the size of $\rho(t-1)$ propelling $\rho(t)$ in each case is similar. Our procedure is to decompose $\rho(t-1)$ into two factors – company specific and industrywide – and then to examine the extent to which firms i and j react in the same way to one or both of these factors. There are two extreme outcomes it is useful to keep in mind when interpreting the model. The first is where only company specific factors matter and, in this case, it turns out that equation (9.3) applies to each industry member, with each displaying different values of α and λ. The other extreme outcome is where only industry specific factors matter, and in this case, it happens that equation (9.3) also applies to each industry member. The difference is that, in this second case, α and λ take common industrywide values and $\rho(t-1)$ is, on average, identical for each firm. All intermediate cases (i.e., where both company specific and industrywide factors are important) yield an equation somewhat more complex than (9.3).

Consider some firm i in industry I with profit rate $\pi_i(t)$. Denote the long run equilibrium profit rate common to all firms in all industries as π_p and the average profit rate earned by members of industry I as $\pi_I(t)$. Clearly, i's current profit rate is determined by π_p, $\pi_I(t)$, and the dynamic forces within and between industries that generate adjustment toward them. Since, by definition,

$$\rho(t) \equiv \pi_i(t) - \pi_p(t) = [\pi_i(t) - \pi_I(t)] + [\pi_I(t) - \pi_p(t)]$$
$$\equiv \rho(i, t) + \rho(I, t), \tag{9.4}$$

it is natural to model $\rho(t)$ by directly modeling movements in $\rho(i, t)$ and $\rho(I, t)$. The main problem with following this path is exactly the same as was encountered earlier in modeling $\rho(t)$, that is, that many of the factors that induce adjustment toward equilibrium are almost impossible to measure. Actual flows of entry into industries or into strategic groups within industries are often difficult to observe, and both entry and intra-industry mobility need not actually occur to have an effect on profits. The solution to this problem follows a similar path as was traveled in deriving (9.3).

Consider first $\rho(I, t)$, the difference between average industry profits and the common long run rate. It is natural to suppose that $\rho(I, t)$ declines toward zero as new firms enter the industry, as incumbents expand, and as competitors imitate each other's strategies and attempt to preempt rivals. Collectively referring to these actions as entry $E(t)$ and assuming that it occurs whenever $\rho(I, t) > 0$, we have

$$E(t) = \phi\rho(I, t-1) + \mu(I, t). \tag{9.5}$$

The effect of entry is that profits, on average, approach the common economywide norm $\pi^*(t)$. Thus,

$$\Delta\rho(I, t) = \beta_I E(t) + \theta_I \rho(I, t-1) + \epsilon(I, t), \tag{9.6}$$

where $\Delta\rho(I, t) \equiv \rho(I, t) - \rho(I, t-1)$. By construction, $\mu(I, t)$ and $\epsilon(I, t)$ are orthogonal to $\rho(I, t-1)$ and $E(t)$, respectively, and capture *all other (unobservable) forces*. Since $E(t)$ reflects both actual entry and threats of potential entry, it is at least partly unobservable. Using only data on actual entry is liable to lead to bias since the mismeasurement of $E(t)$ that this occasions is correlated to $\rho(I, t-1)$. Hence, it is difficult if not impossible to estimate ϕ_I, β_I, and θ_I. It is, however, possible to assess their combined effects by substituting (9.5) into (9.6) to get

$$\rho(I, t) = (1 + \phi_I \beta_I)\rho(I, t-1) + \beta_I \mu(I, t) + \epsilon(I, t)$$
$$\equiv \lambda_I \rho(I, t-1) + v(I, t). \tag{9.7}$$

Consider now $\rho(i, t)$, the relative profits of some firm i that occupies some niche or strategic position i in industry I. If $\rho(i, t) > 0$, then as firm i is earning returns above those earned on average in the industry, this outcome can be expected to set in motion a competitive response directed at i's strategic position. New firms may threaten or attempt to enter, incumbents in other market niches may contemplate diversification, and firm i may choose to expand capacity and/or preempt rivals. As these actions are directed specifically at i's niche, they must be distinguished from broader, industrywide responses such as entry. Thus, we shall refer to this more specific activity as "mobility" $M_i(t)$ and suppose that

$$M_i(t) = \phi \rho(i, t-1) + \mu(i, t). \tag{9.8}$$

When firm i enjoys a level of profits above the industry average, both mobility directed at i's niche and entry more generally can be expected to occur. Hence,

$$\Delta \rho(i, t) = \beta_i M_i(t) + \gamma_i E(t) + \theta_i \rho(i, t-1) + \epsilon(i, t), \tag{9.9}$$

where $\mu(i, t)$ and $\epsilon(i, t)$ capture unsystematic forces in the manner of $\mu(I, t)$ and $\epsilon(i, t)$. As neither $M_i(t)$ nor $E(t)$ is observable, we follow the same procedure as before, yielding

$$\rho(i, t) = (1 - \phi_i \beta_i + \theta_i) \rho(i, t-1) + \gamma_i E(t) + \beta_i \mu(i, t) + \epsilon(i, t)$$
$$\equiv \lambda_i \rho(i, t-1) + \gamma_i E(t) + v(i, t). \tag{9.10}$$

Equation (9.10) describes firm specific deviations from average industry profitability as a simple autoregressive process like (9.3), augmented by possible additional feedback as the interindustry forces generated by $\rho(I, t) \neq 0$ concentrate particularly on firm i's niche in industry I. Comparing (9.7) and (9.10), it is also evident that the process describing $\rho(i, t)$ differs from that describing $\rho(I, t)$ to the extent that firm i is more or less vulnerable than average to the effects of entry. The speeds of the two processes differ according to the relative strength of entry and mobility. Using (9.5) and then substituting (9.10) and (9.7) into (9.4), we arrive at the desired extension of (9.3),

$$\rho(t) = \lambda_i \rho(i, t-1) + \Gamma_i \rho(I, t-1) + \eta(i, t) \tag{9.11}$$

where $\lambda_i \equiv (1 + \phi_i \beta_i + \theta_i)$ and $\Gamma_i \equiv (\gamma_i \phi_i + \lambda_I) = (\gamma_i \phi_i + 1 + \phi_i \beta_I + \theta_I)$. Equation (9.11) describes $\rho(t)$ as a first order process defined on its two components plus an unknown, unsystematic term $\eta(i, t)$. The mean of $\eta(i, t)$ is the sum of the means of $v(I, t)$ and $v(i, t)$ and is nonzero if there exist long run departures of either average profits in I from that common to all industries or i's profits from those of rivals in I. The two components of $\rho(t)$ that determine its motion are firm and industry specific, and to each there is, in principle, a firm specific response. The response λ_i to the firm specific component of motion $\rho(i, t-1)$ depends on the firm specific factors (summarized by ϕ_i, β_i, and θ_i) that determine the extent of mobility into i's market niche. The response β_i to the industry specific component of motion $\rho(I, t-1)$ depends on how fast entry bids down profits on average in the industry (summarized by ϕ_I, β_I, and θ_I) and takes a firm specific value only if i's strategic position in the industry is unusually vulnerable to entry (i.e., $\gamma_i \neq \gamma$).

Our interest is in assessing the relative importance of firm and industry effects in explaining movements in $\rho(t)$ over time. We propose to do this by examining the extent to which (9.11) exhibits common parameters when applied to individual members i of some industry I. (See the Appendix to Chapter 2.) At one extreme, all firms i in I may exhibit identical values of λ_i, β_i, and innovations $\eta(i, t)$. In this case, aggregating (9.11) and examining industry dynamics through inspection of a representative firm involves no sacrifice of information. On the other hand, a collection of firms that are protected by substantial mobility barriers will be affected by competitive forces to different degrees, and in this case, aggregation of (9.11) is likely to be worse than useless. These two extreme cases generate particular simplifications of (9.11) that each resemble (9.3); intermediate cases where both company specific and industrywide factors are important produce slightly more complex autoregressive processes. All of these simplifications are, however, nested simplifications of (9.11).

V   Firm and industry effects in the United Kingdom

We have applied (9.8) to a sample of 217 large U.K. firms using annual observations on profitability for the years 1951–77. As much of this period saw intense merger activity, there is a clear sample selection bias toward survivors, and we experienced problems in assembling a data series on profits for each firm. The two principal problems involved in using a long series for this population are disappearance through merger and the post-merger swelling of both the assets and profits of the surviving company. In order to minimize the effects of this, the following procedure was used:

1. All companies surviving in the data bank from 1951 to 1977 were identified and used as the basis of the analysis.
2. A "merger" tree was derived from the data bank showing which companies took over which others, making it possible to identify the final location of any disappearing company's assets, where the final location was one of the surviving companies.
3. This tree was then used to aggregate the accounts of all the companies that ended up together. This eliminates the effect of different gearing ratios (or "leverage") on the volatility of profit rates.

The economywide rate of return was defined for all firms in the sample, whether they survived for the whole period or not. Both profits and assets were aggregated across the sample, and the ratio was used as $\pi^*(t)$. Each firm was then allocated to a three-digit industry on the basis of its principal activity (in fact, the classification system of these data is slightly more aggregated than the SIC Minimum List Heading level). Of the 48 industries so chosen, 10 contained only one firm. The industry rate of return, $\pi_I(t)$, was calculated in the same way as $\pi_p(t)$ except that the averaging was done across companies classified to the same three-digit industry. The 38 multifirm industries in our sample were then allocated to models in which the relative importance of firm and industry effects differed.[8]

Of the 38 multifirm industries, firms in just under 35 percent of them showed no common responses to industry or firm specific forces. Since the number of firms per industry varies, another way to summarize these results is to note that roughly 55 percent of the firms covered exhibited common responses to competitive forces as their rivals in the same industry; very few, if any, appeared capable of being subsumed into an "average" or "representative" firm. Roughly 70 percent of the firms in our sample showed different responses to firm specific and industrywide forces. Of these 153 firms, about 59 percent exhibited more sensitivity to $\rho(i, t-1)$ than to $\rho(I, t-1)$. Of the 207 firms in the 38 industries with more than 1 firm, 24 firms in 17 industries (or, about 12 and 45 percent, respectively) showed λ_i not significantly different from zero, whereas 76 firms in 19 industries (or about 37 and 50 percent, respectively) showed β_i not significantly different from zero. Thus, industry specific forces frequently provoked a more substantial response than firm specific ones, suggesting that entry may be stronger and more effective than mobility, or, equivalently, that mobility barriers may be higher than entry barriers. The estimated values of λ_i and β_i exhibited quite a bit of variation in size across the sample, although 50 percent of both the λ_i and the β_i exceeded 0.500, a figure comparable to those displayed in Table 9.1.

Finally, about 66 percent of firms in our sample exhibited an estimated constant not significantly different from zero, with about 17 percent of the significant estimates showing positive values. This evidence is consistent with the notion that returns are not, in general, equalized across all firms and sectors even in the long run. Whereas two-thirds of our sample converged toward a common profitability level, a solid core of firms appear able to maintain some independence from market forces more or less indefinitely. This set of estimates is much higher than those reported in Table 9.1 for equation (9.3) and suggests that estimates of long run equilibrium levels of profits may be sensitive to sample selection in a way

---

[8] Although (9.11) does not involve a lagged dependent variable, it is easy to see departures from white noise generating bias because of the way $\rho(t)$ has been constructed from $\rho(i, t)$ and $\rho(I, t)$. All regressions were examined for serial correlation, and this proved not to be a problem.

that estimates of market dynamics are not. The higher incidence of significant α's in the current sample may also be due in some way to the reduced scope for a profit rate dilution effect of mergers in our (purged) sample.

There are a number of ways to describe the observed interfirm and interindustry heterogeneity of these estimated parameters. Perhaps the simplest is to regress the estimated parameters on various structural variables of interest, looking for simple patterns of association or broad tendencies within the data. It should be emphasized that this is largely a descriptive exercise, and the results are limited to the 60 percent or so of the 38 industries for which we could get satisfactory data.

Consider first "explaining" variations in the response to industry effects. It proved to be almost impossible to account for variations in Γ_i, suggesting that the kinds of factors that often explain average industry profits seem much less suited to accounting for the speed of industry dynamics. Much the same conclusion seems warranted when we look at the possible determinants of the company adjustment rates, λ_i, and the determinants of long run equilibria. Table 9.3 reports the results of regressing these coefficients against various industry variables plus company specific variables. The first three equations explore the determinants of λ_i. It seems clear that most of the rather small explanation achieved is due to industry characteristics, particularly industry concentration and, somewhat less, advertising and imports. This much is not inconsistent with the regression results reported in Table 9.2. Firms in highly concentrated industries appear to adjust much more slowly toward long run equilibrium profit rates. The second three equations in Table 9.3 explore some of the characteristics of these long run equilibria. Here, as in Table 9.2, industry characteristics play almost no role (barring, perhaps, the extent of foreign ownership). However, large, productive, and fast growing firms all earn higher profits in the long run; acquisition-oriented firms in highly capital intensive industries appear to earn lower returns in the long run. The strong correlations between profitability in the long run and growth are consistent with managerial theories of corporate choice, and the inverse relationship with acquisition-oriented methods of growth echo recent results on the efficiency consequences of merger (e.g., Meeks, 1977). This, in turn, reinforces the view that this type of activity may bring more gains to management than shareholders or society at large (e.g., Mueller, 1969). Certainly, it is not inconsistent with the view that the *market for corporate control* is a very imperfect substitute for weak forces of competition in product markets.

VI   Conclusions

In this chapter, we have explored models designed to measure the strength of competitive processes. The problem that arises in attempting to carry

Table 9.3.

	Industry variables							Company variables							
	Constant	SF	CON	DV	AS	GS	IS	ASSETS	MS	ACQ	PROD	GROW	CAPINT	$\bar{R}^2$	N
(1)	60.00 (6.04)	-0.154 (-0.676)	0.185 (1.53)	-0.480 (-1.21)	-775 (2.25)	1.27 (0.35)	-42.9 (-1.67)	—	—	—	—	—	—	0.097	88
(2)	45.366 (4.78)	—	—	—	—	—	—	-0.000006 (0.474)	-0.00035 (0.401)	-0.152 (0.971)	-0.028 (1.09)	15.29 (1.35)	0.491 (1.69)	0.0046	133
(3)	37.22 (2.52)	-0.432 (-1.35)	0.379 (2.17)	0.020 (0.033)	40.7 (0.426)	-24.6 (0.457)	-12.8 (-0.398)	-0.000009 (-0.573)	0.0018 (-1.30)	-0.1679 (0.877)	-0.0004 (0.011)	4.11 (0.274)	0.184 (0.489)	0.0082	83
(4)	0.075 (0.054)	-0.021 (-0.626)	-0.0027 (0.161)	0.0071 (0.126)	18.86 (0.419)	4.64 (0.949)	-3.27 (-0.810)	—	—	—	—	—	—	-0.045	88
(5)	-0.462 (-3.42)	—	—	—	—	—	—	0.000005 (2.51)	0.000028 (0.296)	-0.033 (-2.16)	0.0013 (4.04)	5.92 (3.67)	-0.085 (-2.27)	0.119	132
(6)	-4.37 (-2.35)	-0.081 (-2.08)	-0.0024 (-0.124)	0.060 (0.853)	-2.17 (-0.196)	-1.62 (-0.268)	0.270 (0.063)	0.000004 (3.11)	0.00004 (3.45)	-0.031 (-1.78)	0.0065 (1.56)	5.73 (2.94)	-0.092 (-2.01)	0.154	83

Notes: Company variables (Source: DTI/Cambridge U.K. Quoted Companies Databank): ASSETS = assets in 1973 (in thousand pounds); MS = market share = company sales (1973)/industry sales (1968) at SIC level; ACQ = number of acquisitions, 1951–73; PROD = increase in productivity (rate of change of sales per employee), 1968–73; GROW = (assets 1973 − assets 1951)/assets 1973; CAPINT = assets/employee, 1973. The dependent variable is λ_i in the first three regressions and the constant from equation (9.11) in the second three. All regressions are weighted to correct for the heteroscedasticity arising from using an estimated coefficient as a dependent variable. Numbers in parentheses are t-statistics.

Source: Reproduced from Cubbin and Geroski (1987).

out this kind of exercise is that many of the competitive challenges to which firms respond take the form of threats posed by potential competitors. These challenges are difficult to observe when made and, if they provoke a preemptive response by incumbents, may never result in observable entry attempts. Our solution to this latent variables problem has been to use a noisy signal of such competitive activity, the deviation of profits from the norm, to reflect the extent of the competitive challenge facing firms.

Our basic models have either been first order autoregressions in profits relative to the norm or slightly more complex extensions. For a process,

$$\rho(t) = \lambda\rho(t-1) + v(t) \tag{9.12}$$

(i.e., for which $\alpha = 0$), the size of λ reflects the extent and power of competitive forces. Most of our results suggest that $\lambda \approx 0.50$, a value that implies a 10% deviation of $\pi(t)$ from $\pi^*(t)$ will return to within 1 percent of $\pi^*(t)$ in three years.[9] This suggests a market response to "excess profits" that is neither instantaneous nor excessively slow. However, there is considerable evidence that (particularly for "smaller" firms) $\alpha \neq 0$, suggesting that there are quite a number of firms that enjoy (experience) profits more or less permanently different from the norm. Hence, although the market process appears to work moderately rapidly in the United Kingdom when gauged in terms of λ, the adjustment that occurs often appears to be fundamentally incomplete.

The second broad theme of our results is that competition is a force that does not appear to affect all firms equally. Although there are traces of industry factors (like industry concentration and the extent of product differentiation) that appear to affect λ and traces of common industry forces affecting the profits of all industry members, the fact of the matter is that these "industry effects" do seem to be surprisingly weak. Certainly only company specific factors appear to affect the sizes of α that we observed. At the very least, competition as a process in the United Kingdom appears to be far more localized than three-digit industry classifications suggest.

Are industries in the United Kingdom competitive enough to ensure satisfactory rates of innovation and growth? Although there is not enough information in our data to answer this question satisfactorily, the flavor of our results at least suggests a presumption. It appears that although

---

[9] By way of contrast, Geroski (1986) and Geroski and Masson (1987) provide estimates of λ based on the parameters of equations (9.1) and (9.2) reported in the empirical literature. These estimates are based on actual entry flows and suggest that $\lambda \approx 0.90$. The difference between these estimates and that reported in the text suggests the importance of potential entry as a competitive force.

competition exists in the United Kingdom, it is neither strong nor pervasive enough to rule out a perhaps substantial scope for the exercise of managerial discretion. Although it is possible that managerial preferences for growth may encourage investment in R&D and the exploitation of new innovations, the revealed preferences of most managers for growth via merger suggest that this is not likely to be the case.

CHAPTER 10

The persistence of profits: international comparison

HIROYUKI ODAGIRI AND HIDEKI YAMAWAKI

I   Proportion of surviving and acquired companies

Table 10.1 presents the number and proportion of companies that survived, were acquired, or were liquidated over the observation period in Canada, France, Japan, the United Kingdom and the United States. The samples are those used in the country studies of persistent profitability in this volume. Unfortunately, at present, comparable figures are not available for other countries.

Out of the 458 Japanese manufacturing companies that were listed in the First Section of the Tokyo Stock Exchange in 1964, 399 firms were still listed in at least one of the eight stock exchanges in Japan in 1984. Thus, over the 1964–84 period, 41 Japanese firms disappeared through mergers and 8 firms went into bankruptcy.[1] Ten firms were not listed in any of the stock exchanges in 1984 for other reasons.[2] The proportion of the companies in the sample that survived over the period is thus 87 percent, whereas the proportion of those companies that were acquired is 9 percent. The inclusion of the companies listed in the Second Section of the Tokyo Stock Exchange in 1964 to the sample makes little difference in the proportions of surviving and acquired firms (column 3).

This finding for Japan makes a clear contrast to the situation in the United States and the United Kingdom. In the United States, of the original 1,000 companies in 1950, 583 firms still existed in 1972. Thus, over the 1950–72 period, 58 percent of the original firms survived. On the other hand, 384 firms, or 38 percent, of the original 1,000 firms were acquired over the period. In the United Kingdom, 327 firms out of the original 3,011 firms, or 11 percent, of the original firms survived over 1950–77 period, whereas 1,265 firms, or 42 percent, of the original firms were acquired

---

[1] This includes those firms that declared bankruptcy but eventually succeeded to revive.

[2] Some firms are believed to have been liquidated. There are also some cases where the company is still active but not listed anymore because the number of shareholders has become too few to satisfy the number-of-stockholders requirement of the stock exchange.

Table 10.1. *International comparison of the proportion of surviving, acquired, and liquidated companies*

Status	Japan (1964–84) First Section, Tokyo Stock Exchange	First and Second Sections, Tokyo Stock Exchange	United States (1950–72)	United Kingdom (1950–77)	Canada (1968–82)	France (1965–82)
Survived	399 (87.1)	768 (85.4)	583 (58.3)	327 (10.9)	161 (93.1)	450 (46.1)
Acquired	41 (9.0)	67 (7.5)	384 (38.4)	1265 (42.0)	10 (5.8)	273 (28.0)
Liquidated	8 (1.7)	26 (2.9)	19 (1.9)	115 (3.8)	2 (1.2)	38 (3.9)
Others	10 (2.2)	38 (4.2)	14 (1.4)	1304 (43.3)	0 (0.0)	215 (22.0)
Total	458 (100)	899 (100)	1000 (100)	3011 (100)	173 (100)	976 (100)

Notes: Numbers in parentheses are percentages. The number of firms is based on the status at the end of the observation period in each country. The status of the Japanese firms in the Tokyo Stock Exchange is for 1964.

by 1977.[3] This suggests that the proportion of acquired firms is about 30 percentage points higher in the United States and 35 percentage points higher in the United Kingdom than in Japan. Accordingly, the proportion of surviving firms is higher in Japan than in the United States and the United Kingdom. Obviously this must be reflecting more aggressive takeover activities commonly observed in the United States and the United Kingdom.

On the other hand, the proportions of surviving and acquired companies in Canada resemble those observed in Japan. For the 1968–82 period, 161 firms out of the original 173 firms, or 93 percent, of the original firms survived in Canada. Ten firms, or 6 percent, of the original firms were acquired during the period.

A much greater fraction of firms (28 percent) disappeared through merger in France than in either Canada or Japan. Taking into account the longer time span for the U.S. data than for France (23 vs. 18 years), the relative importance of mergers in explaining disappearances in France is quite comparable to the United States. Once again, liquidations are a small fraction of disappearances.

II   Intertemporal behavior of profits

To provide an overview on the characteristics of the profit data for individual countries, this section first examines the intertemporal behavior of the means and standard deviations of profit rates across firms. The profit rate is defined as after-tax profits plus interest divided by total assets and is not normalized. Table 10.2 reports the summary statistics for Canada, West Germany, Japan, the United Kingdom, and the United States. The left column for each country shows the statistics based on the data used in the individual country study (Canada, 1968–82; Germany, 1961–82; Japan, 1964–82; the United Kingdom, 1951–77; and the United States, 1950–72), whereas the right column reports those based on the data that are comparable among the five countries. The 1964–80 data for West Germany and Japan, the 1964–82 data for Canada, and the 1964–77 data for the United Kingdom are simply a subsample of the entire period, whereas the 1964–80 data for the United States are an extended version of the time-series data used by Mueller (1986). The updating of the U.S. data was made by consulting *Moody's Industrial Manual.* Thus, the number of firms in the U.S. sample differs between these two data sets. The mean, standard deviation, and coefficient of variation of company profit rates

---

[3] For the 1957–69 period, 1,740 firms out of the 3,566 firms, or 48.8% of the original firms, were acquired or liquidated. See Kuehn (1975). This finding is consistent with the one in Table 10.1. For the U.S. result, see also Mueller (1986).

Table 10.2. *Means and standard deviations of time-series profit rates*

	Federal Republic of Germany		Japan		United States		Canada		United Kingdom	
	1961-82	1964-80	1964-82	1964-80	1950-72	1964-80	1968-82	1964-82	1951-77	1964-77
Number of firms (n)	299	299	376	376	551	413	161	129	243	243
Mean (m)	4.833	4.762	6.295	6.374	7.669	8.317	12.999	13.761	9.258	9.789
Standard deviation (s)	3.998	4.096	2.761	2.812	4.600	3.892	9.533	6.036	4.974	5.818
Coefficient of variation (cv)	0.868	0.899	0.459	0.463	0.601	0.462	0.756	0.476	0.537	0.600
Correlation between m and s	−0.518	−0.463	−0.477	−0.662	0.274	0.463	−0.851	−0.801	0.632	0.566

Notes: Profit rates are defined as after-tax profits plus interest divided by total assets. They are not normalized. Mean (m), standard deviation (s), and coefficient of variation (cv) are the average over the time period specified in the second row.

were first calculated for each year using the cross section of sample firms and were then averaged over the observation period.

Table 10.2 yields the following conclusions:

(1) The mean profit rates across firms and over time (m) in Canada, 13.0 for 1968–82 and 13.8 for 1964–82, are the highest among the five countries, followed by those in the United Kingdom, 9.3 for 1951–77 and 9.8 for 1964–77. On the other hand, the mean profit rates in West Germany, 4.8 for both 1961–82 and 1964–80, are the lowest. The mean values in the United States, 7.7 for 1950–72 and 8.3 for 1964–80, are in the middle among the five countries. The Japanese mean values, 6.3 for 1964–82 and 6.4 for 1964–80, are lower than those in the United States.

(2) The mean standard deviation across firms and over time (s) in Japan, 2.8 for both 1964–82 and 1964–80, are the lowest among the five countries, suggesting that the dispersion of profit rates across firms in Japan is the smallest among these countries.[4] On the other hand, the standard deviations in Canada, 9.5 for 1968–82 and 6.0 for 1964–82, are the highest among the five countries. The values in the United States, 4.6 for 1950–72 and 3.9 for 1964–80, are similar to those in West Germany, 4.0 for 1961–82 and 4.1 for 1964–80, and in the middle among the five countries. The standard deviations for the United Kingdom, 5.0 for 1951–77 and 5.8 for 1964–77, are again the second highest in the group.

(3) The finding that the dispersion of profit rates across firms is the smallest in Japan is reinforced by the comparison of the mean values of the coefficient of variation (cv). The coefficient of variation in Japan, 0.46 for both 1964–82 and 1964–80, tends to be lower than those in other countries: 0.90 in Germany for 1964–80; 0.46 in the United States for 1964–80; 0.48 in Canada for 1964–82; and 0.60 in the United Kingdom for 1964–77.

(4) The correlation coefficients between the mean and the standard deviation are found to be positive for the United States (0.27 for 1950–72 and 0.46 for 1964–80) and for the United Kingdom (0.63 for 1951–77 and 0.57 for 1964–77). On the other hand, they are negative for Canada (-0.85 for 1968–82 and -0.80 for 1964–82), West Germany (-0.52 for 1961–82 and -0.46 for 1964–80), and Japan (-0.48 for 1964–82 and -0.66 for 1964–80). This implies that in Canada, West Germany, and Japan, the dispersion of profit rates across companies becomes wider in the years with low profitability,[5] whereas in the United Kingdom and the United States, the dispersion of profit rates becomes narrower in the low-profit years.

---

[4] This conclusion is consistent with the findings in Odagiri and Yamawaki (1986).
[5] We found, at least for Japan, that the profit rates tend to fluctuate in parallel with business conditions. Namely, the profit rate is lower in recession. See Chapter 8 in this volume.

As mentioned earlier, the profit rate examined in this study is defined as the ratio of net profits plus interest payments to total assets, which are evaluated in book value at acquisition costs. To examine if the reevaluation of profit rates at current prices makes any significant differences, we present in Table 10.3 the nominal profit rates for West Germany, Japan, and the United States that are used in this study along with the real profit rates for these three countries that were estimated by Albach (1984) for West Germany, Wakasugi et al. (1984) for Japan, and Holland and Myers (1984) for the United States.[6]

Table 10.3 shows that for all three countries the sample mean for the real profit rate is lower than that for the nominal profit rate. The real profit rate for West Germany and Japan dropped sharply after 1973, reflecting the high inflation rate caused by the first oil crisis, whereas the real rate for the United States fell less drastically after 1973. Thus, the difference between the average real profit rate for 1973–79 and that for 1966–72 is −3.29 for West Germany and −3.36 for Japan, whereas it is −1.23 for the United States. The nominal profit rate tends to show a downward trend for West Germany after 1968 and for Japan after 1970, whereas it tends to move upwardly for the United States after 1970. Reflecting presumably these intertemporal movements, the correlation between the nominal and real profit rates is moderately high for West Germany ($r = 0.68$) and Japan ($r = 0.60$) and significant at the 5 percent level, whereas the correlation is low for the United States ($r = 0.22$ for Mueller's sample) and insignificant.

On the other hand, the average difference between the nominal profit rate and real profit rate is consistent across the three countries. The average difference between the nominal and real profit rates for 1966–72 is 1.48 for West Germany, 1.83 for Japan, and 1.58 for the United States, whereas the average difference for 1973–79 is 3.75 for West Germany, 3.72 for Japan, and 3.91 for the United States.

III   Persistent profitability differences

In this section, we examine the existence of persistent differences in profitability in Canada, West Germany, France, Japan, Sweden, the United

---

[6] The real profit rate for West Germany is defined as after-tax real rate of return on total capital (unweighted) for manufacturing corporations and is obtained from Albach (1984, Table 7-3, p. 282). The real profit rate for Japan is estimated by Wakasugi et al. (1984, Table 9-2, p. 364) and is defined by them as $ROC_W(AT)$. The real profit rate for the United States is obtained from Holland and Myers (1984, Table 2-3, pp. 58–9) and is defined by them as $ROC_W(AT)$.

Kingdom, and the United States. Table 10.4 summarizes the results for the estimations of the autoregressive equation,

$$\Pi_{it} = \hat{k}_i + \hat{\lambda}_i \Pi_{it-1} + u_{it}, \tag{10.1}$$

where the long-run projected profits of firm i are defined as $\hat{\alpha}_i = \hat{k}_i/(1-\hat{\lambda}_i)$, and $1-\hat{\lambda}_i$ is the speed of profit adjustment. A detailed discussion on the theoretical justification of using the autoregressive model to estimate the persistence of profits is given in Chapter 2 of this volume by Geroski. As in the previous analysis, we define the profit rate as after-tax profits plus interest divided by total assets. The profit rate of each company is normalized by deducting the mean profit rate of the sample in each country and is denoted by Π_{it} for firm i in year t. Table 10.4 replicates the estimated results of persistent profitability for the seven countries in the format used in the individual country studies to facilitate an international comparison. The sample of firms in each country was divided into six subsamples according to the order of the initial profit rates (Π_0). Then the mean values of $\hat{\alpha}$ and $\hat{\lambda}$ were calculated for each of the six subsamples. Detailed accounts on the estimation method and the construction of the table are given in the individual country studies.

Table 10.4 yields the following findings:

(1) The ordering of $\hat{\alpha}$ across the six subsamples is in perfect accordance with that of Π_0 in Canada, France, Japan, and the United States (1950–72). On the other hand, in West Germany, Sweden, the United Kingdom, and the United States (1964–80), the ordering of $\hat{\alpha}$ does not necessarily accord with that of Π_0, whereas the mean $\hat{\alpha}$ in subsample 1 is always highest among the six subsamples. This implies, most importantly, that in Canada, France, Japan, and the United States (1950–72) a company earning a higher- (lower-) than-average profit rate in the initial period is expected to earn a higher- (lower-) than-average profit rate in the long run, and the difference in profitability across firms persists. The result also suggests that in West Germany, Sweden, the United Kingdom, and the United States (1964–80) the difference in profitability across firms is less noticeable than in the case of Canada, France, Japan, and the United States (1950–72), but the persistent profit difference exists at least between the most profitable group of firms and the less profitable group of firms. In addition, except for Sweden and the United Kingdom, the mean $\hat{\alpha}$ in subsample 6 is the lowest among the subsamples, suggesting also the persistence of low profitability.

(2) The range of the mean values of $\hat{\alpha}$ is relatively wide in Canada, France, and the United States (1950–72), whereas it is relatively narrow in

Table 10.3. *Comparison of nominal and real profit rates in Federal Republic of Germany, Japan, and the United States*

	Federal Republic of Germany		Japan		United States		
Year	Manufacturing (276 firms)[a] (1)	Manufacturing (222 firms)[b] (2)	Manufacturing (376 firms)[c] (3)	Nonfinancial (848 firms)[d] (4)	Manufacturing (551 firms)[e] (5)	Manufacturing (413 firms)[c] (6)	Nonfinancial corporations[f] (7)
1950					10.65		5.2
1951					8.49		4.5
1952					7.32		4.2
1953					7.41		3.8
1954					7.48		4.2
1955					8.58		5.4
1956					8.53		4.4
1957					7.88		4.2
1958					6.73		3.7
1959					7.77		4.8
1960					7.06		4.5
1961	5.73	3.8	—	—	6.63	—	4.5
1962	5.63	3.5	—	—	6.90	—	5.6
1963	5.45	3.7	—	—	7.07	—	6.1
1964	5.69	3.2	6.82	—	7.79	7.95	6.9
1965	5.77	3.4	6.62	—	8.34	8.54	7.8
1966	5.44	3.4	7.44	5.5	8.65	8.88	7.7
1967	5.31	4.2	7.74	5.8	7.71	8.03	7.1
1968	4.99	5.1	7.65	5.7	7.50	7.79	6.6
1969	4.91	3.1	7.75	5.6	7.28	7.61	5.7
1970	5.03	2.2	7.21	5.2	6.78	7.22	4.7

Year	(1)	(2)	(3)	(4)	(5)	(6)	(7)
1971	4.95	1.7	5.89	4.9	6.82	6.91	5.2
1972	4.57	1.7	5.96	4.1	7.02	7.29	5.7
1973	4.70	0.4	7.24	1.6	—	8.06	5.4
1974	4.78	−2.0	6.09	0.4	—	8.85	3.7
1975	3.84	0.8	4.33	2.4	—	8.28	4.8
1976	4.23	1.0	5.28	2.3	—	8.68	4.9
1977	3.57	0.8	4.83	2.3	—	8.60	5.4
1978	3.42	1.0	5.33	2.5	—	9.29	5.3
1979	3.54	−0.2	6.21	1.8	—	9.73	4.6
1980	4.30	−1.1	6.56	2.4	—	9.66	4.1
1981	4.24	−0.2	5.64	3.4			
1982	—	—	5.03				
Mean	4.77	1.88	6.30	3.49	7.67	8.32	5.18
Standard deviation	0.75	1.90	1.05	1.75	0.91	0.83	1.11
Simple correlation between	(1) and (2) 0.68		(3) and (4) 0.60		(5) and (7) 0.22		(6) and (7) 0.21

Notes: Columns 2, 4, and 7 are for *real* profit rate series and thus show real rates of return on total capital. Simple correlation between columns 3 and 4 is estimated for 1966–81. The real rate of return was estimated by Albach (1984, Table 7-3, p. 282) for West Germany, by Wakasugi et al. (1984, Table 9-2, p. 364) for Japan, and by Holland and Myers (1984, Table 2-3, pp. 58–9) for the United States.

[a] See Chapter 6.
[b] From Albach (1984).
[c] See Chapter 8.
[d] From Wakasugi et al. (1984).
[e] See Chapter 3.
[f] From Holland and Myers (1984).

Japan, Germany, and the United Kingdom. The United States (1964–80) is in the middle.

(3) The proportion of regression equations that have $\bar{R}^2$ greater than 0.1 (row A) or significant $\hat{\lambda}$ (rows D and E) is lowest in the United States for 1950–72, whereas the proportion in the United Kingdom is the highest. These proportions in the rest of the countries lie between these two extreme cases, whereas the proportions in West Germany, Japan, and the United States (1964–80) are relatively higher than those in Canada, France, and Sweden. This implies that the profit rate of most U.S. firms exhibits no significant trend toward the mean profit rate in the 1950–72 period, and the variation over time of the profit rate is a random movement around the mean for most firms in the same period. On the contrary, particularly in West Germany, Japan, and the United Kingdom, the profit rate tends to adjust systematically toward the long-run levels.[7] This argument is reinforced by the comparison of the correlation coefficient between $\hat{\alpha}$ and the initial profit rate (Π_0) across countries. The correlation coefficient for the United States for 1950–72, 0.58, is among the highest, whereas that for Germany, 0.24, is the lowest. The correlation coefficients for Canada (0.45), France (0.36), Japan (0.31), and the United Kingdom (0.34) lie between those for the United States (1950–72) and Germany. However, the coefficient for Canada is much higher than those for France, Japan, and the United Kingdom. The correlation coefficient for the United States for the 1964–80 period, 0.28, is much lower than that for the 1950–72 period and is close to the German figure. Thus, these findings would give some justification for the argument that the persistent differences in company profitability are most evident in the United States for 1950–72.

(4) The result for West Germany shows that the extent of persistent profitability is less evident. The $\hat{\alpha}$ in the first subsample, 0.48, is small compared to the initial profit rate for the sample, 4.57, though it is the largest among the six subsamples in Germany. As mentioned earlier, the correlation between $\hat{\alpha}$ and Π_0 for Germany is the lowest among the countries in Table 10.4.

(5) The difference in the results between Japan and Germany seems to be small. The range of the mean values of $\hat{\alpha}$, the speed of adjustment, and the proportion of equations that have significant $\hat{\alpha}$ and $\hat{\lambda}$ are all similar between Japan and Germany. The correlation of $\hat{\alpha}$ with Π_0, or $\bar{\Pi}$, is somewhat larger for Japan, but the difference is small compared to the difference with the United States (1950–72). In addition, the U.K. result appears to resemble the Japanese and German results.

---

[7] Row D in Table 10.4 shows that in more than 70% of the sample firms λ was found to be significantly positive for West Germany, Japan, and the United Kingdom.

Table 10.4. *International comparison of the persistence of profits*

Subsample	Canada, 1968–82 (161 firms)			Federal Republic of Germany, 1961–82 (290 firms)			France, 1965–82 (450 firms)			Japan, 1964–82 (376 firms)		
	$\hat{\alpha}$	$\hat{\lambda}$	Π_0	$\hat{\alpha}$	$\hat{\lambda}$	Π_0	$\hat{\alpha}$	$\hat{\lambda}$	Π_0	$\hat{\alpha}$	$\hat{\lambda}$	Π_0
1	7.912	0.341	14.410	0.480	0.515	4.574	6.40	0.543	8.50	0.7369	0.6325	3.4095
2	2.669	0.295	4.460	0.353	0.282	1.655	1.72	0.392	2.90	0.2824	0.4579	1.1582
3	1.833	0.208	1.034	0.466	0.337	0.186	−0.06	0.330	−0.20	0.1476	0.4563	0.4219
4	−0.016	0.233	−1.542	0.243	0.427	−0.851	−1.35	0.244	−1.50	−0.1913	0.3917	−0.2445
5	−1.206	0.252	−4.885	−0.361	0.394	−1.768	−1.64	0.322	−3.30	−0.6326	0.4447	−1.1735
6	−10.801	0.465	−12.774	−1.138	0.398	−3.705	−3.29	0.368	−6.60	−0.7571	0.4053	−3.5742
A		76 (47.2)			160 (55.2)			223 (49.6)			250 (66.5)	
B		33 (20.5)			53 (18.3)			NA			62 (16.5)	
C		23 (14.3)			50 (17.2)			NA			56 (14.9)	
D		83 (51.6)			204 (70.3)			204 (45.3)			285 (75.8)	
E		0 (0.0)			0 (0.0)			5 (0.1)			1 (0.3)	
F		0			0			5			1	
G		0.454			0.244			0.359			0.305	
H		NA			0.736			0.789			0.869	

Table 10.4 (cont.)

Subsample	United Kingdom, 1951–77 (243 firms)			United States						Sweden, 1967–85 (43 firms)		
				1950–72 (551 firms)			1964–80 (413 firms)					
	$\hat{\alpha}$	$\hat{\lambda}$	Π_0	$\hat{\alpha}$	$\hat{\lambda}$	Π_0	$\hat{\alpha}$	$\hat{\lambda}$	Π_0	$\hat{\alpha}$	$\hat{\lambda}$	Π_0
1	1.911	0.574	9.081	4.6789	0.1214	5.4944	1.485	0.575	5.618	4.083	0.825	14.314
2	0.892	0.449	3.827	1.5139	0.1664	2.0933	0.785	0.490	1.405	0.959	0.694	6.318
3	0.138	0.446	1.559	0.1721	0.2121	0.4196	-0.694	0.458	0.051	1.360	0.870	-4.774
4	-0.577	0.457	-0.415	-0.4646	0.2547	-0.8739	-0.230	0.417	-1.151	-0.464	0.846	-4.990
5	-1.051	0.472	-2.057	-1.6377	0.2015	-2.2439	-1.270	0.468	-2.168	-4.057	0.748	-5.225
6	-0.666	0.548	-4.209	-2.8270	0.1419	-4.6637	-2.227	0.412	-3.773	-1.971	0.711	-5.642
A		228 (93.8)			117 (21.2)			259 (62.7)			14 (32.5)	
B		37 (15.2)			125 (22.7)			66 (16.0)			7 (16.2)	
C		37 (15.2)			149 (27.0)			137 (33.2)			8 (18.6)	
D		185 (76.1)			152 (27.6)			255 (61.7)			17 (39.5)	
E		0 (0.0)			0 (0.0)			1 (0.2)			1 (2.3)	
F		1			0			0			0	
G		0.339			0.582			0.275			0.603	
H		NA			0.916			0.398			0.674	

Notes: Numbers in parentheses are percentages.

A = number of cases for which $\bar{R}^2 > 0.1$
B = number of cases for which $\hat{\alpha}$ is significantly positive (10% level, two-tailed test)
C = number of cases for which $\hat{\alpha}$ is significantly negative (10% level, two-tailed test)
D = number of cases for which $\hat{\lambda}$ is significantly positive (10% level, one-tailed test)
E = number of cases for which $\hat{\lambda}$ is significantly negative (10% level, two-tailed test)

(6) The Canadian results appear to show more proximity to the U.S. result for 1950–72. Both the proportion of regression equations that have significant $\hat{\alpha}$ and $\hat{\lambda}$ and the correlation coefficient between $\hat{\alpha}$ and Π_0 are in the middle between those for Japan and Germany and those for the United States for 1950–72. The range of the mean $\hat{\alpha}$ is the widest.

(7) The French result seems to be similar to the Canadian one in terms of the estimates of $\hat{\alpha}$ and the proportion of companies with $\bar{R}^2$ greater than 0.1 and significant $\hat{\lambda}$. We need to note, however, that Canadian and French studies differ from others in their inclusion of nonmanufacturing companies in the sample. In both countries, mining companies earn the lowest profits. Hence, among the manufacturing companies, the dispension of the profit rate is expected to be smaller than the table shows.

(8) The U.S. result for 1964–80 shows some important differences with the result for 1950–72. The mean value of $\hat{\alpha}$ in subsample 1 in the 1950–72 sample, 4.68, is much higher than that in the 1964–80 sample, 1.49, though the initial profit rates in these two samples are rather similar, 5.49 for the 1950–72 sample and 5.62 for the 1964–80 sample. Furthermore, the correlation coefficient between $\hat{\alpha}$ and Π_0 is much higher in the 1950–72 sample than in the 1964–80 sample. To see whether these differences between the two U.S. results are caused by the difference in the samples, we selected 397 firms from the original samples for which time-series profit data are available for both periods (1950–72 and 1964–80). Table 10.5 shows mean values for $\hat{\alpha}$, $\hat{\lambda}$, and Π_0 for the two periods that are estimated from the sample of the 397 U.S. firms and grouped into six subsamples. The results are basically the same as those in Table 10.4. Thus, in Table 10.5 the mean value for $\hat{\alpha}$ in subsample 1 in the 1950–72 period, 4.29, is much higher than that in the 1964–80 period, 1.57. In addition, for the 1964–80 period the ordering of $\hat{\alpha}$ does not agree with that of Π_0, whereas for the earlier 1950–72 period it does. These results suggest that the difference in the U.S. results between the 1950–72 period and the 1964–80 period is caused mainly by the difference in the observation periods rather than the difference in the samples. Therefore, we conclude that the extent of the persistent difference in company profitability in the United States is less significant in the 1964–80 period than in the 1950–72 period.

Notes to Table 10.4 *(cont.)*

F = number of cases with $\hat{\lambda} > 1$ (In calculation of average $\hat{\alpha}$ and $\hat{\lambda}$ in subsamples and of correlation coefficients in rows G and H, $\hat{\lambda}$ was set equal to 0.95 in these cases.)

G = correlation coefficient between $\hat{\alpha}$ and Π_0

H = correlation coefficient between $\hat{\alpha}$ and $\bar{\Pi}$ (average of the normalized profit rate for the entire period)

NA = not available

Table 10.5. *The persistence of profits in the United States: comparison of results for 1950–72 and for 1964–80*

Subsample	United States, 1950–72 (397 firms)			United States, 1964–80 (397 firms)		
	$\hat{\alpha}$	$\hat{\lambda}$	Π_0	$\hat{\alpha}$	$\hat{\lambda}$	Π_0
1	4.2881	0.1290	6.2568	1.5716	0.5726	5.6878
2	1.1709	0.1674	2.2428	0.5659	0.4809	1.4390
3	0.1265	0.2282	0.2843	−0.4166	0.4769	0.0819
4	−0.8969	0.2185	−1.2178	−0.2320	0.4044	−1.1067
5	−0.9637	0.2355	−2.6916	−0.7117	0.4810	−2.1730
6	−2.5269	0.1631	−5.7028	−2.2096	0.4307	−3.7285

Based on these findings, one may conclude that the extent of persistent differences in company profitability is most striking in the United States for 1950–72 in the sense that (i) the firm with a high (low) initial profit rate tends to find the profit rate to decline (increase) in the long run but the extent of the decline (increase) to be smaller; (ii) the projected long-run profit rate is highly correlated with the initial or average profit rate; and (iii) the tendency of convergence toward the mean profit rate is more often insignificant. On the other hand, the persistence of profitability seems to be least evident in Germany. Canada, Japan, France, and the United Kingdom appear to be in the middle between the United States (1950–72) and Germany. However, the Japanese and U.K. results are much closer to the German one, whereas the Canadian and French results tend to show more proximity to the U.S. result for 1950–72. The U.S. result for 1964–80 appears to show less significant evidence for the persistence of profitability than the result for 1950–72.

IV   Comparison by industry

To see how the estimated values of the long-run profit rate vary across industries, Table 10.6 presents the means of $\hat{\alpha}$ by industry for the six countries, Canada, West Germany, France, Japan, the United Kingdom, and the United States (1950–72 and 1964–80). We selected 16 industries that could be matched closely among the six countries. However, for some industries, the concordance of industries among these countries is not perfect. For instance, synthetic fiber is classified in the textile industry

Table 10.6. *Means of $\hat{\alpha}$ by industry*

	Canada (1968–82)		Federal Republic of Germany (1961–81)		France (1965–82)		Japan (1964–82)		United Kingdom (1951–77)		United States			
											1950–72		1964–80	
	$\hat{\alpha}$	n	$\hat{\alpha}$	n	$\hat{\alpha}$	n	$\hat{\alpha}$	n	$\hat{\alpha}$	n	$\hat{\alpha}$	n	$\hat{\alpha}$	n
Food	1.631	20	0.230	47	0.06	49	−0.930	27	0.439	36	−0.061	61	−0.007	40
Textile and clothes	−2.434	5	−0.436	36	−2.18	15	−0.874	40	0.328	12	−1.615	15	−0.938	7
Paper and pulp	1.614	10	−2.155	12	−0.08	16	−0.007	15	−1.028	27	−0.735	17	0.169	8
Chemicals	—	—	—	—	1.56	30	0.126	55	−0.208	1	2.634	17	−0.456	11
Pharmaceuticals	1.666	6	0.516	34	12.52	6	1.465	14	0.137	7	5.904	9	4.552	8
Petroleum refining	1.445	9	−0.710	5	5.04	9	−0.435	8	−0.197	3	0.923	18	0.766	18
Rubber products	0.423	1	−0.130	9	−2.70	2	0.274	6	−3.126	5	−2.098	3	−1.761	7
Cement, stone, ceramic, and glass	−1.124	10	0.026	31	2.44	22	0.365	21	1.516	13	2.525	17	−1.481	8
Iron and steel	1.029	8	−0.450	13	−0.82	13	0.395	28			−1.514	30	−1.722	9
Nonferrous metals	3.411	2	−0.803	9	−1.41	8	0.408	20	0.861	3	0.560	12	−0.252	7
Metal products	3.534	7	−0.125	5	0.49	23	−1.099	8	4.058	1	−1.015	17	−1.095	8
Machinery and tools	−1.078	2	0.179	51	0.25	31	−0.389	44	0.686	34	2.136	30	0.511	19
Electrical equipment	1.312	10	0.370	16	0.05	34	0.013	40	2.531	11	2.922	19	2.121	6
Shipbuilding	—	—	−0.688	7	−2.95	2	−0.259	4	−4.857	3	−4.916	4	−2.507	4
Cars and other transportation equipment	0.813	5	1.338	9	−0.13	34	0.074	25	1.366	5	0.029	28	−1.632	16
Precision instruments	—	—	1.127	7	−0.73	3	1.134	10	—	—	3.576	10	0.173	5

in Japan, but it is in the chemical industry in Germany. Also, the car and transportation equipment industry includes only cars and trucks in France, but it includes cars and bicycles in Germany, cars, bicycles, and railroad vehicles in Japan, and all these plus aircraft in the United States. Furthermore, a company with diversified products had to be assigned into the industry of its primary product without regard to the company's other products. Therefore, the comparison made in this section should be interpreted with some qualifications.

One of the most significant characteristics of the industry means of $\hat{\alpha}$ observed from Table 10.6 is that the pharmaceutical industry commands a high positive profitability in most countries. The industry has the highest projected long-run profit rate in France, Japan, and the United States. Although pharmaceuticals are combined with chemicals in Canada and Germany, the combined industry in both of the two countries also commands relatively high profits. The mean $\hat{\alpha}$ in the electrical equipment industry is also positive in all the six countries, though the value is not so high as in the pharmaceutical industry and varies across countries. Similarly, the cement, stone, and glass industry has a positive $\hat{\alpha}$ in all the countries except Canada and the United States (1964–80).

Another characteristic common to the six countries is that companies in the shipbuilding industry are losing money in the long run. The mean $\hat{\alpha}$ in this industry is negative in all the countries. The mean $\hat{\alpha}$ for the textile industry is also negative in all the countries except the United Kingdom. Other industries where the mean $\hat{\alpha}$ tends to be negative are iron and steel (except for Canada and Japan), rubber products (except for Canada and Japan), and paper and pulp (except for Canada and the United States, 1964–80).

The performance of the technology-intensive industries except pharmaceuticals tends to be similar across the countries except France. The performance of French industries tends to be poorer compared to the rest of the countries. The mean value of $\hat{\alpha}$ in the electrical equipment industry is relatively high in Canada, Germany, the United Kingdom, and the United States but is low in France. Similarly, the precision instrument industry in Germany, Japan, and the United States (1950–72) has a high long-run profit rate, whereas this industry in France has a negative long-run profit rate. The mean $\hat{\alpha}$ for the car and transportation industry is positive in all the countries except France and the United States (1964–80).

The Canadian firms also show some distinctive patterns in their performance. The firms producing food, nonferrous metals, metal products, and paper and pulp are performing well compared to other industries in

Canada and to the counterparts in other countries.[8,9] This finding seems to reflect Canada's comparative advantage in natural resources.

These findings suggest that the projected long-run profit rate varies across industries, and the pattern tends to differ across countries. Thus, the pattern of the projected long-run profit rate across industries is rather similar among West Germany, Japan, the United Kingdom, and the United States, whereas Canada and, to a lesser extent, France show distinctive national characteristics.

V   Summary

This chapter has reported an international comparison of the persistent difference in company profits. The international comparison among Canada, West Germany, France, Japan, Sweden, the United Kingdom, and the United States was made by using the estimated results obtained in the individual country studies. This chapter found, most importantly, that the extent of the persistent differences in company profitability is most evident in the United States for the 1950–72 period. On the other hand, the persistence of profitability was found to be least evident in West Germany. We found that the results in Canada, Japan, France, and the United Kingdom lie between the U.S. result for 1950–72 and the result in West Germany. However, the Japanese result tends to be much closer to the German result, whereas the Canadian and French results tend to show more proximity to the U.S. result for 1950–72. We also found that the strong persistent profitability observed in the United States for the 1950–72 period becomes less significant for the 1964–80 period.

[8] The food industry in Germany has a positive and moderate long-run profit rate. However, this owes mostly to a high profitability of the beer-brewing companies.

[9] Note that we are comparing the normalized profit rates and the normalization is made as a deviation from the mean in each country; therefore, a higher normalized profit rate in a Canadian firm than, say, a Japanese firm does not necessarily imply a higher nonnormalized rate in the former.

CHAPTER 11

The persistence of profits in perspective

PAUL A. GEROSKI AND DENNIS C. MUELLER

I   Introduction

Competition is a dynamic process involving innovation and adaptation, survival, and failure; its outcome is a variety of products and prices that evolve in complex ways over time and are produced by a changing collection of firms. The particular patterns of evolution exhibited by different industries depend on both exogenous factors and the degree of competition present at any particular time. There are, of course, numerous ways to evaluate the strength of market competition, but for fairly obvious reasons, most attention has focused on profitability. From the point of view of the corporate strategist, profits are both an index of current success and a source of funds to finance the kinds of strategic investment that help to ensure the continuance of that success. From the point of view of public policy, profits provide a rough indication of the divergence of prices from marginal cost and thus of the difference between current market performance and the competitive ideal. And finally, from the point of view of those interested in analyzing market dynamics, profits are an important piece of the puzzle of explaining the evolution of competition. Profits at any time reflect the current degree of competition in a market, and because high profits attract entry, current profits also cause changes in the degree of competition, thus affecting its intensity in the near future.

Using profitability as an indicator of market performance is not, however, completely straightforward, and there are at least three different notions of profitability that command attention. Most accessive are *current* profits at any particular time, and one could use differences in current profitability between different firms in the same industry or different industries in the same country to make inferences about differences in the degree of competitiveness in each situation. The difficulty with this procedure is that current profits reflect the effects of numerous purely transitory factors (including the effects of systematic short run disequilibrium dynamics) that contain no useful information on the intensity of competition. A more satisfying concept is long run, or *permanent,* profits. Although not directly observable, estimates of permanent profitability can be constructed from any econometric model that clearly distinguishes between the short and long run effects of various exogenous factors on profitability. Measures of permanent profits yield valuable information on the tendencies in the competitive process, on the ultimate implications of movements in current profitability, and on its exogenous determinants. Yet, however interesting it is to speculate on the long run consequences of various changes in exogenous factors, such an exercise is of limited interest if short run dynamics are weak and only gradually propel the system toward its long run state. Indeed, any concern with competition as a process (rather than as an equilibrium state with certain normatively appealing properties) focuses attention on such dynamics and, in particular, on the degree to which a given level of profitability persists in remaining at a distance from its ultimate long run level. That is, the *persistence* of profits reflects both the strength of competition as a process that drives profits toward their long run equilibrium values and the extent to which these long run values differ from zero.

These three different measures of profitability are obviously linked, and indeed, to make estimates of permanent profits or of the speed of adjustment of profits to their permanent levels, one must start with an observable like current profitability. However, there are a number of good reasons for pushing beyond current profits and trying to construct useful estimates of permanent profits and adjustment speeds. From the point of public policymakers, high current profits provide no compelling case for antitrust concern. A persuasive case for intervention exists only if such high levels of profitability are permanent or if they persist for long periods of time. From the point of view of corporate strategists, measures of the permanent component of profits reflect the long run potential of the firm's current strategy, and measures of the speeds of adjustment of profits reflect the intensity of imitation by rivals, giving the firm an estimate of the kind of time it has available to adapt to the consequences of current success or failure. Finally, for those interested in the nature of market dynamics, measures of permanent profits directly reflect the height of barriers to entry, whereas measures of the rates at which profits converge on their permanent levels reflect the speed with which competitive forces like entry react to the existence of excess profits and the effect that entrants have on profitability subsequent to entry.

Given the interest in and importance of calculating measures of persistence, it is important to devote time and energy to the process of making inferences about these from data on current profits. The main problem to be faced in constructing models of profitability is that many of the determinants of profitability are difficult to observe with accuracy. This is particularly the case with completely latent factors like the threat of entry. As discussed in Chapter 2, this type of problem can be overcome and a simple solution is an autoregressive profits equation,

$$\pi_{it} = \alpha_i + \lambda_i \pi_{it-1} + \mu_{it}, \tag{11.1}$$

where π_{it} is the profits of firm i at time t, π_{ip}, $\alpha_i/(1-\lambda_i)$, is the level of profits i will realize in the long run, and λ_i reflects the persistence with which profits differ period by period from their long run level. This long run level, π_{ip}, depends on the barriers to entry and intramarket mobility that protect firm i's niche in the market. The λ_i, in contrast, reflect the numerous factors influencing the short run adjustments of a firm or its market to disequilibria. In a sense, π_{ip} measures permanent differences in profit *levels* across firms over time, and λ_i (or more accurately $1-\lambda_i$) measures permanent speeds of adjustment to disequilibria. Estimates of (11.1) applied to time series data for particular firms yield estimates of π_{ip} and λ_i in a straightforward way, and it is in terms of these two parameters that we shall review the findings of this book.

II   Interpreting the results

This volume has reported the results of applying models like (11.1) together with more sophisticated variants to data on firms in seven countries. A brief summary tabulation of the salient features of these data is contained in Chapter 10, and in what follows, we propose to develop some of the broader implications of those results.

A   *Permanent profits*

In every country, permanent differences in profitability across firms, and in the United States also across industries, were observed. The subsample of firms with the highest initial profits had highest long run projected profits in every single country. The subsample with the lowest initial profits had the lowest projected profits in every country save Sweden, where it was the second lowest initial profit group that had the lowest profits.[1] Firms with above (below) normal profits at a given point in time can be expected to earn above (below) normal profits into the indefinite future. Despite this common pattern of permanent departures from average profits across the countries, however, important differences exist between countries in the extent to which profits persist permanently. These differences are readily apparent when one compares the fraction of initial

---

[1] Each subsample in Sweden has only 11 firms in it, so that one or two firms can shift a subsample.

profits that are projected to persist indefinitely across the several countries. Table 11.1 gives the ratio of projected initial profits for the highest and lowest initial profit subgroups. Two clusters of results exist. Canada, France, and the United States (1950–72) all have substantial degrees of persistence. If we regard the initial point in time for each study as essentially randomly selected, then for Canada, France, and the United States between 50 and 85 percent of the differences in profit rates from the average of their highest and lowest profit firms are projected to persist indefinitely. In contrast, for West Germany, Japan, and Sweden these percentages range from 15 to 35 percent.

Over much of the 1950–72 period many markets in the United States were relatively free from import competition. This protection could help explain the relatively higher estimates of profits persistence in the United States, measured as ratios of π_p to initial profit differences, for the 1950–72 period than for the 1964–80 period. More took place in the troubled seventies than merely a rise in import competition, however, and so the relative importance of this explanation is not clear.

Canada experiences relatively high levels of import penetration but also has rather high tariffs. These tariffs plus the high levels of concentration in Canadian industries may account for the relatively strong persistence of above normal profits in Canada.

Japan, on the other hand, has an economy whose internal markets are generally thought to be protected from foreign competition. But the degree of persistence measured for this country resembles that of the more open West German, Swedish, and U.K. economies. The estimates of permanent rents for France are much closer to those of Canada and the United States than they are to those of its Common Market neighbor, West Germany. Industry concentration levels are somewhat higher in France than in West Germany (Yamawaki, Weiss, and Sleuwaegen, 1986), and in Chapter 7 Jenny and Weber note that the industries with high permanent rents are typically quite concentrated. Concentration has been found to be positively related to profitability across industries in both France (Jenny and Weber, 1976) and West Germany (Neumann, Böbel, and Haid, 1979). Thus, the somewhat higher average concentration levels in France than in West Germany become a possible explanation for the greater degree of profits persistence in France. But concentration cannot be the whole story, since concentration levels are even higher in Japan than in France or Germany.[2] We conclude that no single variable (imports, tariff levels, concentration) stands out as *the* explanation for the cross-national differences observed. Unfortunately, the small number of countries in our study precludes a more systematic examination of this issue.

---

[2] Observation based on comparable data compiled by Peter Murrell.

Table 11.1. *Long run projected profit rates relative to initial period profit rates*

| | Canada | | Federal Republic of Germany | | | France, | Japan, | Sweden, | United Kingdom, | United States, π_{at} | |
	π_{at}	π_{bt}	π_{at}	π_{bt}	V	π_{bt}	π_{at}	π_{bt}	π_{at}	1950–72	1964–80
Highest initial profit rates	0.55	0.49	0.15	0.19	0.21	0.62	0.22	0.29	0.21	0.85	0.26
Lowest initial profit rates	0.84	0.71	0.31	0.32	0.15	0.48	0.21	0.35	0.16	0.63	0.59

Notes: Estimates of π_{at} are based on accounting profits after taxes divided by total assets; π_{bt} estimates based on accounting profits before taxes divided by total assets; V estimates based on the market value of the firm divided by total assets.

Japanese corporations have not succeeded in translating their spectacular success in capturing international markets into permanently high profit margins. The degree of permanent profits persistence in Japan is about the same as in the United Kingdom. It is interesting in this regard that the three countries that appear to have the most competitive economies, as measured by the relative size of permanent to initial profits, are Japan, West Germany, and the United Kingdom. The latter's products have generally been thought to be uncompetitive on world markets, whereas Japan's products have had spectacular success in all parts of the world. West German industries have fallen somewhere in between doing very well in the early part of the sample period, less well in recent years. Yet all three countries look about the same in terms of the relative size of their permanent rents, and all come fairly close to the norm expected of an economy at a long run competitive equilibrium.

Some effort to go beyond the measurement of permanent departures from average profits and account for its causes was made in nearly all of the country studies. The richest data base existed for the United States, where it was found that a firm's market share and product differentiation were important explanations for differences in the permanent profit levels of firms. Firm growth rates were also positively correlated with π_p. Similar results were found at the industry level in the United States, where permanent differences in industry profit levels were related to concentration, entry barriers, product differentiation, and industry growth rates. In Japan, it was again found that firm market share (or rank in its industry) and advertising were positively related to persistent profitability. Advertising intensity was significantly related to profitability in Germany but not in the United Kingdom; proxies for market share in both the United Kingdom and West Germany proved to be statistically insignificant. It is possible that the U.K. proxy also measures the extent of diversification, however, which was found to be negatively related to profitability in Germany and the United States (Mueller, 1986, ch. 7).

Thus, it seems that successful product differentiation, where success is measured by market share and product differentiation is measured by industry R&D or advertising, leads to persistent differences in profitability (see also Jacobsen, 1988). This suggestion is reinforced by other studies that have found the combination of market share and product differentiation to be important in explaining profitability (e.g., Ravenscraft, 1983). The role played by product differentiation may also explain some of the differences in the patterns of results observed across countries. Television advertising is a major vehicle for product differentiation in the United States and Canada but is severely restricted by the state's control of the television networks in West Germany. Brand images are thus more difficult to establish in West Germany, and fewer consumer products with significant market power are found in Germany than in Canada, the United Kingdom, and the United States. In those industries where product differentiation is important in Germany (e.g., automobiles and beer), several companies with apparently permanent above normal profits do exist, but much of the German production is concentrated in capital goods industries that compete on international markets. Both Sweden and Japan are also heavily dependent on their export markets. In internationally open markets, establishing the kind of buyer loyalty and market position that can be established for goods facing only domestic competitions is difficult, and indeed, this difficulty may be part of the explanation for the greater degrees of persistence in the United States than in Germany, Japan, and Sweden.

Beyond this rather speculative generalization about the importance of product differentiation, the other main conclusion to be drawn from the country studies is that firm characteristics are more important than industry characteristics in accounting for differences in long run profit levels. This result comes through most clearly for Japan, the United Kingdom, and the United States where firm specific variables explain a higher proportion of the variance in π_{ip} than industry variables that, in some cases, make no statistically significant individual or collective contribution. This conclusion is only clearly contradicted in Canada, although the variables used to measure firm characteristics in this country are not the same as those used in the other countries. Thus, as a final generalization, one might say that although both firm and industry characteristics are important elements of the explanation of profits, firm attributes are somewhat more important in explaining the long run equilibrium values of company profits and industry characteristics are more important in explaining the adjustment process in reaching the equilibrium.

B   *The persistence of short run deviations of profits from their permanent levels*

There are two issues that must be faced when examining the persistence of profits: why the adjustment of market forces to excess returns may not be instantaneous and why the rate of erosion in excess profits differs for different firms. The two questions are, in fact, highly interrelated. Costs of adjustment depend on both the internal structure and functioning of firms (e.g., see the classic discussion in Penrose, 1959) and on the kinds of obstacles included in structural factors like entry and mobility barriers on the one hand and the response of incumbents to attempted entry or intraindustry mobility on the other. One way or the other, the existence of such adjustment costs means that profits will not be instantaneously driven to their long run levels. Profits will adjust rather gradually to shocks that displace them from equilibrium, and this means that one will observe a systematic relation between profits in t and those in $t+1$. That the internal structure and functioning of different firms differs and that different firms face different entry and mobility barriers imply that disequilibrium profits of different firms are unlikely to persist to the same degree. It is, however, important not to confuse persistence in profits caused by a slow adjustment of market forces to excess returns with the kinds of intertemporal linkages in profits that business cycle factors can create. Since these returns are likely to be transitory and not related to competitive dynamics, it is important to purge the data of their effects. Of the several ways that one can do this, we have elected to measure profits as a deviation from the sample means of all firms in each country in each year.

That adjustment costs depend on entry barriers suggests that the degree of the persistence in profits will be related to industry characteristics; that mobility barriers or factors internal to the firm affect adjustment costs indicates that firm specific characteristics may be important. In fact, both firm and industry specific characteristics were found to be important in explaining different speeds of adjustment across firms, although industry factors were somewhat more important than firm factors in accounting for observed differences between firms. In Japan, the United Kingdom, and the United States, industry characteristics proved to be somewhat more important in explaining λ than firm characteristics. Whether the common industry factors that affect the adjustment process are related to the business cycle is difficult to tell. Hints that business cycle factors may be important are contained in the firm level results for the United States. Compared to the period 1964–80, 1950–72 was a rather tranquil period of economic activity. Thus, one would expect business cycle factors to have a greater effect on the adjustment process in the period 1964–80 than for the later period. Larger λ_i's were observed for the later period consistent with the hypothesis. Sweden underwent a significant structural transformation over the period 1967–85. One might expect such a massive adjustment to changed market conditions to take some time to work itself out. The large estimated λ_i's indicate a considerably slower adjustment process for Sweden than for the other countries. Also interesting in this connection is the smoothing effect of profits taxation. In two countries, λ_i's were estimated for both before- and after-tax data. In both cases, the mean λ_i's were lower using after-tax profit data than for before-tax data, indicating that after-tax profit rates return to their equilibrium values more quickly than their before-tax counterparts. Mean λ_i's for before- and after-tax profit data were respectively 0.36 and 0.30 for Canada and 0.48 and 0.39 for West Germany.

Impediments to entry can be expected to be greater than impediments to exit. Some firms have an incentive to undertake measures to impede entry, but no firms have an incentive to block exit.[3] The greatest incentive to block entry exists for those firms with the highest profit rates. Thus, one might expect the adjustment process to work most slowly for these firms, and this was, in fact, consistently observed. The highest λ_i's were observed for the subsamples of firms with highest initial profit rates in Germany, France, Japan, and the United States (1964–80). Highest mean λ_i's were also observed for the highest initial profit firms in the United States for the 1950–72 period, when profits were measured as a relative deviation from the mean (Mueller, 1986, ch. 2). As the chapter on Canada makes clear, exit barriers in the minerals and natural resources industries were important in this country over the period under study, and the lowest initial profit group had the highest λ_i's. But the second highest λ_i's for Canada were found in the highest initial profit group. Thus, the behavior of the λ_i's across the different subgroups of firms in each country does generally accord with what one expects if the height of λ is dependent on entry and exit barriers. The results for the United States at the industry level of aggregation (Chapter 4) also indicate that the speeds of adjustment of industry profits to their long run equilibrium levels varied with entry and exit conditions in the predicted manner.

With the exception of Sweden, the mean estimated value of λ_i in all other countries averaged around 0.5 or lower. Read literally, these estimates imply that a departure of profits from their normal level of, say, 10 percent would be reduced to a departure of about 1 percent in just over three years. Put differently, if $\alpha_i = 0$ in equation (11.1), then the half-life of profits above the norm is log(half) divided by log(λ_i), or if $\lambda_i \simeq 0.5$, about one year. Although this is appreciably faster than econometric estimates from structural models suggest (e.g., Geroski and Masson, 1987), there are good reasons to think that these are, nevertheless, upper bound estimates of the speed of market processes. In particular, many accounting practices – like profits taxation – tend to "smooth" profits data, thereby importing a degree of convergence toward the norm independent of any competitive pressures. Thus, it appears that the competitive process works no faster than three to five years on average in eliminating "short run" deviations from permanent profits. Although not slow, this process can by no means be thought of as instantaneous.

Three further remarks are worth making on generalizations of (11.1) discussed in Chapter 2 with which various authors have experimented. Models that have decomposed profits relative to the norm into firm and industry specific components (see Cubbin and Geroski, 1987) have discovered that

---

[3] Labor unions or local communities may raise exit barriers, however.

the dynamics of profits relative to the norm are, on the whole, driven by firm specific factors that ensure that firm specific performance relative to the industry norm persists longer than average industry performance relative to the all-manufacturing norm. Models that have allowed adjustment speeds of profits above the norm to differ from those applying to profits below the norm have provided very weak indicators that the two speeds of adjustment often differ. However, since most firms in most samples were generally either above or below the norm for most of the sample period, differences in λ_i due to asymmetric adjustment are hard to distinguish from differences due to firm specific factors like mobility barriers or internal firm structure. Finally, models that have extended (11.1) to allow for longer, more complex dynamics have generally produced estimates suggesting that the simple first order model, equation (11.1), adequately captures most of the interesting dynamics to be observed. This, in turn, suggests that the competitive process is a fairly simple one, involving no real hint of overshooting or other forms of instability.

C   Summary

The basic properties of the data that are common to the various countries in the sample can be usefully summarized in a way that is not model dependent: That profit differences between firms persist permanently suggests that there are cross-sectional variations in outcomes to be explained. That market dynamics are fairly quick suggests that the strictly time series properties of profits data are of somewhat less compelling interest. That is, it is (roughly speaking) the case that the between firm variation in profits is larger and more important than are those within firm variations in profits over time.

III   Some pitfalls

It would be injudicious to draw overly strong conclusions from these results despite their striking consistency across the seven countries covered in this study. Still, it would also be unwarranted to dismiss these results on the grounds that the model is too simple or that the data are flawed in one of a number of ways. To assess the significance of what has been found, it is necessary to explore each of the major potential weaknesses in what has been done and determine exactly what – if any – biases have been created.

A   The model

The model is a fairly simple one, no more than a reduced form. As such, it has advantages and disadvantages. On the plus side, it is a solution to a latent variables problem that, in principle, is likely to bedevil efforts to assess the precise character of competitive dynamics. The consequence is that our efforts to characterize the dynamics are not conditional on the precise details of how entry, potential or actual, is measured. Further, the model is fairly simple in structure and does not involve a variety of complicating features that often make estimates unrobust. The major drawbacks of using this reduced form model are created by ambiguities that arise from two sources. First, our interpretation of the data rests on the structure of the model, a structure that cannot be adequately evaluated when only the reduced form is estimated. Second, the reduced form coefficient reflects the effects of combinations of the original structural parameters, which themselves remain unidentified. As a consequence, it is hard to decide whether, for example, the persistence of profits that we observe is due to a slow response by entrants to profit signals or to a weak effect that entrants have on profits.

It is hard to say what these strengths and weaknesses add up to on balance. It is clear that the model is fairly robust, and it seems to account for the broad features of the data in a satisfactory way. Further, the estimates reported seem to be quite consistent with those that have been generated using at least one particular structural model (e.g., Geroski, 1988) and using nonparametric methods (e.g., Geroski and Toker, 1988). We tentatively conclude then that our conclusions are not (terribly) model specific.

B   Measuring current profits

As we noted in the Appendix to Chapter 1, accounting measures of profitability are subject to possibly large measurement errors when treated as economic returns on capital. Indeed, it is possible that accounting and economic profits measured at any given time will diverge noticeably, making inferences about the latter using estimates of the former hazardous. It is not clear, however, how serious this problem really is. On the one hand, persistently high accounting profits (e.g., profits in excess of the firm's rate of growth) imply persistently high economic profits (in the same sense) [see Edwards et al. (1987) and references therein]. And on the other hand, accounting profits are readily observable and do play a major role in many of the important decisions made by agents. To explain the important dynamic movements and interfirm or interindustry variations in observables is an important and worthwhile task; to move from such estimates to normative judgments is, of course, inherently more speculative.

Economic theory offers the most solid theoretical underpinnings for the relationship between long run equilibrium profit levels and various market structure variables. Here the relationships between market share, product differentiation, and our measures of equilibrium profits in several of the country studies accord well both with what theory predicts and what other researchers have found. These results suggest at least a positive association between our measures of permanent profits and true economic profits. There are also good reasons to expect the process of adjustment to equilibrium to be more governed by industry factors than firm-related factors, and this has tended to be the case in our results. Thus, our measures of profitability have behaved broadly, as one would expect economic profits to behave. Although not a test of propositions regarding the determinants of economic profit, these results are at least consistent with both theory and previous results.

Nevertheless, accounting differences may be responsible for the poor explanatory power of our models of the differences between π_{ip} and λ_i across firms, industries, and countries. The only way to test whether this is so is to compare our results to those obtained using measures of true economic profitability. Some industrial economists have claimed that the market value of a firm is a better measure of these economic rents than current accounting profits. To the extent that this is so, it is interesting to contrast the results for West Germany when market value is used as the numerator in the performance measure and before- and after-tax profits are used (Chapter 6). They are very similar. A comparison of Germany with France and Canada in Table 11.1 reveals that for Germany the values of V are much closer to those of π_{at} and π_{bt} than are the values of π_{at} and π_{bt} for Germany to the values for Canada and France. Assuming the observed values of V to be true values, this implies that comparisons of accounting profit measures across the three countries may be at least qualitatively correct. A far smaller proportion of above and below normal returns tend to persist in West Germany than they do in Canada and France.[4]

The differences between the V and π_{at} and π_{bt} for Germany are also interesting. For the lowest initial profit group, the long run projected profit rates measured as a percentage of the initial values are double the corresponding ratio for the V's. In contrast, if the market perfectly forecasted future market values, this ratio would be 1.0. Thus, for the lowest initial market value companies, the stock market is a poorer predictor of long run projected value than current accounting profits. On the other hand, at the top end of the profit (or V) scale, the stock market is a slightly better predictor of long run equilibrium values. The mean values of λ_i for π_{at}, π_{bt}, and V for West Germany were 0.39, 0.48, and 0.62, respectively,

---

[4] Connolly and Schwartz (1985) also report qualitatively similar results when Tobin's q is used to test for profit persistence over time as when accounting profit rates are used.

suggesting that stock market values exhibit the slowest speed of adjustment. This is surprising since the capital market literature would lead one to expect instantaneous adjustments to new information and thus a λ of zero. The result may reflect the delays in adjustment occasioned by capital market agents when they overreact to events.

These arguments do not, of course, solve the problem of how useful accounting profits are as indicators of economic profits. Whether they strengthen one's confidence in accounting profit data or weaken it in market value data is, perhaps, a matter of taste. But the results, at least for Germany, seem to suggest that accountants, capital markets, and economists are all measuring roughly similar phenomena.

C   Mergers and sample selection

A second set of problems with the country studies in this volume arises from the possibility of a sample selection "bias" and the lack of treatment of mergers. Of necessity, we have focused upon only surviving companies over the sample period. At least two other groups of firms require examination to obtain a complete picture of the dynamics of economic markets: those entering and those leaving the population. The closest we have come to examining these companies has been to include them among the "unobservables" that influence the intertemporal movements of profits. To observe them directly would take an expenditure of resources that is probably greater than the already large efforts that went into this project. It is an endeavor recommended to those long on time and of long purse.

What we can do here is merely to conjecture about the possible biases that arise from ignoring these two categories of companies. Consider first the newcomers. They start with a zero return. Some will see their returns skyrocket, others may rise for a short time and then plummet, and still others may disappear almost as soon as they arrive. For those that survive, it is possible that the λ_i's estimated from the autoregressive profits equation would be much larger than for the companies we studied. Newly created firms undoubtedly would be further away from their long run equilibrium positions than mature, established firms and may pass through a "life cycle" of rising and falling profits that generates large values of λ_i. Thus, the most reasonable expectation for new firms that eventually survive is that the estimates of their speeds of adjustment may be lower than for the samples with which we have worked.

Now consider the effect on our estimates of long run equilibrium profit rates of omitting newcomers. With respect to those that survive, the most reasonable assumption is that newcomers will have long run equilibrium profit rates distributed in about the same way as old survivors do, and thus no significant distortions are introduced into our results with respect to the equilibrium values by omitting the newcomers that survive. All survivors were once newcomers, and there is no obvious reason to expect yesterday's newcomers who survived until today to look different from today's newcomers that survive until tomorrow. The projected returns of those who did not survive would certainly be negative had they survived. Thus, looking at the equilibrium profit projections of surviving companies paints a rosier picture of profits persistence than would be obtained if one examined the trajectories of firms that came and went during the sample period. This point does not, however, negate the fact that significant fractions of firms that survive earn above normal returns.

Consider now the companies that existed at the beginning but not at the end of the period and that would, therefore, have been part of our samples had they survived. Those that were liquidated undoubtedly followed downward spiraling profit paths that would generate possibly high λ_i's if they did not expire too quickly and certainly low or negative π_{ip}'s. However, the data for Canada, France, Japan, the United Kingdom, and the United States indicate that liquidated companies comprise less than 3.3 percent of the population of firms from which our samples are drawn. The preponderance of disappearances were the result of acquisitions. What would the profit trajectories of the acquired firms have been had they not been acquired? This is a question no research can definitely answer. Data do exist in most countries on the profits of some acquired companies prior to their acquisition, and these could be used to project their profits at the time of acquisition to see whether they differ systematically from otherwise similar unacquired companies. To date no study of this type has been done. What is worse, the existing literature on acquisitions does not paint a clean picture of the characteristics of acquired companies. Some studies find that they are performing relatively poorly at the time they are acquired, some find them performing better than average, and still others find their performance indistinguishable from that of otherwise similar firms (see Boyle, 1970; Singh, 1971; Mueller, 1980; Harris, Stewart, and Carleton, 1982; Ravenscraft and Scherer, 1987, ch. 3). Thus, it is difficult to guess what the performance of acquired firms would have been in the absence of their acquisition, and so the direction of any bias from omitting these companies remains in doubt.

A clear bias against finding differences in long run equilibrium values of profits across firms is introduced by the averaging effects of mergers. Evidence of this effect was reported for the United States and was apparent for the United Kingdom in the greater number of π_{ip}'s found to be significantly different from zero from a subsample of companies purged of mergers than was observed in the full sample. One-third of the measured erosion of the initial profit differences across firms in the United States was attributed to the averaging effect of mergers. Merger activity was even more intense in the United Kingdom, and can be expected to have had an even more dramatic effect driving estimates of long run projected returns in that country toward the sample mean. In no other country were mergers as important a source of growth as in the United Kingdom and the United States, but mergers occurred in all of them and may be expected to have imparted some regression-to-the-mean effect to the results for all countries. Thus, the extent to which individual company profit rates in given markets persist permanently is probably underestimated by our projections. Similarly, internal diversification should have an averaging effect on our estimates of equilibrium profit rates. A single product firm with a profit rate far above the average is more likely to earn a lower rate of return on any new activity than a higher one. Firms have become more diversified in all countries, and this diversification process should have accelerated the conversion of firm profit rates on the mean.

Beyond the averaging effects of mergers and diversification, there are their synergistic effects. Based on the results for Germany, the United Kingdom, and the United States (Mueller, 1986, ch. 7), these appear to be small. The only effort made to isolate the effects of mergers on long run projected profits was for the United States, and it too appeared to be nil or negative (Mueller, 1986, ch. 8). Once again, the existing literature on mergers is of little help since observers are of differing views as to what mergers' effects have been.[5]

To understand the intertemporal relationships between mergers and profitability, fresh modeling of the determinants and effects of mergers is required (Pakes, 1987). The empirical estimation of such a model would undoubtedly require profits data for both the acquiring and acquired companies over an extended time series prior to the merger and for the same two companies, now divisions of a larger firm in a vertical or conglomerate acquisition, after the merger. Such data were gathered for a few years by the Line of Business Program of the U.S. Federal Trade Commission. But this program was stopped, and no comparable program exists anywhere else in the world. The complete modeling of merger–profitability interrelationships over time appears a long way off.

[5] For positive interpretations, see Benston (1980), Brozen (1982), Jensen and Ruback (1983), and Halpern (1983). More skeptical evaluations are presented by Steiner (1975, ch. 8), Mueller (1977, 1987), Scherer (1980, pp. 138–41), and Rhoades (1983).

D   *"Dry-wells" biases*

In the Cournot model of competition, the height of rents in the industry supplying spring water is inversely related to the number of sellers in the industry. In the absence of impediments to entry, new sellers of spring water will appear until all of the rents are gone. The results of this book indicate that permanent rents (positive and negative) are earned by some companies in every country we studied. Impediments to entering some markets exist. No firm can earn above normal returns selling spring water, but it may be possible that it will earn a permanent rent if it sells Perrier. The importance of product differentiation in explaining persistent differences in profitability across firms was apparent in the empirical results for several countries and across industries in the United States and to some extent in the mere identities of the persistently profitable firms and the products that account for their success.

However, to the extent that product differentiation explains the differences in profits observed, a different form of modeling of the competitive process may be required. Indeed, a different, more Schumpeterian form of competition is to be presumed. Instead of thinking of the competitive process as continuous, with output and capital expanding by increments until output reaches the point where price equals marginal cost, a discontinuous, lumpy view of investment is required. Each potential supplier of water makes an expenditure to find a spring or to advertise the spring water already found. Some of these expenditures will be successful, others come up dry; the rents of the market are distributed in an uneven, perhaps almost random, way to the quickest, luckiest, or most talented investors. The others receive nothing. Many observers regard the persistent rents received by a few firms as the necessary social cost of inducing the investments that created the rents in the first place. They see the competitive process as yielding an outcome such that each industry earns zero profits and not such that each firm earns zero profits by equating price and average costs. The rents earned by the successful investors are seen as being offset by the losses of the unsuccessful.[6] This view of competition resembles that of the rent-seeking literature (e.g., Posner, 1975). Indeed, rent-seeking and rent-creating activities go hand in hand. Whereas the lure of persistent profits first induced the investments leading to the development of Perrier, these rents now induce investments by others to duplicate or surpass Perrier's success. Should the combination of taste and image that has produced Perrier's success prove to be

---

[6] Several of those attending the conference in Berlin of March 1987 expressed this view. See, also Littlechild (1981).

unmatchable, these other investments will prove to have been wasted. On the other hand, if a new and superior product is found, there may be a net social gain. Unfortunately, the literature contains no proof that the gains from this form of competition exceed or even just balance the social costs.[7,8]

The dry-wells model of competition (for every well that produces oil society must drill 100 dry ones), even if valid, does *not* imply that our estimates of permanent rents are inaccurate or biased. What it does suggest is that caution must be exercised in drawing any inferences about the efficacy of the competitive process of the needed policies to improve it from the existence of these rents.

IV   Final thoughts

The existence of monopoly rents are a clear signal of the existence of a monopoly "problem." If the π_{ip} and λ_i estimates in each country implied that all monopoly rents quickly disappeared, then there would be no scope for public policy. But some permanent rents (positive and negative) appear to exist in every industry and in every country, and although the adjustment process appears to be fairly quick on average across the several countries, in some instances the λ's do imply a slow adjustment to the estimated long run equilibria. Whether the existence of these rents constitutes a sufficient condition for policy action depends on four factors: (1) the magnitude of the misallocation of resources implied by the measured rents; (2) the costs to both the firms and the enforcement agencies of eliminating the monopoly positions that create these rents; (3) the social waste from expenditures to protect and capture these rents; and (4) benefits from new products and processes brought about through the creation of monopoly rents.

The first two factors raise no issues of controversy or novelty in antitrust enforcement. What is the cost (in terms of efficiency loss) of the existence of monopoly? What are the costs of eliminating it? Every country in this study, and most of those among the developed, industrialized nations, have some form of monopoly commission, fair trade commission, or similar organization charged with curbing the social costs of monopoly and promoting the social benefits from competition. The analyses

[7] Quite to the contrary, see Spence (1976), Lancaster (1975), Marris and Mueller (1980).

[8] Kessides's results in Chapter 4 indicate that differences in profits across industries are not eliminated by rent-seeking investments by the firms *within* the industry. It is, of course, possible that "outsiders" are also making investments to break into an industry with high permanent rents, and if these were counted, the returns to investment in any particular industry would be normal.

in this volume suggest that the first place for these organizations to look for a monopoly problem is among the firms with high π_{ip} and λ_i values.[9] The competition or antimonopoly policies of every country are built on the presumption that the Cournot model describes the competitive process. *The* monopoly problem consists of too few sellers, producing too little output at too high of a price. The solution to this problem is to increase the number of sellers, and/or their output and thereby bring down industry price. In those markets where static competition with a relatively homogeneous product is a reasonable approximation, this policy remains a reasonable approach to the problem. But some markets are better characterized by a Schumpeterianlike model of dynamic competition. Products are heterogeneous and nonprice, investment modes of competition predominate. In these markets, more sellers may not lessen "the monopoly problem" and might even worsen it. An appropriate policy to apply to these markets must address the third and fourth factors listed in the preceding, but as yet, no country's antitrust authorities have given much evidence that they are even aware that other factors are involved.[10]

---

[9] For a discussion of the economic approach to antitrust built around these two questions, see Long, Schramm, and Tollison (1973).

[10] The cereals case, brought by the U.S. Federal Trade Commission in the mid-seventies, indicated an appreciation of these issues and a novel attempt to attack them under existing law. It was killed by the Reagan Administration shortly after it took office. See Schmalensee (1978) and Scherer (1979).

References

Adelman, M. A. and Stangle, Bruce E., "Profitability and Market Share," in F. M. Fisher, ed., *Antitrust and Regulation: Essays in Memory of John J. McGowan,* Cambridge, MA: MIT Press, 1985, pp. 101–13.

Albach, Horst, "The Rate of Return in German Manufacturing Industry: Measurement and Policy Implications," in D. M. Holland, ed., *Measuring Profitability and Capital Costs: An International Study,* Lexington, MA: Lexington Books, 1984.

"Profitability of German Corporations," in D. M. Holland, ed., *Corporate Profits,* Cambridge, MA: MIT Press, 1985.

"Investitionspolitik erfolgreicher Unternehmen," *Zeitschrift für Betriebswittschaft,* July 1987, *57,* pp. 636–61.

Alchian, A., "Uncertainty, Evolution and Economic Theory," *Journal of Political Economy,* June 1950, *58,* pp. 211–22.

Amemiya, T., "Qualitative Response Models: A Survey," *Journal of Economic Literature,* December 1981, *19,* pp. 1483–1536.

Bain, Joe S., *Barriers to New Competition,* Cambridge, MA: Harvard University Press, 1956.

Baldwin, John and Gorecki, Paul K., *Entry and Exit to the Canadian Manufacturing Sector, 1970–1979,* Discussion Paper 25, Ottawa: Economic Council of Canada, 1983.

Baumol, William J., Panzar, John C., and Willig, Robert D., *Contestable Markets and the Theory of Industry Structure,* San Diego, CA: Harcourt Brace Jovanovich, 1982.

Benston, George J., *Conglomerate Mergers: Causes, Consequences, and Remedies,* Washington, D.C: American Enterprise Institute for Public Policy Research, 1980.

"The Validity of Profits–Structure with Particular Reference to the FTC's Line of Business Data," *American Economic Review,* March 1985, *75,* pp. 37–67.

Bowman, Edward H., "A Risk/Return Paradox for Strategic Management," *Sloan Management Review,* Spring 1980, *21,* pp. 17–31.

Boyle, Stanley E., "Pre-merger Growth and Profit Characteristics of Large Conglomerate Mergers in the United States, 1948–68," *St. John's Law Review,* Spring 1970, special edition, *44,* pp. 152–70.

Breusch, T. S. and Godfrey, L., "A Review of Recent Work on Testing for Auto-Correlation in Dynamic Simultaneous Models," in D. Curtis, R. Nobay, and D. Peer, eds., *Macroeconomic Analysis: Essays in Macroeconomics and Econometrics,* London: Croon Helm, 1981.

Brozen, Yale, "The Antitrust Task Force Deconcentration Recommendation," *Journal of Law and Economics,* October 1970, *13,* pp. 279–92.

"Bain's Concentration and Rates of Return Revisited," *Journal of Law and Economics,* October 1971a, *14,* pp. 351–69.

"The Persistence of 'High Rates of Return' in High-Stable Concentration Industries," *Journal of Law and Economics,* October 1971b, *14,* pp. 501–12.

Concentration, Mergers and Public Policy, New York: Free Press, 1982.

Caves, R. and Porter, M., "From Entry Barriers to Mobility Barriers: Conjectural Decisions and Contrived Deterrence to New Competition," *Quarterly Journal of Economics,* May 1977, *91,* pp. 241–61.

Caves, Richard E., Porter, Michael E., Spence, Michael, with Scott, John T., *Competition in the Open Economy,* Cambridge, MA: Harvard University Press, 1980.

Clark, John M., *Competition as a Dynamic Process,* Washington, DC: Brookings Institution, 1961.

Comanor, William S. and Wilson, Thomas A., "The Effect of Advertising on Competition: A Survey," *Journal of Economic Literature,* June 1979, *17,* 453–76.

Connolly, Robert A. and Schwartz, Steven, "The Intertemporal Behavior of Economic Profits," *International Journal of Industrial Organization,* December 1985, *3,* pp. 379–400.

Cournot, Augustin A., *Researches into the Mathematical Principles of the Theory of Wealth,* New York: Macmillan, 1927, original publication, 1838.

Cowling, K. and Waterson, M., "Price–Cost Margins and Market Structure," *Economica,* August 1976, *43,* pp. 267–74.

Cubbin, J., "Industry Structure and Performance: The Empirical Work," mimeo, Queen Mary College, 1986.

Cubbin, J. and Geroski, P., "The Convergence of Profits in the Long Run: Inter-firm and Inter-industry Comparisons," *Journal of Industrial Economics,* 1987, *35,* pp. 427–42.

Cyert, Richard M. and DeGroot, Morris M., "An Analysis of Cooperation and Learning in a Duopoly Context," *American Economic Review,* March 1973, *63,* pp. 24–37.

Demsetz, Harold, "Industry Structure, Market Rivalry, and Public Policy," *Journal of Law and Economics,* April 1973, *16,* pp. 1–9.

"Two Systems of Belief about Monopoly," in Harvey J. Goldschmid, H. M. Mann, and J. F. Weston, eds., *Industrial Concentration: The New Learning,* Boston: Little, Brown, 1974, pp. 164–84.

"Barriers to Entry," *American Economic Review,* March 1982, *72,* pp. 45–57.

Domowitz, Ian, Hubbard, R. Glenn, and Petersen, Bruce C., "Business Cycles and the Relationship between Concentration and Price–Cost Margins," *Rand Journal of Economics,* Spring 1986, *17,* pp. 1–17.

Edwards, Jeremy, Kay, John, and Mayer, Colin, *The Economic Analysis of Accounting Profitability,* Oxford: Oxford University Press, 1987.

Encaoua, D. and Geroski, P., "Price Dynamics and Competition in Five Countries," *OECD Economic Studies,* 1986, *6,* pp. 47–74.

Fisher, Franklin M. and McGowan, John J., "On the Misuse of Accounting Rates of Return to Infer Monopoly Profits," *American Economic Review,* March 1983, *73,* pp. 82–97.

Gabel, H., "A Simultaneous Equation Analysis of the Structure and Performance of the U.S. Petroleum Refining Industry," *Journal of Industrial Economics,* September 1979, *28,* pp. 89–104.

Gale, Bradley J. and Branch, Ben S., "Concentration versus Market Share: Which Determines Performance and Why Does It Matter?" *Antitrust Bulletin,* Spring 1982, *27,* pp. 83–106.

Geroski, P. A., "Simultaneous Equations Models of the Structure–Performance Paradigm," *European Economic Review,* 1982, *19,* pp. 145–58.

"The Empirical Analysis of Entry: A Survey," mimeo, University of Southampton, 1983.

"Do Dominant Firms Decline?" in D. Hay and J. Vickers, eds., *The Economics of Market Dominance,* Oxford: Basil Blackwell, 1986.

"Innovation, Technological Opportunity, and Market Structure," mimeo, University of Southampton, 1987.

"The Effect of Entry on Profit Margins in the Short and Long Run," mimeo, London Business School, 1988.

Geroski, P. and Jacquemin, A., "Dominant Firms and Their Alleged Decline," *International Journal of Industrial Organization,* March 1984, *2,* pp. 1–28.

"The Persistence of Profits: A European Comparison," *Economic Journal,* June 1988, *98,* pp. 375–89.

Geroski, P. and Masson, R., "Dynamic Market Models in Industrial Organization," *International Journal of Industrial Organization,* March 1987, *5,* pp. 1–14.

Geroski, P. and Murfin, A., "Entry and Industry Evolution: the U.K. Car Industry, 1958–83," mimeo, University of Southampton, 1987.

Geroski, Paul A. and Toker, S., "Pricing and New Products: Cellular Phones in the U.K.," mimeo, London Business School, 1988.

Gort, Michael and Klepper, Steven, "Time Paths in the Diffusion of Product Innovations," *Economic Journal,* September 1982, *92,* pp. 630–53.

Grant, Robert M., Jammine, Azar, and Thomas, Howard, "The Relationship Between Diversification and Profitability Among British Manufacturing Firms," paper presented at EARIE meetings, August 1986.

Halpern, Paul, "Corporate Acquisitions: A Theory of Special Cases? A Review of Event Studies Applied to Acquisitions," *Journal of Finance,* May 1983, *38,* pp. 297–317.

Hannan, T., "Limit Pricing and the Banking Industry," *Journal of Money, Credit and Banking,* November 1979, *11,* pp. 438–46.

Harris, Robert S., Stewart, John F., and Carleton, Willard T., "Financial Characteristics of Acquired Firms," in Michael Keenan and Lawrence J. White, eds., *Mergers and Acquisitions: Current Problems in Perspective,* Lexington, MA: Lexington Books, 1982, pp. 223–41.

Hirschey, Mark, "The Effect of Advertising," *Journal of Business,* April 1981, *54,* pp. 329–39.

Holland, Daniel M. and Myers, Steuart C., "Trends in Corporate Profitability and Capital Costs in the United States," in D. M. Holland, ed., *Measuring Profitability and Capital Costs: An International Study,* Lexington, MA: Lexington Books, 1984.

Hymer, Stephen H., *The International Operations of National Firms,* Cambridge, MA: MIT Press, 1976.

Imai, Ken'ichi, "Iron and Steel," in K. Sato, ed., *Industry and Business in Japan,* White Plains, NY: M. E. Sharpe, 1980.

Jacobsen, R., "The Persistence of Abnormal Returns," *Strategic Management Journal,* September–October 1988, *9,* pp. 415–30.

Japan Fair Trade Commission, *Nihon no Sangyo Shuchu – Shona 38-41 Nen* (Industrial Concentration in Japan: 1963-1966), Tokyo: Toyo Keizai Shinpo Sha, 1969.

Jenny, F. and Weber, A.-P., "Profit Rates and Structural Variables in French Manufacturing Industries," *European Economic Review,* February 1976, *7,* pp. 187–206.

Jensen, Michael C. and Ruback, Richard S., "The Market for Corporate Control: The Scientific Evidence," *Journal of Financial Economics,* April 1983, *11,* pp. 5–50.

Johnston, J., *Econometric Methods,* 2d ed., New York: McGraw-Hill, 1972.

Kessides, Ioannis, "Advertising, Sunk Costs, and Barriers to Entry," *Review of Economics and Statistics,* February 1986, *48,* 84–95.

"Market Structure and Sunk Costs: An Empirical Test of the Contestability Hypothesis," Working Paper No. 88-50, University of Maryland, 1988a.

"Do Firms Differ Much: Some Additional Evidence," mimeo, University of Maryland, College Park, 1988b.

Khemani, R. S., "The Extent and Evolution of Competition in the Canadian Economy," in D. G. McFetridge, ed., *Canadian Industry in Transition,* Royal Commission on the Economic Union and Development Prospects for Canada, Ottawa: Supply and Services, 1986.

Khemani, R. S. and Shapiro, D. M., "The Determinants of New Plant Entry in Canada," *Applied Economics,* November 1986, *18,* pp. 1243–57.

Kirzner, Israel M., *Competition and Entrepreneurship,* Chicago: University of Chicago Press, 1973.

Klepper, Steven and Graddy, Elizabeth, "Industry Evolution and the Determinants of Market Structure," mimeo, Carnegie-Mellon, 1984.

Kmenta, Jan, *Elements of Econometrics,* New York: Macmillan, 1971.

Kuehn, Douglas, *Takeovers and the Theory of the Firm,* London: Macmillan, 1975.

Kuenne, Robert E., "Towards an Operational General Equilibrium Theory with Oligopoly: Some Experimental Results and Conjectures," *Kyklos,* 1974, *27,* pp. 792–820.

Lancaster, Kelvin, "Socially Optimal Product Differentiation," *American Economic Review,* September 1975, *65,* pp. 567–85.

Lecraw, D. J., and Thompson, D. N., *Conglomerate Mergers in Canada,* Study No. 32, Royal Commission on Corporate Concentration, Ottawa: Supply and Services, 1978.

Levy, David, "The Speed of the Invisible Hand," *International Journal of Industrial Organization,* March 1987, *5,* pp. 79–92.

Lindenberg, Eric and Ross, Stephen, "Tobin's q Ratio and Industrial Organization," *Journal of Business,* January 1981, *54,* pp. 1–32.

Littlechild, S. C., "Misleading Calculations of the Social Costs of Monopoly Power," *Economic Journal,* June 1981, *91,* pp. 348–63.

Litvak, I.A. and Maule, C. J., *The Canadian Multinationals,* Toronto: Butterworths, 1981.

Long, William F., "Market Share, Concentration, and Profits: Intra-Industry and Inter-Industry Evidence," unpublished, Federal Trade Commission, 1982.

Long, William F., Schramm, Richard, and Tollison, Robert D., "The Economic Determinants of Antitrust Activity," *Journal of Law and Economics,* October 1973, *16,* pp. 351–64.

Lynk, William J., "Information, Advertising, and the Structure of the Market," *Journal of Business,* April 1981, *54,* pp. 271–303.

McNulty, Paul J., "Economic Theory and the Meaning of Competition," *Quarterly Journal of Economics,* November 1968, *82,* pp. 639–56.

Marris, Robin, *The Economic Theory of Managerial Capitalism,* Glencoe, IL: Free Press, 1964.

Marris, Robin and Mueller, Dennis C., "The Corporation, Competition, and the Invisible Hand," *Journal of Economic Literature,* March 1980, *18,* pp. 32–63.

Martin, Stephen, "Market, Firm, and Economic Performance," Monograph Series in Finance and Economics, NYU Graduate School of Business Administration, 1983.

Meeks, Geoffrey, *Disappointing Marriage: A Study of the Gains from Merger,* Cambridge: Cambridge University Press, 1977.

Mizon, G., "Model Selection Procedures," in M. J. Artis and A. R. Nobay, eds., *Studies in Current Economic Analysis,* Oxford: Blackwell, 1976.

Mood, A., Graybill, F., and Boes, D., *Introduction to the Theory of Statistics,* London: McGraw-Hill, 1974.

Mueller, Dennis C., "A Theory of Conglomerate Mergers," *Quarterly Journal of Economics,* November 1969, *83,* pp. 643–659.

"The Effects of Conglomerate Mergers: A Survey of the Empirical Evidence," *Journal of Banking and Finance,* December 1977, *1,* pp. 315–47.

ed., *The Determinants and Effects of Mergers: An International Comparison,* Cambridge: Oelgeschlager, Gunn, and Hain, 1980.

Profits in the Long Run, Cambridge: Cambridge University Press, 1986.

The Corporation: Growth, Diversification and Mergers, Chur: Harwood Academic Publishers, 1987.

National Science Foundation (NSF), *Science Indicators 1976,* Washington, DC: Government Printing Office, 1977.

Nelson, Richard R. and Winter, Sidney G., *An Evolutionary Theory of Economic Change,* Cambridge, MA: Harvard University Press, 1982.

Neumann, Manfred, Böbel, Ingo, and Haid, Alfred, "Profitability, Risk and Market Structure in West German Industries," *Journal of Industrial Economics,* March 1979, *27,* pp. 227–42.

Newman, M., "Strategic Groups and the Structure–Performance Relationship," *Review of Economics and Statistics,* August 1978, *60,* pp. 417–27.

Niosi, Jorge, *Canadian Multinationals,* Toronto: Garamond Press, 1985.

Odagiri, Hiroyuki, "Market Share and the Persistence of Profits in Japan: An Empirical Study for Japanese Firms," Discussion Paper No. 320, Institute of Socio-Economic Planning, University of Tsukuba, 1987.

Odagiri, Hiroyuki and Yamawaki, Hideki, "A Study of Company Profit-Rate Time Series: New Results for Japan and an International Comparison," CEPS Working Documents, No. 17 (Economic), Brussels: Center for European Policy Studies, 1985.

"A Study of Company Profit-Rate Time Series: Japan and the United States," *International Journal of Industrial Organization,* March 1986, *4,* pp. 1–23.

Orr, Dale, "The Determinants of Entry: A Study of the Canadian Manufacturing Industries," *Review of Economics and Statistics,* February 1974, *56,* pp. 58–66.

Oster, S., "Intra-industry Structure and the Ease of Strategic Change," *Review of Economics and Statistics,* August 1982, *64,* pp. 376–83.

Pakes, Ariel, "Mueller's *Profits in the Long Run,*" *Rand Journal of Economics,* Summer 1987, *18,* pp. 319–32.

Penrose, Edith T., *The Theory of the Growth of the Firm,* New York: Wiley, 1959.

Porter, M., "The Structure within Industries and Companies Performance," *Review of Economics and Statistics,* May 1979, *61,* pp. 214–28.

Posner, Richard A., "The Social Cost of Monopoly and Regulation," *Journal of Political Economy,* August 1975, *83,* pp. 807–27.

Qualls, David, "Stability and Persistence of Economic Profit Margins in Highly Concentrated Industries," *Southern Economic Journal,* April 1974, *40,* pp. 604–12.

"Market Structure and the Cyclical Flexibility of Price–Cost Margins," *Journal of Business,* April 1979, *52,* pp. 305–25.

Quandt, R., "Tests of Equilibrium and Disequilibrium Hypotheses," *International Economic Review,* June 1978, *19,* pp. 435–52.

"Econometric Disequilibrium Models," *Econometric Reviews,* 1982, *1,* pp. 1–63.

Ravenscraft, D., "Structure–Profit Relationships at the Line of Business and Industry Level," *Review of Economics and Statistics,* 1983, *65,* pp. 22–31.

Ravenscraft, David J. and Scherer, F. M., "Life After Takeover," *Journal of Industrial Economics,* December 1987, *36,* pp. 147–56.

Rhoades, Stephen A., *Power, Empire Building, and Mergers,* Lexington, MA: Lexington Books, 1983.

Rugman, Alan M. and McIlveen, John, *Megafirms,* Toronto: Methuen, 1985.

Salinger, M. A., "Tobin's-Q, Unionization, and the Concentration–Profits Relationship," *Rand Journal of Economics,* Summer 1984, *15,* pp. 159-70.

Saxonhouse, Gary R., "Estimated Parameters as Dependent Variables," *American Economic Review,* March 1976, *66,* pp. 178-83.

"Regressions from Samples Having Different Characteristics," *Review of Economics and Statistics,* May 1977, *59,* pp. 234-7.

Scherer, F. M., "The Welfare Economics of Product Variety: An Application to the Ready-to-Eat Cereals Industry," *Journal of Industrial Economics,* December 1979, *28,* pp. 113-34.

Industrial Market Structure and Economic Performance, 2nd ed., Chicago: Rand McNally, 1980.

Schmalensee, Richard, "Entry Deterrence in the Ready-to-Eat Breakfast Cereal Industry," *Bell Journal of Economics,* Autumn 1978, *9,* pp. 305-27.

"Do Markets Differ Much?" *American Economic Review,* June 1985, *75,* pp. 341-51.

"Competitive Advantage and Collusive Optima," *International Journal of Industrial Organization,* December 1987, *5,* pp. 351-67.

Schumpeter, Joseph A., *The Theory of Economic Development,* Cambridge, MA: Harvard University Press, 1934.

Capitalism, Socialism and Democracy, 3rd ed., New York: Harper & Row, 1950.

Schwalbach, Joachim, "Entry by Diversified Firms into German Industries," *International Journal of Industrial Organization,* March 1987, *5,* pp. 43-9.

"Diversifizierung, Risiko und Erfolg industrieller Unternehmen," mimeo, Berlin, 1988.

Schwalbach, Joachim, Grasshoff, Ulrike, and Mahmood, Talat, "The Dynamics of Corporate Profits," IIM Discussion Paper IIM/IP 87-1, Berlin, 1988.

Scott, John T., "Corporate Finance and Market Structure," in R. E. Caves, M. E. Porter, M. Spence, with J. T. Scott, eds., *Competition in the Open Economy,* Cambridge, MA: Harvard University Press, 1980, pp. 325-59.

Scott, John T. and Pascoe, George, "Beyond Firm and Industry Effects on Profitability in Imperfect Markets," *Review of Economics and Statistics,* May 1986, *68,* pp. 284-92.

Shapiro, D. M., *Foreign and Domestic Firms in Canada,* Toronto: Butterworth, 1980.

Shapiro, D. M. and Khemani, R. S., "The Determinants of Entry and Exit Reconsidered," *International Journal of Industrial Organization,* March 1987, *5,* pp. 15-26.

Shepherd, William G., "The Elements of Market Structure," *Review of Economics and Statistics,* February 1972, *54,* pp. 25-37.

The Treatment of Market Power, New York: Columbia University Press, 1975.

The Economics of Industrial Organization, 2nd ed., Englewood Cliffs, NJ: Prentice-Hall, 1985.

Shubik, Martin, with Levitan, Richard, *Market Structure and Behavior,* Cambridge, MA: Harvard University Press, 1980.

Simon, H., "Theories of Decision Making in Economics and Behavioral Sciences," *American Economic Review,* June 1959, *49,* pp. 253-83.

Singh, Ajit, *Take-overs: Their Relevance to the Stock Market and the Theory of the Firm,* Cambridge: Cambridge University Press, 1971.

Smirlock, M., Gilligan, T., and Marshall, W., "Tobin-Q and the Structure–Performance Relationship," *American Economic Review,* December 1984, *74,* pp. 1051-60.

Smith, Adam, *The Wealth of Nations,* New York: Random House, 1937, original publication, 1776.

Spence, Michael, "Product Differentiation and Welfare," *American Economic Review,* May 1976, *66,* pp. 407-14.

Statistics Canada, *Inter-Corporate Ownership,* Ottawa Catalog No. 61-508, various years.

Steiner, Peter O., *Mergers: Motives, Effects, Policies,* Ann Arbor: University of Michigan Press, 1975.

Strickland, Allyn D. and Weiss, Leonard W., "Advertising, Concentration, and Price–Cost Margins," *Journal of Political Economy,* October 1976, *84,* 1109–21.

Teece, David J., "Towards an Economic Theory of the Multi-product Firm," *Journal of Economic Behavior and Organization,* March 1982, *3,* pp. 39–63.

Uekusa, Masu, *Sangyo Soshiki Ron* (Industrial Organization), Tokyo: Chikuma Shobo, 1982.

Wakasugi, Takaaki, Nishina, Kazuhiko, Kon-ya, Fumiko, and Tsuchiya, Moriaki, "Measuring the Profitability of the Non-financial Corporate Sector in Japan," in D. M. Holland, ed., *Measuring Profitability and Capital Costs: An International Study,* Lexington, MA: Lexington Books, 1984, pp. 345–86.

Weiss, Leonard W., "The Concentration–Profits Relationship and Antitrust," in H. J. Goldschmid, H. M. Mann, and J. F. Weston, eds., *Industrial Concentration: The New Learning,* Boston: Little, Brown, 1974.

Corrected Concentration Ratios in Manufacturing – 1972, Washington, DC: Federal Trade Commission, 1981.

von Weizäcker, C. C., *Barriers to Entry,* Berlin: Springer-Verlag, 1980.

Winter, S., "Economic Natural Selection and the Theory of the Firm," *Yale Economic Essays,* 1964, *4,* pp. 255–72.

Wrigley, L., "Divisional Autonomy and Diversification," D.B.A. Thesis, Graduate School of Business Administration, Harvard, 1970.

Yamawaki, Hideki, "Market Structure, Capacity Expansion and Pricing: A Model Applied to the Japanese Iron and Steel Industry," *International Journal of Industrial Organization,* March 1984, *2,* pp. 29–62.

"A Comparative Analysis of Intertemporal Behavior of Profits: Japan and the United States," Discussion Paper IIM/IP 87-2 (February), International Institute of Management, Berlin, 1987.

"The Steel Industry," in R. Komiya, M. Okino, K. Suzumura, and K. Sato, eds., *Industrial Policy in Japan,* Tokyo: Academic Press, 1988, ch. 10.

Yamawaki, Hideki, Weiss, Leonard W., and Sleuwaegen, Leo, "Industry Competition and the Formation of the European Common Market," mimeo, Science Center Berlin, 1986.

Index

213